MW00817479

Strategies for SUCCESS with English Language Learners

Virginia Pauline Rojas

ASCD® LEARN. TEACH. LEAD.

Alexandria, Virginia USA

1703 North Beauregard Street

Alexandria, VA 22311-1714 USA

Telephone: 1-800-933-2723 or 1-703-578-9600

Fax: 1-703-575-5400

Website: www.ascd.org

Author

Virginia Pauline Rojas

ASCD Staff

ASCD's Executive Director is Gene R. Carter.

Content Production

Ann Cunningham-Morris, *Director, Program Development*

Eugenia Hu, *Project Coordinator*

Manual Production

Gary Bloom, Director, *Design and Production Services*

Mary Beth Nielsen, *Manager, Editorial Services*

Catherine Guyer, *Senior Graphic Designer*

Judy Ochse, *Senior Associate Editor*

Dina Murray Seamon, *Production Specialist/Team Lead*

ASCD is a community of educators, advocating sound policies and sharing best practices to achieve the success of each learner. Founded in 1943, ASCD is a worldwide education association with headquarters in Alexandria, Virginia, USA.

ASCD publications present a variety of viewpoints. The views expressed or implied in this manual should not be interpreted as official positions of the Association.

Copyright 2007 by the Association for Supervision and Curriculum Development, 1703 North Beauregard Street, Alexandria, Virginia 22311-1714. All rights reserved. Materials of this guide are intended for use in meetings, professional development opportunities, classrooms, and school community gatherings. For this purpose, materials in the guide may be reproduced. Any other used of these materials is prohibited, unless written permission is granted by ASCD.

Printed in the United States of America

ASCD Stock No.: 111061

ISBN: 978-1-4166-1189-9

22 21 20 19 18   8 9 10 11 12

Strategies for SUCCESS with English Language Learners

About the Author

Virginia Rojas, an ASCD Faculty member and independent consultant in the area of English as a second language, works in schools around the globe and with school districts throughout the United States. She is recognized for her leadership and commitment to the development of second language proficiency among school populations, especially within an inclusionary and collaborative context. It is her belief that strategies that assist English language learners in K–12 settings are beneficial for all learners, and that ESL and classroom teachers need to work together to provide seamless language development and academic achievement programs. She is hopeful that the Understanding by Design curriculum model can provide an avenue for this collaboration in ways that will build equity into the instructional process.

Rojas is a former classroom teacher, a New Jersey State Department of Education central office director, and an Associate Professor at The College of New Jersey. She teaches for the Teacher Training Center for International Educators (www.thettc.org) in London during the summers.

ASCD © 2007. All Rights Reserved.

Acknowledgments

Thank you to the following persons who hold stock on these pages:

To all English language learners—
because of them my understanding of learning is so much deeper.

To teachers who "own" English language learners—
because it really does matter.

To Ann Cunningham-Morris of ASCD for driving me—
because the journey was so valuable.

Most important, to my husband, Tom, for rewarding me with everything
a woman could want in this life. This is dedicated to you.

ASCD © 2007. All Rights Reserved.

SECTION ONE

Challenge, Vision, and Response

SECTION ONE

Challenge, Vision, and Response

The Challenge:

Understanding English Language Learners and Programs

"What do I do with these kids? They don't speak a word of English and I don't speak any other language. I don't think they are getting anything out of this class because all they do is stare at me. In the halls they speak their own language with one another, and at night they go home and don't hear another word of English. How are they ever going to pass this class, never mind the state test at the end of the year? I need help!"

Sound familiar? The number of English language learners in the United States has increased 95 percent in the past decade alone, and the number is expected to grow. Approximately 4.7 million designated English language learners attend public schools (Office of English Language Acquisition, 2002). It is predicted that by the 2030s, English language learners will account for about 40 percent of the school-age population. Yet very few teachers have been trained to address the needs of these students, and the questions they ask are the same as they asked decades ago: Who are English language learners and what are effective ways for schooling them? What kind of educational program brings about the best results? What are sound practices for facilitating English language acquisition? How can English language learners have academic success in subject areas? How do we teach English language learners in our classrooms?

The No Child Left Behind Act (NCLB) poses the challenging mission to schools and educators to ensure that English language learners are making adequate annual progress toward mastery on standards-based, high-stakes assessments. State and local education agencies are responsible for ensuring these targets. This mandate requires programs and curricula that help English language learners be competitive with their English-proficient peers and that provide teachers the capacities for providing quality instruction to a widely diverse population.

A Typology of English Language Learners

School districts vary in the composition of their English language learner population. One district may have an exclusive population of one language and cultural background—perhaps all—born in the United States but with little or no access to social or academic English until entering school. Another district might have students coming from every corner of the world, representing a multiplicity of languages and cultures. Many arrivals may be immigrants, while others may be visitors; some may have strong schooling and literacy skills, while others may not. Further variability exists within these English language learning populations, so much so that what distinguishes them from one another is even greater than what distinguishes them from students who have English as a primary language (Clegg, 1996; Lachat, 1999).

One such distinction relates to the reasons why English language learners come to the United States. A widely held belief is that most immigrants, similar to those of past generations, are looking to make a new home. Although this may be somewhat true, some families expect to return to their native countries once whatever situation compelled them to leave has

improved. In today's increasingly global economy, numerous families live abroad to work with multinational organizations or companies. Finally, and most surprisingly perhaps, is that the fastest-growing number of English language learners in U.S. schools today are not those who are newly arrived but those who were born here and therefore are second- or third-generation immigrants (Houk, 2005).

English language learners also differ in the types of experiences they have had and the degrees of proficiency they have in their primary languages. Some experiences have been restricted, meaning that there has been modest exposure to the "register of schooling" (Cummins, 2000). Indeed, a number of English language learners enter U.S. schools without prior education in their home country or in their primary language. Others have strong or enriched literacy skills in their primary language and, therefore, are skilled in the types of activity and discourse particular to school—an essential factor for successful second language schooling (Clegg, 1996; Collier, 1995; Cummins, 2000).

Exposure to and experience with English varies among this population as well. Although English is a frequently taught language around the globe, the materials and methods used do not often lead to fluency even after years of study. The study of English may be compulsory, and although students may know the formal grammar of the language, they may not feel comfortable using it or even have the desire to own it. A common expectation is that children born in the United States will naturally come to school proficient in English. But this is not always the case, as it depends on how much English their parents may speak or how much English they are exposed to in their

ASCD © 2007. All Rights Reserved.

neighborhoods. Linguistic minorities born in the United States are often proficient in the social domains of English language usage but not with the academic or literacy skills requisite for school.

Examples of students within this framework are as follows:

• Abraham, a 16-year-old, arrived from a refugee camp in Tanzania. He is originally from Sudan and is considered to be one of the "lost boys," a group who escaped the genocide of tribal warfare. In school, he completed the equivalent of 3rd grade and has basic literacy skills in Arabic, Sudan's official language. He also speaks his tribal language with his friends. Abraham was studying English at the camp while waiting to come to the United States, and he is able to communicate socially on a limited basis. Because of the years of schooling he missed, he is underprepared academically. He says he will never return to his homeland.

• Aiko is 10 years old and has arrived with her family from Japan. Her father has been temporarily transferred to the United States with his company. At first, he was going to come alone, but then he decided to bring his family so the children could learn English. Aiko speaks a few words already, though her preference is to read it, which she does reasonably well. Aiko attends Japanese Saturday school to study Japanese and mathematics because her father does not want her to fall behind her Japanese peers. Aiko's mother speaks no English.

• Fabian was born in the United States and is entering kindergarten this year. His parents are immigrants from Mexico, speak Spanish but have had limited schooling, and speak enough English to communicate in their factory jobs. As Fabian's father learns more English, he tries to speak it with his son because he hopes this will help in

school. Fabian speaks Spanish with his mother, converses in Spanish and English with his father and his playmates, and watches television in English. He often translates for his mother in public. Sometimes he mixes the two languages while speaking, though he is able to separate them when speaking with Spanish-only or English-only speakers.

• Irina was born in the United States to parents who speak Ukrainian, Russian, German, and English. She began school in the United States but returned to the Ukraine after one year. Her parents have returned to the United States for now but one day hope to return to their homeland. Both are professionals and work in English. They speak Ukrainian at home with their children, though they often help with schoolwork in English. Irina is quickly retrieving her early years of English and is quite literate in her primary language. She plans to study Russian and German as soon as she is able to.

A summary of these distinguishing characteristics appears in Figure 1.

Additional misunderstandings complicate perceptions of English language learners. One dominant belief is that issues relevant to English language learners and special-needs students are one and the same. Although some English language learners do have special needs, the percentage does not exceed the percentage of special-needs students in the general student population. Another misconception rests on the notion that because English language learners do not know English, they may not know much or be expected to know anything at all until they master English (Valdés, 2004). Students who have been schooled in their own language know a lot—just not in English—and what they know can

 © 2007. All Rights Reserved.

Figure 1.
Distinguishing Attributes of English Language Learners

Status	Primary Language(s) Experiences and Proficiency	English Experiences and Proficiency
Newly arrived to U. S.	Immigrant with restricted or enriched literacy experiences and access to formal schooling in primary language(s) Visitor with restricted or enriched literacy experiences and access to formal schooling in primary language(s)	No previous experience with English Social exposure to English Formal academic study of English Compulsory academic study of English
Born in U. S.	Immigrant parents with restricted or enriched literacy experiences and access to formal schooling in primary language(s) Visitor with restricted or enriched literacy experiences and access to formal schooling in primary language(s)	Restricted access to English socially or academically Enriched access to English socially but restricted access academically Enriched access to English socially and academically

bridge their transfer to academic success while they are acquiring English. Finally, acquiring another language through schooling is a variable process, and not all students can be expected to do it at the same rate, in the same way, or to the same degree of proficiency. The need to document English language learners' actual achievements, both linguistically and academically, is crucial to clarify these issues. Clearly, the differences among English language learners are considerable and complex, and schools should not make blanket decisions about their educational needs or programs (Clegg, 1996).

A Typology of Programs

Four attributes characterize the types of programs available for schooling English language learners. Two indicate whether or not the students are separated from or included in mainstream classrooms. Elemen-

tary programs tend to separate English language learners part of the day to provide what is considered specialized instruction. Upper-school programs sometimes separate them until they are fluent enough to join their English-proficient peers and classrooms. The underlying premise of separate programs is that students' lack of English fluency is a deficiency that needs to be remedied before they are permitted into the mainstream (Clegg, 1996). English language learners are perceived to be a problem to be fixed by specialists, somewhat analogous to the medical model of patient and doctor.

The other two attributes designate the languages of instruction—that is, whether or not the students' primary languages will be used in addition to English, or English will be the exclusive language of instruction. Programs that use students' primary languages to varying degrees honor the complex interplay of language, cognition, and culture and understand that bilingualism

ASCD © 2007. All Rights Reserved.

and underachievement are not synonymous. The underlying intention signals an ethos of additive bilingualism for students; that is, they acquire English in addition to their primary languages. In contrast, programs emphasizing the use of English as the exclusive medium of instruction hint at subtractive bilingualism or the loss of students' primary languages. The ultimate goal is for English language learners to fit into the school, and not vice versa (Baker, 1995; Clegg, 1996; Reed & Railsback, 2003). Figure 2 classifies the program types within this framework, and each program is further explained in the text that follows.

Bilingual and Dual Language Education Program Types

Early-exit or transitional bilingual education uses students' primary languages for a limited number of years to promote their mastery of academic material while they are learning English. Late-exit or developmental bilingual education is ongoing and has as its ultimate goals primary language maintenance through subject matter and English mastery. One-way dual language education is a stronger form of primary language instruction in that it is positioned as an enrichment model rather than a compensatory model for English language learners; hence, the expected outcome is full bilingual proficiency. Regrettably, bilingual education programs are often surrounded by confusion and emotionally charged attacks in the United States because they are perceived as an excuse for language-minority students not to acquire English. This backlash persists despite research that supports the bilingual approach as an effective program for schooling English language learners (Collier, 1995; Thomas & Collier, 2002).

In response to the very vocal "English-only" movement against bilingual education in the United States, some ethnic groups are establishing an alternative program known as heritage schools, which preserve students' primary cultures and languages. A few heritage schools aim to compensate for perceived shortcomings in U.S. education by offering courses in literature, history, math, and even SAT preparation. Ironically,

Figure 2.
A Typology of Program Options for English Language Learners

	English + Primary-Language Instruction	English Language Instruction Exclusively
Separate provision	Early-exit or transitional bilingual education Late-exit or developmental bilingual education One-way dual language or enrichment bilingual education Heritage schools	Newcomer programs ESL pull-out program taught traditionally Content-based ESL pull-out program SDAIE, CALLA, and sheltered instruction (SIOP)
Inclusive provision	Two-way dual language or bilingual immersion	Collaborative sheltered immersion

a small number of ethnic schools have begun to accept "others" for language immersion programs that are accredited by public schools. These "others" are English-speaking students who aspire to become bilingual.

Several U.S. school districts are experimenting with dual language immersion programs, putting proficient English speakers in the same classes with English language learners. Two-way immersion, two-way bilingual, and dual language programs embrace the goals of immersion programs for the English-proficient cohort and those of developmental bilingual education for English language learners. These programs employ each group's primary language for academic instruction at certain points during the school day. The amalgamation of the program types aims for bilingualism for both groups of students and promotes two languages as an enrichment experience for all rather than a compensatory measure for a few. A growing number of dual language programs in the United States and Canada show that educational excellence and second language acquisition are not mutually exclusive. When compared with other program models, two-way dual language programs account for English language learners' lead in long-term K–12 achievement on standardized tests in English reading over native English speakers' results (Collier, 1995).

English as a Second Language Program Types

The most frequently implemented English language instructional programs separate English language learners from their academic peers. Newcomer programs are often established for older English language learners and are designed to meet the needs of academically underprepared students. These programs are intended to help students acquire English and requisite skills, including acculturation into the school system. English as a second language (ESL) pull-out programs vary widely in their organization. Many English language learners are pulled out for short periods of time, while others go to ESL classrooms for up to half of their school day, at times missing core academic subjects. Traditionally, pull-out programs have grouped students by their English proficiency levels in order to deliver a language-led or grammar-based curriculum. Current approaches now offer subject matter in ways that make the content accessible to students while also promoting English language acquisition and development. These include specially designed academic instruction in English (SDAIE), the cognitive academic language learning approach (CALLA), and sheltered-instruction programs (Chamot, 2005; Echevarria, Vogt, & Short, 2000).

A number of school districts across the country are restructuring mainstream classrooms by having ESL and mainstream teachers collaborate to integrate English language learners into classrooms with their English-proficient peers in order to work toward language acquisition and academic achievement simultaneously (Barnett, 1993; Carrasquillo & Rodriguez, 2002; Clegg, 1996; Rojas, 1999). An overriding aim of these inclusive efforts is to dispel the prevailing deficit perspective as well as to promote "ownership" of English language learners by all classroom teachers. Theoretically, the case can be made that these experiences qualify as immersion programs, because English is used as the medium of instruction and because the goals include proficiency in

ASCD © 2007. All Rights Reserved.

the target language in addition to students' primary languages, mastery of subject matter, and cross-cultural understanding (Curtain & Pesola, 1994). Unless school districts have this vision and provide professional development efforts to build the capacities of mainstream teachers, however, immersion is more akin to submersion—a situation in which most English language learners sink rather than swim (Samway & McKeon, 1999). The same can be said for mainstream teachers who suddenly find themselves in a class with English language learners for the first time.

The Vision:

Building Capacities of All Teachers to Support English Language Learners

An Inclusive Model of Responsibility

Neither separate programs nor unprepared mainstream classes are suitable instructional environments for English language learners, especially when there is little articulation between the two. The questions of who "owns" English language learners, and why, resonate in this context. Bilingual and ESL teachers feel a need to protect students from what they perceive as potential harm in mainstream classes. Classroom teachers feel mystified by students who do not share the language of the classroom, and these teachers are often ill-equipped to support English language learners' academic achievement. The longer these sensitivities endure, the longer schools delay implementing an ecological model of responsibility, in which second language *and* mainstream teachers own English language learners.

Evidence suggests that separate bilingual and English as a second language programs may serve as safe havens from countless mainstream classes. Stories abound of teachers who expect too much or too little from English language learners, to the point where students are either silenced or ignored. Callous attitudes persist about different ethnic or linguistic groups, and at times teachers or peers make remarks or show behaviors accordingly. But these should not be reasons to justify the practice of separate programs. Rather, these questions should be asked: Why do schools sanction mainstream classrooms that do not make those entrusted to their care feel wanted or safe

ASCD © 2007. All Rights Reserved.

(Cummins, 1994)? Why should it be the exclusive responsibility of bilingual or ESL classrooms and teachers to nurture and support English language learners?

Evidence also suggests that separate programs do not necessarily offer the kind of environment English language learners want. Often, students say that ESL classes are too easy, are unrelated to what they need to succeed in their academic classes, or are nothing more than makeshift tutorials. Indeed, if it is true that English language learners feel so comfortable in withdrawal programs, then why do they or their families frequently want to get out at the first chance they have? Although the intention of separate programs is to provide the skills and confidence needed to succeed in the mainstream, research calls attention to effects of such programs that are not language-related: English language learners feel stigmatized, deficient, removed from the everyday happenings of school life, and separated from their social peer groups (Carrasquillo & Rodriguez, 2002; Clegg, 1996; Harklau, 1994).

In addition to adverse social effects, separate programs can prove academically disadvantageous. English language learners do not always have access to their grade-level curriculum, and this sets them back even further. Withdrawal classes can not provide the same intellectual challenges or conceptual understandings as mainstream classes simply because most ESL teachers are not content-area teachers (Bunch, Abram, Lotan & Valdés, 2001). For English language learners well educated in their own language, a cursory offering of watered-down content is unresponsive. It is equally dismissive for those who lack primary language literacy skills or who are underprepared academically. Building academic

equity for English language learners is not accomplished through the lowering of standards but through the design of instructional strategies and scaffolds to help students attain what is expected.

The incessant practice of "fixing" English language learners with special programs is paradoxical. Bilingual classes are meant to educate English language learners in their primary language until they acquire enough English to move into the mainstream. However, a political backlash against what is perceived as un-American has always plagued the implementation of bilingual programs, and even now states continue to dismantle them. ESL classes teach students the school language to prepare them for entry into mainstream programs. But the traditional pull-out classes do not work as well as was intended in preparing English language learners for academic success or in closing the achievement gap between them and their English-proficient peers (Thomas & Collier, 2002). The current shift toward designing content-based ESL curriculum and sheltered-instruction content classes is a better approach. Such programs honor the prior learning and absolute capacities of English language learners to acquire English and academic content simultaneously. But English language learners can not remain in sheltered-instruction programs forever.

It takes 4–10 years of institutional support for English language learners to acquire the level of academic language proficiency needed to catch up with their English-proficient peers (Cummins, 2000; Thomas & Collier, 2002). Delaying their entrance into mainstream classes prevents schools from fulfilling the commitment to provide an environment where English language learners can thrive. Why, after all, should schools go to all the trouble of re-creating separate classrooms when mainstream classes are available right next door (Clegg, 1996)? Wouldn't it be just as effective to integrate English language learners into mainstream classes, where they could acquire social and academic English in natural settings alongside their peers? Wouldn't schools be better served to invest in the professional development of mainstream teachers and language education specialists so they could collaboratively teach one curriculum to English language learners? As the number of English language learners continues to increase around the country, wouldn't it make more sense to prepare the mainstream for them rather than the other way around?

Collaborative Sheltered Immersion

Getting mainstream classrooms ready for English language learners should not be interpreted to mean that bilingual and ESL teachers or classrooms are no longer necessary. Nor does it mean that English language learners can be thrown into mainstream classes without modifications or support systems in place; after all, unsupported mainstream classrooms are what led to separate programs in the first place. English language learners have distinct learning needs that warrant specialized instruction, and mere exposure to and interaction with the English language is not enough for student success (Hadaway & Young, 2006). However, a vision of increasing the responsiveness of mainstream classrooms to English language learners can begin with putting into practice as many principles as possible from those English language program models that are success-

ful—namely, sheltered-instruction and immersion programs.

One essential principle of both programs is their conceptual understanding of bilingualism. Teachers are well-informed about the process of second language acquisition and fully understand the interconnectedness of the primary language to English. The use of students' primary languages as tools for learning is not perceived as detrimental to the acquisition of English, and the academic capabilities of students who have been schooled in their home language are not underestimated. Sheltered-instruction and immersion teachers do not see the home languages of students as interference or as barriers to the acquisition of English; they do not view parents of English language learners as obstacles to be overcome. They do possess knowledge about the languages and cultures of their students; in fact, a number of sheltered-instruction teachers are somewhat proficient in at least one language other than English, and most, if not all, immersion teachers are bilingual and bicultural themselves.

Sheltered-instruction and immersion teachers grasp the complexity of the second language acquisition process. They are aware that English language learners go through developmental stages, make errors along the way, pick up chunks of language without knowing what it all means, and rely on sources of input—speakers of the language—to make it comprehensible. They appreciate errors as predictable components of the second language acquisition process and do not assume that all errors originate from students' primary languages or that they are immutable. Sheltered-instruction and immersion teachers realize that the second language acquisition

ASCD © 2007. All Rights Reserved.

process is not linear but more developmentally zigzag in nature and that it is a stronger force than any attempts made by teachers or texts to logically "sequence" the language points to be mastered (Collier, 1995). Finally, they know that second language acquisition is a dynamic, creative, innate process best developed through contextualized and meaningful activities, and that many variables play upon the second language acquisition process and account for the differences that exist among second language learners.

Because these differences are accepted and understood, sheltered-instruction and immersion teachers are skilled at integrating language and challenging academic instruction. Both approaches provide grade-appropriate content and expect and support rigorous levels of performance. To accommodate the range of knowledge, skills, language proficiencies, and learning styles of students, teachers use instructional strategies and assessment procedures that presuppose diversity, such as the following:

✓ Visual aids, modeling, demonstrations, vocabulary previews, adapted texts, and multicultural materials.

✓ Highly interactive classrooms using cooperative learning, peer tutoring, and flexible groupings.

✓ Language instruction integrated with challenging academic instruction.

✓ Tasks that emphasize problem solving and discovery learning and that appropriate a conscious fostering of reading and writing opportunities as part of a wider reorientation to the role of language in all learning.

✓ Outcome- and performance-based assessments that make use of multiple measures and observational contexts (Carrasquillo & Rodriguez, 2002; Collier,

1995; Clegg; 1996; Cloud, Genesee, & Hamayan, 2000; Echevarria, Vogt, & Short, 2000; Gibbons, 2002; Tharp, Estrada, Stoll Dalton, & Yamauchi, 2000).

Combining the principles of sheltered instruction and immersion can result in an inclusive and collaborative sheltered immersion program model. For the vision to become reality, however, schools have to commit to ending the ESL deficit programs where English language learners are considered aberrations subject to compensatory intervention and move toward establishing partnerships among classroom and ESL or bilingual teachers (Carrasquillo & Rodriguez, 2002). The paradigm suggested in this ASCD Action Tool conceives of all teachers as teachers of English language learners and as teachers of language, regardless of subject matter or grade level. As a first step toward realizing this vision, Figure 3 contrasts the characteristics of unresponsive and responsive classrooms.

Fortunately, the criteria for providing responsive learning environments for English language learners are similar to many of those for all students. Much of the academic literature today speaks to teachers about the need to shift away from the practices of unresponsive classrooms to create learning-centered environments (Wiggins & McTighe, 2005). Yet classrooms do not look much different than they did decades ago. If the questions involved were only about English language learners, they would probably continue unresolved. The debate, however, has more important implications for what schools are to become for each and every student. What is needed in schools for English language learners is a framework that addresses this essential question: Are English language learners acquiring English over time, steadily, and in

Figure 3.

Contrasting Unresponsive and Responsive Mainstream Classrooms for English Language Learners

Unresponsive Mainstream Classroom: Submersion ("sink or swim")	Responsive Mainstream Classroom: Collaborative Sheltered Immersion
An ethos of subtractive bilingualism exists; i.e., students' primary languages are perceived as detrimental to English language acquisition.	An ethos of additive bilingualism flourishes; i.e., students' primary languages are honored as beneficial to and necessary for English language acquisition.
Parents are perceived as problematic or disinterested.	Involvement of parents is obvious, especially in development of the primary language.
Students' cultural backgrounds and experiences are perceived as irrelevant and at times are dismissed as inferior.	Connections are made to students' cultural backgrounds and experiences to bridge development of new concepts, knowledge, and skills.
English language learners are perceived as remedial or learning disabled and are expected to be "fixed" by specialists; "fixing" can mean that students complete low-level tasks in tiresome contexts.	The school ecology provides a facilitating environment for language acquisition and academic achievement; students engage in academically rigorous tasks in low-anxiety contexts.
Low expectations for achievement are evident in "watering down" of content, materials, or tasks as a means to provide equity.	High expectations for achievement are evident in providing access to grade-level content, materials, and tasks; equity is built into the instructional process.
There is little to no articulation between mainstream and ESL or bilingual programs, curriculum, or teachers.	Mainstream and ESL or bilingual teachers work collaboratively to provide inclusive instruction using one curriculum—from planning through implementation and reflection.
Content (what students know) and skills (what students can do linguistically) are separated and removed from context with little to no understanding of the centrality of language to learning.	Content (what students know) and skills (what students can do linguistically) are integrated and taught in appropriate contexts with the understanding that learning and language are inseparable.
Literacy is viewed and implemented within a learning-to-read-and-write framework; reading and writing are taught separately from content as skills prerequisite to the acquisition or sharing of new information and concepts.	Literacy is viewed and implemented within a reading-and-writing-to-learn framework; reading and writing across the curriculum is an overriding goal for acquiring new information and then synthesizing it to share new concepts with peers.
Language development opportunities are provided through traditional language learning means (i.e., grammar and vocabulary as objects of study in hierarchically sequenced segments).	Opportunities for both informal and formal language development are systematically provided through the study of genres (i.e., linguistic markers and vocabulary for different types of text).
Assessment is seen as evaluative; i.e., assessment *of* learning or a single piece of evidence to see "who got it"; assessments are often selected-response tests of passive knowledge.	Assessment is seen as informative; i.e., assessment *for* learning so students can show "what they got" through open-ended performance tasks. Teachers can assist learners to "get more" because tasks are multistep and require coaching over extended time.

ASCD © 2007. All Rights Reserved.

Unresponsive Mainstream Classroom: Submersion ("sink or swim")	Responsive Mainstream Classroom: Collaborative Sheltered Immersion
Feedback to students is often provided after instruction; students are assigned scores based on percentage correct, and scores are averaged over a specified period of time for a grade.	Feedback to students is provided before instruction through rubrics or checklists, which specify performance expectations along with instructional strategies, to assist students to attain expectations; the achievement grade is based on the final level of performance.
Instructional plans are disconnected from the assessment process; strategies might be related to learning targets, might be activities unrelated to specific targets, or might be prescribed from texts.	The backward-planning model for instruction is used to target strategies that will enable learners to complete previously designed performance assessment tasks.
Overreliance on teacher-centered and whole-class instruction is evident; more often than not, it appears to be the teacher who is "doing" and the doing consists only of talking.	Emphasis on learners as makers of meaning and builders of knowledge is evident; instructional strategies are purposefully aligned with skills so that it is the students who are "doing" and the doing involves negotiation of meaning.
English language learners are grouped by language proficiency level (e.g., Level 1, 2, 3, etc.), thereby having limited opportunities for interaction with students of mixed proficiencies.	English language learners engage in collaborative learning through grade-level groupings with students of mixed language proficiencies and students whose primary language is English.
Teachers use traditional instructional arrangements and methods, including single text, single tasks for students to complete, and single instructional frameworks or strategies; students who do not "fit" do not do well.	Teachers use a wide repertoire of instructional arrangements and methods, including multiple materials, a choice of tasks for students to complete, a variety of instructional frameworks, and strategies to support a range of knowledge and skill levels within the class.
Struggling learners fail or are referred to additional "fix-it" specialists for intervention.	Scaffolding strategies or ways of supporting struggling learners are built into the backward-planning instructional model.
Students' language is characterized by literal-level discourse, often in response to yes/no and either/or types of questioning; students' responses are often *scripted*, indicating that students are merely parroting what teachers and texts say.	Students' language is characterized by descriptive, persuasive and critical-level discourse produced in response to divergent, open-ended questions; students *generate* responses, indicating that they find ways to name their developing cognitive world.
Evidence of language performance is measured by students' capacities to recall what has been learned in a given context (i.e., coverage-focused evidence).	Evidence of language performance is measured by students' capacities to transfer use to new situations and challenges (i.e., results-focused evidence).

 © 2007. All Rights Reserved.

ways that will allow them to meet the same subject-area standards as their English-speaking peers?

A Standards-Based and Assessment-Driven Learning Environment

The current emphasis on the use of standards and authentic or performance assessments to reform curriculum and instruction lays the groundwork for responsive learning environments for all students. Teachers articulating what students should know and be able to do at grade-level junctures, collecting evidence of attainment of this knowledge and skills, and providing instruction to help students achieve are the cornerstones of the standards and assessment movements. Integrating curriculum, assessment, and instruction pinpoints students' achievement in relation to expectations and, in so doing, offers an equitable window of opportunity for students who have traditionally been left behind. Standards and assessments require that schools break free of assumptions that attribute lack of success to lack of ability by focusing instead on the ongoing and unwavering preparation of students for academic success. Theoretically, schools are obliged to provide access to the quality of instruction necessary for students to complete the assessment tasks as evidence of standards' attainment.

No doubt having the same expectations and ensuring access to high-quality instruction presents a challenge to diversely populated schools. Many educators argue that not all students can meet the same standards and, therefore, to hold them accountable puts an extra burden on them and their teachers. In the case of English language learners, critics of the standards movement are distressed by students held accountable for performance before they acquire English. The critics reiterate how factors outside of school prevent English language learners from achieving, regardless of what is made available for them in schools. They worry that the shift to higher expectations and the accountability of high-stakes tests is not paralleled by a provision of a more responsive learning environment. Ultimately, they question how the results will be used and whether or not standards will support or further suppress English language learners.

Naturally, advocates hope for the more optimistic of these outcomes. They argue that English language learners are vulnerable to educational failure if denied academic instruction until they become English proficient, and that such students can learn when provided with equal access to challenging curriculum, resources, and high-quality instruction (Lachat, 1999; Laturnau, 2003). If teachers are challenged by English language learners, then it is up to school leaders to build their capacities with the necessary tools. Supporters of standards highlight their advantages for English language learners: access to challenging curricula and the raising of expectations; the use of authentic assessment tasks as evidence of what students know and can do over time; the purposeful design of instructional practices offering multiple paths to learning; additional support for learning through the use of scaffolding strategies; sustained literacy development through content-based ESL curriculum; communication with parents; the changing dynamics of classrooms from teacher-directed to learning-centered; and increased collaboration

ASCD © 2007. All Rights Reserved.

between classroom and second language teachers (Graves & Fitzgerald, 2003; Lachat 1999, 2004; Laturnau, 2001, 2003).

The preK–12 standards recently revised by Teachers of English to Speakers of Other Languages underscore this collaborative intention (TESOL, 2006). The standards do not stand alone but connect second language acquisition to academic subject areas. They provide English language learners immediate access to challenging, grade-level content and create a concrete vision of academic success by describing the language proficiencies needed to attain the same high-level standards in content areas as English-proficient students. The five standards are shown in Figure 4.

Given the expanded scope of the revised TESOL standards, states are collectively compelled to shift into a new way of thinking—a paradigm shift—so English language learners can benefit from large-scale school improvement and accountability efforts. Clearly, the standards focus not only on developing academic language proficiency but, more importantly, doing so through specific content areas. Evident are the expectations that English language learners will gain enough proficiency to carry out school tasks as competitively as their English-proficient peers and that programs will implement the methodology needed to help them do so (Garcia, 2003; Peregoy & Boyle, 2005; Young & Hadaway, 2006). Several changes in how teachers provide services, assess students, and plan instruction can help make this happen.

If the intent of the standards-based movement is to be realized and English language learners are to attain grade-level content standards, then ESL programs have to reorganize to commit to delivering grade-level curriculum in all subject areas. Traditionally, the tendency has been to group students by their language-proficiency levels. For example, ESL classes in a middle school might cluster one group of 6th, 7th, and 8th graders together as "beginners"

Figure 4.
Revised ESL Standards Emphasizing Content-Area ESL Curriculum and Instruction

PreK–12 English Language Proficiency Standards in the Core Content Areas
Standard 1: English language learners communicate for social, intercultural, and instructional purposes within the school setting.
Standard 2: English language learners communicate information, ideas, and concepts necessary for academic success in the area of **language arts.**
Standard 3: English language learners communicate information, ideas, and concepts necessary for academic success in the area of **mathematics.**
Standard 4: English language learners communicate information, ideas, and concepts necessary for academic success in the area of **science.**
Standard 5: English language learners communicate information, ideas, and concepts necessary for academic success in the area of **social studies.**

ASCD © 2007. All Rights Reserved.

and another group as "intermediates." Such groupings originated to facilitate the delivery of a language-led curriculum model—that is, a syllabus based on a hierarchy of grammatical forms and vocabulary needs. The notion of language levels has been around a very long time, and ESL teachers might find it difficult to conceive of instructing mixed-level proficiency classes. However, equally difficult—if not almost impossible—is to instruct a content-based ESL curriculum if students are not grouped by grade levels. Proficiency-grouped classes with linguistically sequenced curricula will have to defer to a grade-level and content-based curriculum model, and ESL and classroom teachers need to learn to use their respective TESOL and subject-area standards concurrently.

Many school districts rely on a commercially available or district-designed English language proficiency test as a means of identifying, placing, and exiting English language learners for support services. Most of the instruments continue to be language-based rather than content-based and therefore do not present accurate portraits of how students will function within the academic context of subject-area curriculum. English language learners may pass the screening test but are not always able to cope with the demands of the mainstream curriculum; others exit ESL programs with high scores on such tests and then struggle in unsupported classrooms. Monitoring the progress of English language learners' linguistic development and academic achievement must move beyond the once-heralded ESL proficiency test and even the practice of labeling students as either in or out of support programs if the spirit of the standards movement is to be upheld.

Standards and their respective grade-level expectations are inherently organized as a developmental language continuum against which data can be continuously collected to inform schools about how English language learners are doing linguistically and academically. Teachers can administer classroom-based tasks to diagnose the linguistic and academic skills of students upon their entrance to school. Subsequent performances on formative and summative assessments, as well as standardized or large-scale assessments, will provide ongoing information on students' progress toward the attainment of language and academic standards. Figure 5 provides an overview of this standards-based assessment framework with some examples.

The scenario of classroom and second language teachers collaboratively using classroom-based assessments allows English language learners to prove their capacity to live up to the same standards as their peers. When teachers explicitly delineate their expectations of quality and systematically plan instruction, English language learners can perform well on tasks, regardless of how high those expectations may be. The advantages of using performance tasks to provide evidence of standards' attainment are as follows:

✓ Students can display what they know and can do in a variety of ways within the context of classroom instruction.

✓ Language growth and academic achievement are profiled over time in the specific contexts.

✓ Developmental progress is as inherent to the performance assessment as are the principles of language acquisition, learning, and instructional support.

✓ Learners are provided with opportunities and strategies for improving their

ASCD © 2007. All Rights Reserved.

Figure 5.

A Tool for Identifying and Monitoring ELL Linguistic Development and Academic Attainment

		Language Proficiency				Academic Achievement			
		Listening	Speaking	Reading	Writing	Language Arts	Math	Science	Social Studies
Classroom-Based Assessments	Diagnostic	listening comprehension exercises, observation checklists, anecdotal records, student interviews, running records, miscue analyses, retellings, reading logs, journals, writing samples, vocabulary and spelling records, metacognitive self-assessments, teacher-student conferences				**Language Arts:** journals, descriptions, poems, essays, logs, graphic organizers, oral presentations, conferences **Math:** word problems, diagrams, graphs, charts, self-reflections, spreadsheets **Science:** conclusions, notes, experiments, lab reports, inquiry projects, illustrations **Social Studies:** summaries, reports, opinions, comparisons, time lines, editorials, lists, logs, political cartoons, debates			
	Formative								
	Summative								
Standardized Assessments	District	rating scales; analytic, holistic, or task-based rubrics criterion- or norm-referenced tests with selected- or constructed-response item formats				rating scales; analytic, holistic, or task-based rubrics criterion- or norm-referenced tests with selected- or constructed-response item formats			
	State								
	National								

Source: From *Assessing English Language Learners: Bridges from Language Proficiency to Academic Achievement,* by M. Gottlieb, 2006, Thousand Oaks, CA: Corwin Press, and *Understanding by Design, 2nd ed.,* by G. Wiggins and J. McTighe, 2005, Alexandria, VA: Association for Supervision and Curriculum Development. Adapted with permission.

performance as they move from one level of performance quality to another.

✓ Teachers increase their capacity to instructionally coach students to these higher levels of performance.

Students can assemble portfolios of the actual evidence of their linguistic and academic growth over time, organized by specific standards and performance indicators with entries to document their attainment, and they can share them with their parents, other students, and teachers and administrators. Reflection on the extensive range of knowledge, skills, and dispositions required to succeed in an academic setting, along with the range of assessments that provide evidence of attainment, enhances appreciation for the challenges English language learners face. In putting together the portfolio, they and their teachers reflect upon learning content in a second language as well as set goals to further their language proficiency and academic achievement. Teachers' commentaries and students' self-reflections crystallize ways in which the students can continue to make progress.

The benefits of portfolios to mark the achievements of English language learners

ASCD © 2007. All Rights Reserved.

are numerous. They align mainstream and ESL curricular efforts, emphasize the metacognitive development of learners, naturally extend from real-life learning activities, focus on higher-order thinking and problem solving, openly disclose rating criteria, and nurture the potential for cultural sensitivity and the reciprocity between teacher as learner and learner as teacher. Portfolios heed the call for a responsive learning environment in which the question becomes this: How can we assess English language learners in ways that go beyond perceptions of what they can't do?

This entire process creates a concrete vision for English language learners' success if educators use the established criteria not just to appraise performance but, ultimately, to guide the instructional process. Within that vision, teachers target instructional strategies and educational resources to provide students with opportunities to achieve the identified outcomes. They generate a repertoire of instructional strategies to guide students toward performance; each assessment task requires an instructional checklist so that if one strategy doesn't work another is readily available. Classroom and ESL teachers unite best practices from their respective disciplines to design whole-class learning experiences and to support the efforts of individual English language learners, depending on their proficiency and skill levels (Hawkins, 2005). Additionally, ESL teachers offer insights into appropriate cultural and linguistic accommodations (Lachat, 2004). Any difficulties encountered by students yield to a redirection of classroom experiences to ensure that instructional conditions help them meet or approximate the expected behaviors of the

assessment tasks and, consequently, of the standards.

Traditions die hard, however, and the vision of mainstream and second language teachers working together to support English language learners' success requires new roles, responsibilities, and capacities. Collaborative sheltered immersion does not mean that ESL teachers pull aside English language learners to repeat everything the classroom teacher says and does; nor does it mean that ESL teachers function as instructional aides for classroom teachers. What it does mean is that two professionals use standards as the basis for designing evidence-based assessment tasks, feedback instruments, and instructional strategies. It is within the discussions of what students should know and be able to do, and how well they should be able to do, where a living tool kit of best practices matures. By actively engaging in explicit conversations about language development and content-area learning, classroom and ESL teachers move out of isolationist mode and into focused discussions. No other conversations about English language learners can be as important or as powerful as these.

Connecting Second Language Acquisition, Learning, and Scaffolding to Collaborative Sheltered Immersion

The vision of classroom and ESL teachers working together to include English language learners in mainstream classrooms is consistent with current views that the teaching of language and content can be integrated to boost academic achievement and that students' academic development can not be put on hold while they are learning English (Echevarria, Vogt, & Short,

ASCD © 2007. All Rights Reserved.

2000; Houk, 2005; TESOL Standards, 2006). The mainstream curriculum is an ideal resource for a focus on learning through language and about language simultaneously not only for English language learners but for all students (Gibbons, 2002). The acquisition of a second language is similar to developing literacy in a first language in that both involve growing capacity to use language in varying contexts with more abstract and complex tasks. Classrooms that are not equipped to address the second language acquisition or learning needs of English language learners are similarly neglectful of many English-proficient students (Schleppegrell & Colombi, 2002).

Seminal theories of second language acquisition, literacy, learning, and cognitive development provide instructional insights to pave the way for addressing the content-based language acquisition and literacy needs of all students. Figure 6 summarizes these theories and their instructional implications.

As the metaphor suggests, scaffolding involves the building of instructional structures to support English language learners as they advance to higher-level proficiencies, skills, concepts, and understandings. Scaffolding does not change the complexity of what is to be learned but breaks it into manageable parts for learners. Teachers face the responsibility of selecting the appropriate scaffolding strategies to help students accomplish tasks within their range of learning and in ways that move

them progressively forward. Teachers must also monitor students' transfer of developing proficiencies, skills, concepts, and understandings; otherwise, neither they nor their students will have evidence of what can be done that couldn't be done before. In the end, of course, the strength of any instructional tool can be measured only by its effect on student performance.

Scaffolding strategies run the gamut in the academic literature. Two models seem useful to begin addressing the linguistic and academic needs of English language learners: one aims to integrate language development and content instruction in sheltered-instruction programs, while the other targets the improvement of students' reading comprehension skills. Both models are summarized in Figure 7.

The context of the revised TESOL standards, along with the expanding ownership of English language learners in envisioned collaborative sheltered-immersion programs, warrants a more comprehensive model of scaffolding. A central issue for scaffolding English language learners in K–12 school settings focuses on the intersection of the development of language proficiency, literacy and content skills, and content concept and understandings. In exploring the issue, a major question arises: Which types of scaffolding strategies best support these domains? This ASCD Action Tool offers another scaffolding typology, organized around this question and along the continuum presented in Figure 8.

Figure 6.
Seminal Theories and Their Instructional Implications

Theories	Instructional Implications
Cummins (2000, 1979) distinguishes between basic interpersonal communication skills (BICS) and cognitive academic language proficiency (CALP) to describe the growing domains of language proficiency in school settings—that is, the "register of schooling."	As English language learners engage in increasingly complex tasks, they improve their language proficiency skills; in the same way, they have more potential to engage in increasingly complex tasks as their linguistic proficiency increases.
According to Krashen (1992), one condition for second language acquisition is human interaction in which learners receive comprehensible input beyond their current stage of competence. Input, intake, output, and feedback are used to describe the second language acquisition process within a cognitive psychology paradigm (Gersten & Hudelson, 2005).	English language learners require increasingly challenging instruction, but they need to be suitably supported through the instructional process. Ways to support learners include making oral and written text comprehensible, providing a low-anxiety learning environment with opportunities for practice, and coaching to higher levels of performance along the way.
Cambourne (1988) identified seven conditions to create learner engagement and guide learners toward mastery: immersion, demonstration, expectation, responsibility, use, approximation, and response. Applying these conditions to the literacy learning process is especially useful for English language learners (Houk, 2005).	English language learners need to be immersed in the oral and written discourse of content-area study in order to have authentic demonstrations of language construction and usage. Teachers need to hold high expectations for learner performance. Learners assume responsibility when they have opportunities to use and practice their developing capabilities, especially when they are free to approximate or make developmental errors. The quality and timeliness of the feedback or response they receive from more skilled or knowledgeable others is critical to their ongoing progress.
Vygotsky's (1986) zone of proximal development signals the difference between students' capacities to perform on their own and with assistance from someone else. His social constructivist view of learning lays the foundation for the gradual release of responsibility in the instructional model (Clark & Graves, 2005).	Learning is developmental and interdependent. The more abstract and cognitively challenging the curriculum, the more students require support. Ultimately, students progress from teacher- or peer-reliant learning situations to assume more responsibility for independent learning. The process is characterized by teacher modeling, guided practice, independent practice, and transfer or application.
Gibbons (2002) uses the term *scaffolding* to propose a process for ensuring comprehensibility in instructing English language learners in content areas. The process, comprising four stages, uses various strategies and approaches for lesson presentation and delivery, teacher-student interaction, and modification of texts and other instructional materials.	The teaching of English language learners can be integrated across subject areas of the curriculum through the use of pedagogically sound instructional approaches and scaffolding strategies.

ASCD © 2007. All Rights Reserved.

Figure 7.
Scaffolding Typologies

Sheltered-Instruction Scaffolds Echevarria, Vogt, & Short (2004)	Reading Comprehension Scaffolds Clark & Graves (2005)
Verbal scaffolding: Teachers use prompting, questioning, and elaboration to facilitate students' movement to higher levels of proficiency, comprehension, and thinking.	**Moment-to-moment verbal scaffolding:** The teacher's role is to ask probing questions and elaborate student responses in the course of instruction.
Procedural scaffolding: A process-oriented instructional approach going from explicit to modeling to guided to independent.	**Instructional frameworks:** Teachers foster content learning to guide and improve students' understanding and learning as they read texts.
Instructional scaffolding: Specific instructional supports (e.g., graphic organizers).	**Instructional procedures:** Reading comprehension strategies that foster students' independence and transfer.

Figure 8.
Types of Scaffolding to Support Proficiencies, Skills, Concepts, and Understandings

Language Proficiencies	Literacy/ Content Skills	Content Concepts	Content Understandings

Time-Honored ESL Scaffolds	Literacy Scaffolds	Instructional Framework Scaffolds
Second language teachers' repertoire of strategies to help English language learners access and make meaning while they acquire language.	A repertoire of instructional strategies to foster the academic literacy development of second- and first-language students alike.	A repertoire of instructional models to facilitate the development of conceptual knowledge and understandings in a linguistically diverse classroom.

ASCD © 2007. All Rights Reserved.

The Response:

Understanding and Using This ASCD Action Tool Effectively

What Is This ASCD Action Tool?

This ASCD Action Tool is a compilation of strategies that can address the expectations created by the revised TESOL standards as well as the No Child Left Behind Act. Its intent is twofold:

1. To help English language learners obtain and create meaning, increase academic literacy skills, and gain access to the concepts and understandings of core content areas.

2. To help classroom and ESL teachers work together to build their repertoire of instructional strategies for supporting English language learners in K–12 school settings.

Ultimately, the use of the strategies in this manual should be deliberate; that is, classroom and ESL teachers should collaboratively select the most appropriate strategies and then monitor their effect on the language development and academic achievement of English language learners across curriculum areas. In the interim, however, and for whatever barriers lie in the way of this collaboration, either teacher may select a strategy to use as an appropriate place to begin.

Why Use This ASCD Action Tool?

The revised TESOL standards call for new and sophisticated skills for teachers. ESL teachers, for example, are used to addressing the demands of the first

ASCD © 2007. All Rights Reserved.

standard: English language learners communicate for social, intercultural, and instructional purposes within the school setting. But they are not used to supporting English language learners across all content areas as delineated in the remaining four standards. In fact, only recently have teacher preparation courses focused on content-based ESL curriculum, reading and writing strategies in content areas for English language learners, or instructional frameworks that are intended to increase students' access to and performance in academic subject areas. Likewise, classroom teachers who are used to teaching content are unprepared to do so with English language learners. Indeed, the majority of teachers lack the training to help linguistically diverse students succeed academically (Hadaway & Young, 2005). Together, teachers' skill sets can join into an instructional model to help English language learners do what they might not otherwise be able to do.

Imagine that all mainstream teachers—not just those in certain states—were required to study ESL-related courses as a part of their preparation program. Imagine the difference if a few courses helped teachers understand the linguistic and cultural variables that affect the academic success or failure of students. Imagine the difference if a course or two focused on specific ESL strategies. Now imagine just one of those courses being taught completely in another language so that classroom teachers might empathize with just how difficult it is to endure a submersion or immersion environment. Imagine the difference it would make if afterwards teachers had to make a list of all the strategies that helped them feel safe enough to take the required risks to learn

in another language—and then were required to transfer those into their own classrooms.

Imagine, too, that all ESL teachers—not just those that have mainstream classroom experience or licensure—were required to study the concepts and understandings of specific content areas rather than just basic vocabulary or cursory facts. Imagine the difference if they had to find meaningful ways to assist English language learners to further develop those content concepts and understandings even if (or maybe most especially when) the students were absolute "beginners." Imagine the difference if they had to do that when teaching large, heterogeneously grouped classes with many learners having remedial, behavioral, or special needs. Imagine ESL teachers being required to make a definitive strategy list of ways to help each of these students solve math word problems, complete scientific investigations and lab reports, and read overwhelmingly difficult amounts and types of texts in order to prepare oral and written responses and interpretations.

Now imagine these two groups of teachers making a professional commitment to come together to use their respective expertise for the sake of including and ensuring the success of English language learners. Imagine classroom and ESL teachers being able to support one another as they face the daily challenges involved in collaborating. Imagine administrators being able to use this process as a visible model of professional development and helping classroom and ESL teachers see the invisible power of efficacy. Imagine that putting all of these necessary pieces together to scaffold successful learning experiences and instruction for English language learners was not too much to ask for.

How Should This ASCD Action Tool Be Used?

The work of collaborating to help English language learners ultimately requires classroom and ESL teachers to use the three stages of the Understanding by Design (UbD) curriculum model (Wiggins & McTighe, 2005). The first stage requires teachers to articulate desired results of instruction—that is, exactly what English language learners need to know and be able to do academically and linguistically within classroom contexts. In the case of collaborative sheltered immersion, content teachers specify the skills, concepts, and understandings inherent to the core subject areas, while ESL teachers identify the linguistic functions or language skills needed to communicate information, ideas, and concepts. In the second stage, teachers mutually determine what assessment tasks will be accepted as evidence of the specific knowledge and behaviors identified earlier. The third stage begins as classroom teachers plan learning experiences and instruction to enable students to work toward the completion of the assessment tasks, and it finishes as ESL teachers build appropriate scaffolds to support English language learners of varying proficiency levels during the learning experiences and instruction. Figure 9 applies UbD and scaffolding for English language learners.

Undoubtedly, implementing a performance-based and backward planning instructional model is a paradigm shift requiring time and energy as well a commitment to new ways of assessing and instructing. Think of it as an opportunity for English language learners to provide evidence of what they do know and can do by completing demanding tasks but not using perfect English. Think of it as an opportunity for classroom and ESL teachers to clarify what English language learners need to know and be able to do so that grading and instructional policies are consistent. Most important, think of it as an opportunity to examine and discuss beliefs and attitudes about the language acquisition and academic achievement of English language learners, and ultimately to develop a shared vision about the use of classroom assessments and instructional practices.

A place to begin, if you are feeling overwhelmed at the moment, is to identify weekly tasks that you currently use in your classroom. Pinpoint what concept students need to know and understand about the content as a result of completing the task you plan to use in your instruction. Look through the strategies in the next section of this manual and decide whether one might be useful for your content and task— specifically, a possible cooperative learning, differentiation, or coteaching strategy to employ. Either you or an ESL teacher can list the language demands of the task: What essential vocabulary is needed to grasp the concept? What oral, reading, and writing skills are required? Look through the literacy scaffolding strategies and select those that would help your students. Be sure to check the "Why use it?" section to ensure that students are practicing the skills (i.e., benchmarks or performance indicators) you want them to practice or improve. Even if you are unable to get through these sections, please do not forgo looking through the time-honored ESL scaffolds for any ideas or strategies to help you and your English language learners as you get to know one another's strengths and weaknesses.

Section three, Strategies for Working Together, offers ideas to help organize

ASCD © 2007. All Rights Reserved.

Figure 9.
Applying Understanding by Design (UbD) and Scaffolding for English Language Learners

UbD Stage I: Identify Desired Results	
What we want students to know and be able to do (conceptual knowledge, understandings, and skills required by subject areas)	*What we want students to be able to do linguistically (precise language functions or skills needed to be able to communicate ideas, information, and concepts in core subject areas)*
Content Standards: English Language Arts Mathematics Science Social Studies	**Literacy or TESOL Standards:** Listening Speaking Reading Writing
Content Benchmarks: Grade-level expectations, benchmarks, or performance indicators	**Literacy or TESOL Benchmarks:** Grade-level expectations, benchmarks, or performance indicators

UbD Stage II: Determine Acceptable Evidence
Design assessment tasks as evidence of what students know and are able to do (formative assessment = benchmarks; summative assessment = standards).
Design feedback instruments (e.g., checklists, rating scales, rubrics) to monitor students' performance levels and to plan the use of tools to boost performance levels through instructional coaching.

UbD Stage III: Plan Learning Experiences and Instruction	
Design learning experiences and instructional strategies to develop students' subject-matter skills, concepts, and understandings.	Design learning experiences and instructional strategies to facilitate language acquisition and development (i.e., target specific instructional strategies to the desired skills, benchmarks, or performance indicators so students are practicing and improving language behaviors).

UbD + ELL Stage IV: Plan Scaffolding for English Language learners		
Time-Honored Scaffolds	**Literacy Scaffolds**	**Instructional Framework Scaffolds**
ESL teachers' repertoire of tools to help English language learners make meaning for and in mainstream classrooms.	A joint repertoire of instructional strategies to foster the academic literacy development of English language learners for and in mainstream classrooms.	A joint repertoire of instructional approaches to facilitate English language learners' access to content concepts and understandings in mainstream classrooms.

movement toward a collaborative sheltered-immersion approach as follows:

1. A **Scaffolding Success for English Language Learners school or district self-assessment checklist** and a **Responsive English Language Learner Classroom rating scale** to guide school leaders and classroom teachers on determining conditions that are in place as well as those that need to be further developed for the implementation of a collaborative sheltered-immersion approach.

2. A **proposal for an expanded assessment framework tool** to monitor English language acquisition and academic achievement.

3. A **backward design teaching framework template** clarifying the roles and responsibilities of classroom and ESL teachers in the collaborative sheltered-immersion partnership; examples of task-based rubrics as tools for equitable grading of English language learners; and an example of a coplanned backward design instructional unit with an accompanying rubric.

4. A **task planner template for coteaching,** with four examples.

5. An example of a **professional development rubric** to help set expectations and outcomes for teachers involved in collaborative sheltered immersion.

References

Baker, C. (1995). *A parent's and teacher's guide to bilingualism.* Clevedon, United Kingdom: Multilingual Matters.

Barnett, J. (Ed.). (1993). *One classroom—many languages: Issues and strategies for teachers.* South Australia: Centre for Applied Linguistics, University of South Australia.

Bunch, G. C., Abram, P. L., Lotan, R. A., & Valdés, G. (2001). Beyond sheltered instruction:

Rethinking conditions for academic language development. *TESOL Journal, 10*(2/3), 28–33.

Cambourne, B. (1988). *The whole story: Natural learning and the acquisition of literacy in the classroom.* Richmond Hill, Ontario: Scholastic-TAB.

Carrasquillo, A. L., & Rodriquez, V. (2002). *Language minority students in the mainstream classroom* (2nd ed.). Clevedon, United Kingdom: Multilingual Matters.

Chamot, A. U. (2005). The cognitive academic language learning approach (CALLA): An update. In P. A. Richard-Amato, & M. A. Snow (Eds.), *Academic success for English language learners: Strategies for K–12 mainstream teachers* (pp. 87–102). White Plains, NY: Pearson Education.

Clark, K. F., & Graves, M. F. (2005). Scaffolding students' comprehension of text. *The Reading Teacher, 58*(6), 570–580.

Clegg, J. (Ed.). (1996). *Mainstreaming ESL: Case studies in integrating ESL into the mainstream curriculum.* Clevedon, United Kingdom: Multilingual Matters.

Cloud, N., Genesee, F., & Hamayan, E. (2000). *Dual language instruction: A handbook for enriched education.* Boston: Heinle & Heinle.

Collier, V. P. (1995). Promoting academic success for ESL students: Understanding second language for school. *NJTESOL/BE* (available from Bastos Book Co., P.O. Box 433, Woodside, NY 11377).

Cummins, J. (1979). Cognitive academic language proficiency, linguistic interdependence, the optimum age question and some other matters. *Working Papers on Bilingualism, 19,* 197–205.

Cummins, J. (1981). The role of primary language development in promoting educational success for language minority students. In C. F. Leyba, *Schooling and language minority students: A theoretical framework* (pp. 3–49). Los Angeles: Evaluation, Dissemination, and Assessment Center, California State University.

Cummins, J. (1994). Knowledge, power, and identity in teaching English as a second language. In F. Genesee (Ed.), *Educating second language children.* Cambridge, United Kingdom: University Press.

ASCD © 2007. All Rights Reserved.

Cummins, J. (2000). Academic language learning, transformative pedagogy, and information technology: Towards a critical balance. *TESOL Quarterly, 34*(3), 537–547.

Curtain, H., & Pesola, C. A. B. (1994). *Languages and children: Making the match.* White Plains, NY: Longman.

Echevarria, J., Vogt, M. E., & Short, D. (2000). *Making content comprehensible for English language learners: The SIOP model.* Boston: Pearson Allyn & Bacon.

Echevarria, J., Vogt, M. E., & Short, D. (2004). *Making content comprehensible for English language learners: The SIOP model* (2nd ed.). Boston, MA: Pearson Education.

Garcia, G. (2003). *English language learners: Reaching the highest level of English literacy.* Newark, DE: International Reading Association.

Gersten, B. F., & Hudelson, S. (2005). Developments in second language acquisition research and theory: From structuralism to social participation. In P. A. Richard-Amato, & M. A. Snow (Eds.), *Academic success for English language learners: Strategies for K–12 mainstream teachers.* White Plains, NY: Pearson Education.

Gibbons, P. (2002). *Scaffolding language, scaffolding learning: Teaching second language students in the mainstream classroom.* Portsmouth, NH: Heinemann.

Gottlieb, M. (2006). *Assessing English language learners: Bridges from language proficiency to academic achievement.* Thousand Oaks, CA: Corwin Press.

Graves, M. F., & Fitzgerald, J. (2003). Scaffolding reading experiences for multilingual classrooms. In G. Garcia, *English learners: Reaching the highest level of English literacy* (pp. 96–124). Newark, DE: International Reading Association.

Hadaway, N. L., & Young, T. A. (2005). Changing classrooms: Transforming instruction. In T. A. Young & N. L. Hadaway (Eds.), *Supporting the literacy development of English learners.* Newark, DE: International Reading Association.

Harklau, L. (1994). ESL vs. mainstream classes: Contrasting L2 learning environments. *TESOL Quarterly, 28,* 241–272.

Hawkins, B. (2005). Mathematics education for second language students in the mainstream classroom. In P. A. Richard-Amato & M. A. Snow (Eds.), *Academic success for English language learners: Strategies for K–12 mainstream teachers.* White Plains, NY: Pearson Education.

Houk, F. A. (2005). *Supporting English language learners: A guide for teachers and administrators.* Portsmouth, NH: Heinemann.

Kagan, S. (1989). *Cooperative learning: Resources for teachers.* San Juan Capistrano, CA: Resources for Teachers.

Krashen, S. D. (1992). *The input hypothesis: Issues and implications.* NY: Longman.

Lachat, M. A. (1999). *Standards, equity, and cultural diversity.* Providence, RI: Northeast and Islands Regional Educational Laboratory at Brown University.

Lachat, M. A. (2004). *Standards-based instruction and assessment for English language learners.* Thousand Oaks, CA: Corwin Press.

Laturnau, J. (2001). *Standards-based instruction for English language learners.* Honolulu, HI: Pacific Resources for Education and Learning.

Laturnau, J. (2003). Standards-based instruction for English language learners. In G. Garcia, *English language learners: Reaching the highest level of English literacy* (pp. 286–306). Newark, DE: International Reading Association.

Mehigan, K. R. (2005). The strategy toolbox: A ladder to strategic teaching. *The Reading Teacher, 58*(6), 552–566.

Office of English Language Acquisition. (2002). *English language learners and the U.S. census 1990–2000.* National Clearinghouse for English Language Acquisition and Language Instruction Educational Programs. Available online: www.ncela.gwu.edu/policy/states/ellcensus90s/pdf.

Peregoy, S., & Boyle, O. (2005). *Reading, writing, and learning in ESL: A resource book for K–12 teachers.* Boston: Pearson Education.

Reed, B., & Railsback, J. (2003). *Strategies and resources for mainstream teachers of English language learners.* Northeast Regional Educational Laboratory. Available online: www.nwrel.org/request/2003may

 © 2007. All Rights Reserved.

Rojas, V. P. (1999). International schools: The challenges of teaching languages overseas. *Learning Languages, 4*(2), 16–23.

Samway, K. D., & McKeon, D. (1999). *Myths and realities: Best practices for language minority students*. Portsmouth, NH: Heinemann.

Schleppegrell, M. J., & Colombi, M. C. (Eds.). (2002). *Developing advanced literacy in first and second languages: Meaning with power*. Mahwah, NJ: Lawrence Earlbaum Associates.

TESOL (Teachers of English to Speakers of Other Languages). (2006). *Revised PreK–12 English language proficiency standards in the core content areas*: *Preview for review and comment*. Available online: www.tesol.org

Tharp, R. G., Estrada, P., Stoll Dalton, S., & Yamauchi, L. A. (2000). *Teaching transformed: Achieving excellence, fairness, inclusion, and harmony*. Boulder, CO: Westview Press.

Thomas, W., & Collier, V. (2002). *School effectiveness for language minority students' long-term academic achievement*. (Final Report). Center for Research on Education, Diversity, and Excellence.

Valdés, G. (2004). Between support and marginalization: The development of academic language in linguistic minority children. *Bilingual Education and Bilingualism, 7*(2/3), 102–131.

Vygotsky, L. S. (1986). *Thought and language* (Rev. ed.). Cambridge, MA: The M. I. T. Press.

Wiggins, G., & McTighe, J. (2005). *Understanding by design* (2nd ed.). Alexandria, VA: Association for Supervision and Curriculum Development.

Young, T. A., & Hadaway, N. L. (Eds.). (2006). *Supporting the literacy development of English learners*. Newark, DE: International Reading Association.

ASCD © 2007. All Rights Reserved.

SECTION TWO

Scaffolding Strategies for
English Language Learners

Scaffolding Strategies for English Language Learners

ASCD © 2007. All Rights Reserved.

Time-Honored Scaffolds

Time-Honored Scaffolds

Frequent Questions and Concerns About English Language Learners

Time-honored ESL scaffolds—the instructional tools of the profession—offered in this section address the questions and concerns classroom teachers most frequently ask and express about English language learners. Commentaries are provided to help classroom teachers develop insights into the linguistic or cultural rationales of the scaffolding tool.

Question: How do we communicate with English language learners?

Concern: Immediate need to communicate in class.

Scaffolding Strategies

- Use many visuals, icons, and concrete classroom objects to initiate communication.
- Use gestures and facial expressions or other charade-like aids to communicate nonverbally.
- Give the students a key ring full of cards with basic phrases and questions you want them to know immediately. On one side, have the phrase written (or pictured for very young learners), and on the other side have visuals or primary language translations. Get parents, siblings, other students, or ESL teachers to help with the translations.
- At first, break questions down so that only yes/no responses are required. Use strategies like paraphrasing and pausing so students can process what is said as you progress from yes/no questions to information questions. As students gain proficiency, scaffold questioning strategies: move back and forth from display or literal to referential or metaphorical questions.
- Learn one or two phrases in students' primary languages so they know how important communicating with them is to you. Ask parents or older siblings to write a few phrases to post around your classroom. Have all students learn some of the phrases so they, too, learn the value of communication in a multilingual world.

Commentary

- An affectively comfortable environment in which students sense that people will find ways to communicate is an important variable in the second language acquisition and acculturation processes.
- Keep in mind that communication goes beyond words and that students' silence does not necessarily mean they are not trying to understand; rather, they are trying to make meaning out of what most certainly feels and sounds like chaos.
- Try to imagine what it was like or would be like to find yourself in a country where you could not communicate. What support did you or would you need: menus with pictures? bilingual resources? people who use gestures?
- If you have traveled to another country, try to recall people's responses if you tried to use a few phrases in their language. Did your efforts facilitate the exchange? Did using the new language help you feel more in control of the situation?
- Think about your own experiences with trying to communicate in another language. Were you successful? If yes, why and how? If not, why not?

ASCD © 2007. All Rights Reserved.

Question: Should we allow English language learners to use their primary languages?

Concern: Having a strategy for learning English and learning in English.

Scaffolding Strategies

- Allow the use of the primary language through bilingual dictionaries, a linguistic buddy to interpret directions and essential information when needed, and translated material. Allow students to complete academic work in the primary language if possible and when necessary.
- Partner beginning-level English language learners with students who share their language. If possible, rotate the linguistic buddies on a weekly basis. Peer teaching and tutoring with same-language partners are useful strategies to help integrate beginning English language learners socially and academically.
- If there is concern that students are overrelying on the use of their primary languages, build in some metacognitive language usage self-assessments to help students understand their own language acquisition patterns. Have students read stories of people who have written about their experiences of schooling in another language to help them reflect on language usage issues.
- Gather insights about their language acquisition by having conferences with English language learners to discuss their feelings and progress. Ask students to keep journals or checklists.
- Encourage older students to use these insights to eventually write a linguistic autobiography about their experiences. The reflective experience can be therapeutic for them and insightful for you.
- Be an advocate—not an adversary—for English language learners and their dual language and cultural development.

Commentary

- A common misconception is that the use of the primary language will interfere with or slow down the acquisition of English, yet research consistently shows that the use of the primary language is essential to the acquisition of English. The primary language (1) helps learners feel secure and comprehend what is going on while they are acquiring English, and (2) helps learners make meaning in the new context.
- Lowering the anxiety of English language learners is essential for their success. When students feel more comfortable and are more proficient in English, they will take risks to use their new language with teachers and students who speak only English. Keep in mind that it is natural for students who share a language to communicate in that language, especially when some of the students are more proficient.

Section Two

 © 2007. All Rights Reserved. 41

- English language learners will acquire language according to their own variable rates. Some may use English almost immediately upon their arrival in the classroom, while others may not use any English for what seems to be too long a time. Even as students become proficient in English, they will need to use their primary language from time to time, depending on the situation, the tasks undertaken, and a multitude of affective and cognitive factors.

- If students prefer to communicate in their primary languages, perhaps we need to probe their feelings to see what they are trying to tell us. We don't want to silence students who are not yet proficient in English by telling them not to use their own language.

- Access to primary language usage supports second language acquisition, literacy, cognitive development, and academic success. Ultimately, these goals should outweigh any ideological beliefs or personal feelings surrounding the issue of primary-language usage.

ASCD © 2007. All Rights Reserved.

Question: What strategies can we use to build background knowledge for academic success?

Concern: Need to build background knowledge, especially for topics that may be culturally new or different, or to help English language learners with limited formal schooling.

Scaffolding Strategies

- Pinpoint connections between what students may already know in their own culture or from previous schooling and what concepts and understandings you want them to learn. Enlist the help of ESL teachers, most of whom have had cross-cultural training. An Internet search can provide you with "cultural capsules"; that is, information briefs on cultural beliefs and behaviors. Finally, students and their families should be used as informants about their own cultures.
- Use visual supports such as photos, illustrations, demonstrations, and videos and instructional techniques such as brainstorming, anticipatory guides, K-W-L charts, quick writes, vocabulary previews, and text surveys to focus on information needed to develop concepts and understandings that may be culturally new or different for students.
- Use cooperative learning strategies (see the Instructional Practices area of this section of the manual) or exploratory small-group discussions to preview and develop concepts and understandings.
- Use differentiation strategies (found in the Instructional Practices area of this section of the manual) such as centers, independent studies, Web-Quests, or jigsaw expert groups to develop concepts and understandings for students.

Commentary

- Instruction that cultivates connections between what students may already know enables meaningful connections to new content. English language learners who have had formal schooling in their primary language often have the academic schemas for schooling. Preparing these students for concepts and understandings in English may simply be a matter of bridging their knowledge through activation strategies or through use of primary-language materials and strategies.
- Students who have had less formal school experience will require more support. Providing opportunities for students to work together (e.g., structured talk with more knowledgeable learners) or to interact with scaffolded instructional materials and tasks can help students develop concepts and understandings or schemas.
- Modeling and scaffolding declarative knowledge (what to learn) and procedural knowledge (how to accomplish tasks) can help underprepared students learn what and how to learn. Modeling can be done by teachers, assistants, or more knowledgeable students.

ASCD © 2007. All Rights Reserved.

Section Two

Question: What do we do if classroom materials are too difficult for English language learners?

Concern: Inappropriate materials.

Scaffolding Strategies

- Provide primary-language books in classrooms and in school libraries. Download primary-language materials from the Internet. Use the shadow reading strategy (reading primary-language materials with English-only materials either sequentially as part of the reading process or simultaneously), depending on students' skills and motivation.

- Enhance comprehension of classroom textbooks by previewing the text with students (e.g., index and table of contents), examining the format of text pages (e.g., headings and subtitles), pointing out visual elements (e.g., illustrations), and modeling how to skim and scan.

- Use picture walks and predictable charts with very young students as a previewing strategy. Many of the strategies used with emergent readers who are proficient in English will work with emergent English language learners as well (see K–2 reading strategies in the Literacy Strategies section that follows).

- Use a variety of materials including illustrated books, dictionaries, graded readers or reference materials, magazines, recorded materials, and student-developed materials as supplements with older learners.

- Use computer software, CD-ROMs, laser videodisks, satellite networks, and the Internet to help students find supportive material in English or primary languages. Bookmark Web sites on classroom topics in students' primary languages.

- Stock baskets with collections of textbooks and nonfiction materials with a range of readability levels so students can read about a study topic (not *toddler* books but books with more illustrations, graphs, and visual supports).

- Adapt or support content material through the use of resource packets, advance organizers, prepared outlines, rewrites, leveled study guides, highlighted text, tabbed sections, taped text or audiotapes, jigsaw text reading, text digests, supplementary readings, and marginal notes. Have other students complete some of these tasks for their own learning and then use their work with English language learners.

- Use differentiation strategies (found in the Instructional Practices area of this section of the manual) to assist students with material that is too difficult. For example, use the jigsaw method in a math or science class to disperse the material within a group, literature circles to have students share different literary works that are thematically related, and multiple references and materials (e.g., primary and secondary sources) in a social studies class.

ASCD © 2007. All Rights Reserved.

- Provide multiple opportunities for students to practice interacting with texts (e.g., talking to the text, sticky notes, think-alouds, pen-in-hand modeling, journey maps, and reciprocal teaching) to increase comprehension of difficult material (see reading strategies in the Literacy Strategies section that follows). The more difficult the text, the more strategies students will need to interact with or about the material.

Commentary

- Shadow-reading enables students to gain understandings in their own language to support the development of concepts and understandings. If possible, send primary-language materials home and ask parents to discuss the topics as a preview or review for instruction.
- Adapting, supplementing, and differentiating classroom material can enable English language learners to have access to content. Reading is a skill that transfers; as literate students become more proficient in English, their capacities to comprehend grade-level texts will increase.
- Students who are underprepared or unable to read in their primary language will need many of the same support strategies that struggling readers in English need. Enlist the help of ESL teachers, reading staff, and media specialists to locate materials that are more comprehensible at first.
- One of the most useful ways to help students who have a range of literacy skills (whether English-proficient students or English language learners) is to have a classroom full of multilevel and engaging materials. Overreliance on one text or one reading series does not create a rich environment for developing literacy.
- Some teachers believe that all students should be able to read the materials provided in class, while other teachers see the necessity of having a multitude of materials for different readers in class. This philosophical distinction is a literacy issue for all students (not only for English language learners) and needs to be resolved by staff and educational leaders.
- In addition to providing a supply of learner-considerate materials, teachers can use instructional strategies to support readers with difficult text. Specifically, teachers can modify materials, use differentiation strategies, or model and employ reading strategies for each stage of the reading process to manage a class of multilevel readers.
- Language acquisition is a social phenomenon and, as such, is greatly enhanced when English language learners have multiple opportunities to interact with other students in structured ways.

Question: How can we help English language learners complete basic classroom tasks?

Concern: Assisting students while holding them accountable.

Scaffolding Strategies

- Model step-by-step strategies that can be used to complete a particular task, demonstrate a process using a think-aloud protocol, and provide concrete examples of the finished task. Give explicit instructions and check for comprehension through student demonstration or retelling. This process approach to designing learning experiences is the essence of scaffolding in that it builds in opportunities for modeling, bridging, contextualizing, schema building, metacognitive development, and text re-presentation.
- Use differentiation strategies (see the Instructional Practices area of this section of the manual) to expand choices and personalize tasks and criteria for success (e.g., Think- Tac-Toe, independent studies, learning contracts, and menus).
- Collaborate with the ESL teacher to modify tasks, depending on the language proficiency levels of the students (beginner, intermediate, advanced). Incrementally challenging tasks should align with the progression of language proficiency.
- Use cooperative learning (see the Instructional Practices are of this section of the manual) to reap its benefits for heterogeneous classes. Strategically grouped students working together can accomplish more difficult tasks than students working alone.

Commentary

- If learners are unable to complete tasks independently, teachers can use any or all of the following instructional options:
  1. Scaffold or break the tasks into doable parts and then use strategies to move students through the tasks (e.g., sorting vocabulary, buddy reading, taking notes, completing an organizer).
  2. Differentiate the assignments by selecting another task as evidence of students' knowledge (e.g., an oral or visual response instead of a written response).
  3. Modify the task in some way (e.g., one paragraph instead of three).
- Modifying tasks should not be interpreted as simplifying tasks but as building scaffolding into the instructional process to support learners to complete the tasks.
- Cooperative learning differs from group work in that it is highly structured. All students have specific roles or responsibilities and are held accountable accordingly. Its benefits include increased academic achievement, improved self-esteem, active learning, social skill development, and opportunities for simultaneous language practice (i.e., more than one student practicing language at a time).

ASCD © 2007. All Rights Reserved.

Question: How can we help students understand lectures or participate in classroom discussions?

Concern: Students' difficulty attending to or using spoken language.

Scaffolding Strategies

- Repeat, rephrase, or paraphrase key concepts or directions when it is evident that students do not understand. Model, pause, clarify, check comprehension, use visuals, and have students do quick "retells" in pairs.
- Give students lecture guides or outlines so they have a structured overview of the content.
- Give students graphic organizers with key words so they can follow the discussion or lecture (see the Literacy Strategies area of this section of the manual). Use organizers that follow the cognitive pattern of the discussions or lectures—for example, concept maps for concept development, Venn diagrams for comparisons, fishbone for cause-effect, Plus-Minus-Intriguing (PMI) charts for expanded thinking, and problem-solution outlines for problem solving.
- Use SMART boards to record notes or make copies of other students' notes so that English language learners can have copies of the major points of the lecture.
- Videotape a couple of your lessons and have colleagues watch them with the sound turned off to see how much they can understand. Ask the viewers to then brainstorm ways to add at least one meaning-enhancing strategy to the discussion or lecture (e.g., key words or icons, gestures and body language, discussion notes).
- Tape record yourself and give the tape to students so they can listen and take notes at their own pace afterwards alone or with the ESL teacher.
- Make sure that lecture or discussion is not the only means for acquiring information in the class. Vary your oral language delivery modes (e.g., modeling, demonstration, visual representations).
- Use 10-2 lectures or discussions interspersed with small-group or pair interaction strategies to process information (e.g., think-pair-share). The 10 represents a small group to which you deliver information or a concept; the 2 represents a cooperative learning strategy (see the Instructional Practices area of this section of the manual) in which students can demonstrate comprehension by reviewing with a partner.
- Increase opportunities for student-student discussions and decrease "teacher talk" through cooperative learning, instructional conversation groups, discussion circles, and small-group interactions with students reporting back to the class. Provide beginning English language learners with cues and structured overviews of the discussions so they can follow along, if not participate right away.

- Use a process approach to encourage more speaking. Allow opportunities for "working talk" (classroom-based practice sessions in small groups) so students can make judgments about what is worth saying and why, and then for "rehearsed talk" (performance-based responses) so students focus on the quality of their spoken responses rather than the quantity (number of times they raise their hand to speak).
- Use random-selection strategies like selecting cards with students' names or the ticket-out-the-door strategy (i.e., students must say something before leaving).
- Provide opportunities for more speaking through real-life speaking tasks (e.g., debates for social studies, readers' theatre or author's day for language arts, small-group problem solving for math, investigative reports for science).

Commentary

- Krashen (1981) coined the term *comprehensible input* to refer to the process of making messages understandable to English language learners. Some of the characteristics of comprehensible oral input include paraphrasing, clear articulation, greater use of high-frequency vocabulary, less sarcasm and slang, and fewer idioms. Nonlinguistic aids include objects, visuals, videos, and movement.
- Cummins distinguished between context-reduced and context-embedded communication as well as cognitively demanding and cognitively less-demanding tasks that students encounter in communication.
- An example of a rich-context, less-demanding task is to follow demonstrated directions (e.g., a physical education teacher showing how to throw a ball). An example of a rich-context, more demanding task is to understand academic presentations with visual support (e.g., a geography lesson using maps and globes or a math lesson using manipulatives). An example of a context-reduced, less-demanding task is to engage in predictable discussions (e.g., answering recall questions about stories read in an elementary language arts lesson). An example of a context-reduced, more demanding task is to make a formal oral presentation independently (e.g., in a middle or high school social studies class). Using this theoretical model can help teachers identify ways to scaffold students through the provision of context and the scaffolding of cognitive demand.
- Producing utterances in another language is referred to as output and usually happens as a result of negotiation of meaning or interaction with others. One knows immediately via the feedback one receives whether or not the output was comprehensible or understood. Continued opportunities for these types of rehearsal and feedback exchanges promote language development. Interaction and negotiation of meaning between participants in small-group situations enhance the processes of second language acquisition.

ASCD © 2007. All Rights Reserved.

- It is important not to force students to speak until they are ready to. Some students will do so almost immediately, while others appear as if they are never going to. When students are ready, they will speak. This is another good time to use the scaffolding process: having students go from nodding, to yes/no responses, to pair shares, to small-group interactions, to oral presentations with a self-selected audience, to one day feeling comfortable and skillful enough to present for a whole-group audience.
- The process for oral language development follows these stages: observation, participation, practice, performance. Students need to observe spoken language, participate in initial exchanges, practice with more extended exchanges, and finally perform independently. Giving students clear criteria and examples of what class participation looks and sounds like helps set the stage.
- It is important to keep in mind that class participation in Western-style classrooms may differ from other cultural styles. Preparing for, rehearsing, and performing oral tasks should always be done in a climate of trust and advocacy.

Section Two

Question: How can we help English language learners with their vocabulary development?

Concern: Understanding of content vocabulary (i.e., concepts and understandings).

Scaffolding Strategies

- Pinpoint content-obligatory vocabulary (terms and phrases indispensable for concepts and understandings) as the focal point of vocabulary development. Identify content-support vocabulary (terms and phrases that are important for concepts and understandings). Work with the ESL teacher to devise personalized vocabulary lists for English language learners and have the students keep vocabulary journals.

- Use categorical frameworks to help students understand the difference between general and technical vocabulary. For example, post a science word wall that distinguishes between general academic vocabulary (e.g., fall to the bottom, rise to the top, stay the same) and technical vocabulary (e.g., sink, rise, remain unchanged). Use the Simon Says, Science Says strategy to have students practice the different terms, or have students use a cooperative learning strategy after they have completed related experiments. Finally, indicate to the students which terms are expected in their lab reports.

- Use vocabulary strategies that are more inductive and interactive in nature, such as open word sorts for science, definition maps for social studies, four-dimensional word study for math, and character maps and word walls for language arts (see the vocabulary strategies in the Literacy Strategies area that follows in this section of the manual).

- Plan explicit vocabulary strategies or have vocabulary-building strategies available in centers or as anchor activities (see the Literacy Strategies area that follows in this section of the manual).

- Provide glossaries and bilingual, picture, or electronic dictionaries to students.

- Gather materials (e.g., visuals and multimedia) to create a context for essential vocabulary. Post symbols or icons with labels around the room. Construct a content-based word wall with students as the unit progresses (elementary school level) or have students keep a portable word wall (middle and high school levels).

Commentary

- Content-area vocabulary falls into four categories: high-frequency words, general academic vocabulary, technical or specialized vocabulary, and low-frequency words. Teachers need to systematically analyze which types of words are needed for each kind of classroom task and make the categories explicit to learners.

ASCD © 2007. All Rights Reserved.

- Direct study of vocabulary in isolation is not effective. Vocabulary must be contextually presented and practiced. Do not give long lists of words for students to look up in dictionaries and then test them on the meanings of the words.
- The process for vocabulary instruction is best planned as "exposure to, practice with, and mastery of." The ultimate goal of vocabulary instruction is transfer; that is, students should be able to recognize meanings of words when they come across them while reading or listening, and they should be able to use an expanding vocabulary in their speaking and writing.
- Vocabulary acquisition is also a social phenomenon. Having students work together with words, terms, or phrases will have a positive effect on all students' conceptual development. Don't make the assumption that students who are English-proficient do not need vocabulary development, especially academic and technical vocabulary.
- Research continually indicates that free voluntary reading or reading extensively in a wide range of genres is essential for developing high levels of vocabulary (and reading comprehension).

Question: How can we help English language learners improve their reading and writing skills in mainstream classrooms?

Concern: Readiness levels of students' literacy skills.

Scaffolding Strategies

- Use read-alouds, shared reading, guided reading, and independent reading as an inherently scaffolded reading process for young English language learners to gradually release responsibility from teacher as reader to learner as independent reader.

- For older students also, plan the reading process as an inherently scaffolded experience. Design prereading strategies to activate background knowledge, build vocabulary, and introduce a skill-building strategy (e.g., predicting, visualizing, self-questioning, or direction setting). Model a during-reading strategy (e.g., comprehending, making connections, determining importance, or summarizing) that students can use to practice the desired reading behavior (see the reading strategies in the Literacy Strategies area that follows in this section of the manual). Have students complete an after-reading task that can assess their understandings or double as a prewriting strategy or a strategy to prepare for speaking.

- Use reading strategies that promote partner or small-group interaction (see the reading strategies in the Literacy Strategies area that follows in this section of the manual). Establish reading study groups to use specific strategies, such as talk-to-the-text, annotation, and color coding. Have the groups respond to the texts through structured conversations and focused talk.

- For beginning English language learners or more proficient ones who are struggling readers, use additional scaffolds in the form of reading strategies that provide guides, outlines, marked texts, and taped readings.

- Confer regularly with English language learners to monitor their sense of strategy usage via metacognitive self-assessments. Share the process with the ESL teacher so students see class-to-class connections.

- Use an analogous writing process for very young writers (e.g., shared writing, interactive writing, guided writing, and independent writing).

- For older students, note that the writing process is an inherently scaffolded experience because of the stages of prewriting, drafting, revising, editing, and sharing (see the writing strategies in the Literacy Strategies area that follows in this section of the manual).

- Provide writing frames for beginning English language learners or more proficient ones who are struggling writers to help them get their ideas down on paper, or allow them to draft their ideas in their primary language first.

- Provide opportunities for students to practice learning strategies to improve their literacy skills (e.g., define them, model them, embed them in reading and writing activities, and then assess their use).

ASCD © 2007. All Rights Reserved.

- Have students keep a writer's notebook to collect ideas for writing.
- Conduct minilessons to focus on the process and the qualities of good writers. Emphasize the importance of how good readers and writers think.

Commentary

- Reading programs for English language learners are similar to those for English-proficient students in that they need to be balanced. Students learn to read (i.e., they receive instruction on the major cueing systems for making meaning from print) and read to learn (i.e., they become immersed in engaging texts of all genres). In selecting texts for emergent English language learners, it is important either to go for texts that have universal cultural appeal or to build background knowledge to help scaffold the reader-to-text connection.
- Students need a process approach to literacy development to guide them through a progression of skill development, refinement, and precision.
- A critical consideration when selecting reading comprehension strategies is to match the strategy with the desired behaviors; in other words, students need to practice the behavior as a result of the strategy. Examples:
  1. Do You Hear What I Hear? for gathering information for nonfiction notebooks in a grade 1 class.
  2. Scintillating Sentences and Quizzical Quotes for understanding the use of dialogue in a grade 3 language arts class.
  3. T-Notes to scan texts for particular information in a grade 7 social studies class.
  4. Anticipation Guides to practice recognizing what is opinion in a grade 9 science class.
- A teaching strategy transforms into a learning strategy when students can independently use it to construct meaning from a text. Conscious attention to one's own learning leads to better control over what needs to be done and how it can get done.
- Students need to be exposed to how texts are constructed and used and they then need opportunities to practice constructing such texts themselves. Connecting reading experiences to speaking or writing is as important for second language acquisition as it is for first language development.
- Two kinds of writing continuums can be used to assist English language learners. One is a continuum of writing behaviors from novice to practitioner to sophisticated (i.e., using performance indicators). Teachers can select writing strategies to coach students through the continuum (coaching = explicit feedback + strategy to use).
- Another continuum establishes domains of writing starting with informal (e.g., lists or letters) and going to more formal (e.g., research reports). As students practice the different tasks, they can list the defining characteristics of each.
- Chances are many English-proficient students would benefit from literacy strategies across the curriculum.

 © 2007. All Rights Reserved.

Question: How do we help English language learners master correct grammar?

Concern: Accuracy and proficiency.

Scaffolding Strategies

- Work with the ESL teacher to plan exposure and explicit instruction in the structure of English through specific subject-area genres in the context of readers' and writers' workshops (i.e., minilessons). Expose students to grammatical features through text types. For example, narrative writing often uses the past tense, descriptive vocabulary (adjectives), and dialogue. Expository writing uses the present tense and technical vocabulary.

- Provide explicit instruction on text features and how they work. Point out how words and phrases are used. Have students discover and discuss the grammatical cues that indicate relationships such as cause and effect, comparison and contrast, and so on.

- Focus on grammatical features that might relate to a specific genre—for example, verb tenses in social studies, auxiliaries in math, verb phrases in science, and sentence structure in language arts.

- Think of instruction for accuracy as a process: expose students to text, model specific features through exemplars, guide students through the joint construction of text, and then have students practice independently for oral presentations and writing assignments. Provide feedback through the process to help students reflect on language usage and form.

- Mirror or paraphrase correct forms in oral exchanges with students; do not overtly correct students, but provide feedback by paraphrasing the form. Address written errors as part of the editing process.

Commentary

- Traditional approaches to the teaching of grammar were skill driven; that is, the emphasis was on "learning" (even mastering) grammar before "using" it. The learning involved the memorizing of facts, as if the accumulation would eventually transfer into usage. Current approaches are context driven, so that the learner develops an understanding of language structure. In other words, grammar teaching does not involve isolated grammar drills; instead, grammar is acquired in the context of actual language use.

- Grammatical instruction is a process: teachers expose students to grammatical features, design tasks so students can practice usage, and then expect improved usage (not mastery) as a result of "using" the grammar. Students acquire grammar through the active construction of knowledge: they explore, hypothesize, try, verify in speaking or writing, and then internalize (i.e., complete the feedback loop).

ASCD © 2007. All Rights Reserved.

- Learners need to have models of how language is used. Every genre has a specific purpose, a particular organizational structure, and characteristic linguistic features or markers (i.e., signal words and phrases) to indicate how words are used.
- English language learners must feel free to approximate increasingly complex structures. Making mistakes is essential to the second language acquisition process. In the early stages, students will make many errors. As they progress and become more proficient, the number of errors will decline. Errors are normal and necessary if students are to experiment with extending their language use. Function and meaning precede form and accuracy.

Question: How can we assess English language learners' subject-matter knowledge without punishing them for their lack of English proficiency?

Concern: Fairness, equity, and excellence.

Scaffolding Strategies

- As the fairest way to assess English language learners, use performance assessment tasks as evidence of what they know and can do. Be clear with the criteria to be used for assessing how well students know and can do. The criteria may be in the form of checklists, rating scales, or rubrics, but they must be grounded in district standards or your expectations (i.e., they must be benchmarks or performance indicators). Provide students with exemplars (samples of student work) for each level of performance so they get a student-generated sense of the expectations.

- Throughout the instructional process, provide improvement- or solution-focused feedback by sharing the expected criteria of performance (e.g., a rubric) and then coaching learners to perform better through teacher and peer conferences that focus on specific strategies for improving performance (i.e., coaching students through the rubric). For example, if students are copying information rather than taking notes while gathering information in the library, it is probably because they do not know how to take notes. Give them some note-taking strategies to move them away from copying and toward appropriate note-taking behaviors. Some examples include Cornell Method of Note Taking, Coding Strategy, Four-Way Reporting and Recording (see the reading strategies in the Literacy Strategies area that follows in this section of the manual).

- Compile portfolios (e.g., anecdotal records, checklists, ratings scales, journals, graphic organizers, drawings, running records, clozes, projects) with ESL teachers to focus on learners' progress. Portfolios can vary in type and purpose, be useful for the instructional scaffolding process (e.g., feedback portfolios), or function as the basis for grading (e.g., accountability portfolios).

- With the ESL teacher, design a long-term, performance-based project for emergent English language learners. Build in interim checkpoints to provide feedback to students about the quality of their work. Differentiate or modify the project assessment tasks as appropriate for students' proficiency or knowledge skills.

- Whenever testing an English language learner, allow extra time for completion. Modify response options as another equity strategy (e.g., allow taped answers rather than written ones, demonstrations, and one-on-one discussions). Use more constructed-response types of test items so students can show what they know and can do.

ASCD © 2007. All Rights Reserved.

Commentary

- Some teachers do nothing different for English language learners and just let the assessment cards fall as they may. Other teachers feel compelled to make assessment requirements as easy as possible for English language learners. Neither option is viable. Teachers need to have high expectations for English language learners and then they need to design assessment and instruction experiences to enable performance as close to the expectation as possible.

- Performance assessment tasks inherently require products or performances from students and provide a sense of joint responsibility, especially when the expectation criteria are clear and the steps toward attainment are doable. In the process, learners have time and opportunity to use and practice their developing language proficiency and knowledge base in functional ways.

- Performance assessments support instruction, assist teachers to make instructional decisions, maximize the window for drawing conclusions from authentic performances, and provide teachers with evidence to monitor student progress and adjust instruction.

- Instructionally logical formative and summative assessment tasks honor the sense of assessment as a tool *for* learning and not just *of* learning. For example, students take notes, plan an outline, draft, make several revisions, and edit a research paper (all formative tasks). They then need to synthesize their ideas into a summative task, such as an oral presentation (using PowerPoint perhaps) to share with classmates.

- Learners must receive purposeful feedback from more knowledgeable others (teachers or peers). The quality of feedback must be relevant, appropriate, timely, and nonthreatening. Above all, purposeful feedback provides insights into what to do next to improve a level of performance.

- Classroom and ESL teachers, working together, design instructional scaffolds to support students along the process of completing a performance-based project. Design considerations include students' proficiency levels, the language and cognitive demands of the tasks, the extent of students' experiences and interactions with the types of tasks represented, the degree of incremental challenge, and the cultural nuances of the task.

Question: How do we grade English language learners?

Concern: Maintaining standards and respecting students.

Scaffolding Strategies

- Use standards-based performance assessments to gather evidence of what students know and can do, along with clear criteria given to students at the outset of instruction (e.g., rubrics) and well-planned instructional scaffolds for support. Weighting each criterion or each task can clarify for students what they can do to have their performance honored accordingly.
- Provide ESL teachers with the expected performance tasks and the rating criteria well before the tasks are to be completed. Together, brainstorm a list of scaffolding options to make each task more doable.
- Differentiate performance assessment tasks by providing choices as to what students can do for a grade.
- Make students a part of the of the assessment process. Nothing helps English language learners achieve more than the knowledge and evidence that their teachers are their strongest advocates.

Commentary

- Some teachers of English language learners grade students using the same system they use for all students; that is, they grade each piece of work and then average the grades at the end of the term. This traditional grading paradigm requires reflection and action within the context of a standards-based curriculum.
- On the other hand, some teachers feel guilty about grading English language learners at all, so instead they focus on effort or behavior until they feel that the students have acquired enough English.
- The increasing use of standards-based performance assessments graded according to externally established criteria allows for a more equitable way of grading, as long as teachers think of assessment and instruction as tools for enabling student learning and achievement—and plan accordingly. English language learners can achieve a level of acceptable performance if teachers provide scaffolds along their instructional path with the end target in sight.

ASCD © 2007. All Rights Reserved.

Question: How do we motivate English language learners?

Concern: Unmotivated students.

Scaffolding Strategies

- Use as many scaffolding strategies as possible to increase the sense of achievement. The more students see that they can do, the more they will want to do.
- Use an inquiry model of learning (students form questions, gather information using many sources, present their findings, and evaluate their own success of their inquiry). An inquiry model not only taps into student-generated learning but also allows for step-by-step scaffolding by teachers, who are liberated from teaching to focus on learning.
- Use active learning strategies to engage students (e.g., role-plays, simulations, songs, problem-solving activities, brain-compatible methods).
- Plan a culture study or a project in which students do research and share information about their own cultural history.

Commentary

- Krashen (1981) notes three affective variables that influence language acquisition: self-esteem, motivation, and level of anxiety. All are interrelated: the level of comfort one feels in a classroom has an effect on the level of efficacy one senses, and a student's sense of efficacy has an effect on his or her level of motivation.
- Social learning theorists indicate that students are motivated by observing others' actions and the consequences of those actions. Translated into classroom practice, this means that students need to develop an understanding of their own learning and have a sense of control over it. When students are aware of what is expected and are provided with strategies for attaining those expectations, chances are they will feel and exhibit more motivation. What we need to help English language learners understand is that they can engage and try without fear of failure.
- Critical pedagogy takes the stance that we are directly shaped by and then, in return, we shape what happens in the world. This transformative conception calls for curriculum that is grounded in the lives and experiences of students. Including students' home cultures in the classroom is important to the lives of English language learners as well as to the lives of their peers.
- Helping learners to make decisions to transform their lives begins with unconditional support.

Section Two

 © 2007. All Rights Reserved.

Question: How can we involve parents of English language learners?

Concern: Uninvolved parents.

Scaffolding Strategies

- Encourage parents to have primary-language conversations with their children each day about school events and activities. Model or send home a list of the kinds of questions parents can ask.

- Encourage parents to read books with their children. Help them find resources through the library, local bookstores, and community services.

- Explain the value of homework (and then make homework tasks valuable). Ask parents to provide a quiet space and to designate a regular time for homework. They should discuss the work in the primary language and help, if possible, or perhaps a sibling or a school-assigned tutor can help.

- Invite parents to attend orientation workshops, parent-teacher meetings, open houses, school performances (especially involving their children), seminars, and English as a second language classes for themselves (geared toward the English they need for understanding and helping their children adjust to school).

- Invite students and their parents to come to school for portfolio nights (i.e., children-led parent conferences) and family learning nights (e.g., children-led centers to share such learning activities as science experiments, story-telling, math games, and mapping-the-world-by-heart activities).

- Be sure to prepare for the kinds of barriers that might prevent parents' involvement by providing such services as translated notices, on-site interpreters, transportation, and child care.

- Encourage your school to hire a parent liaison to make home visits and calls and to provide insights into the linguistic and cultural factors that may affect parental involvement.

Commentary

- Parental involvement can have a significant effect on students' success in school, especially when it comes to literacy and cognitive development. However, teachers often ask parents to speak English to their children in an attempt to increase students' proficiency. In fact, research dictates that parents should interact with their children in the languages in which they are most dominant and comfortable. It is the nature of the parent-child interaction rather then the choice of language that develops literacy-readiness skills. Children who experience elaborated exchanges with their parents come to school with a cognitive maturity that other children may lack. As they acquire English, this level of cognitive development will transfer in English.

ASCD © 2007. All Rights Reserved.

- Parental involvement is multifaceted and reciprocal. Schools need to provide background sociocultural information and training to teachers and school staff so they can work effectively with parents and families (i.e., without being judgmental). Methods of two-way communication need to be institutionalized and not be dependent on the few persons who are bilingual. Outreach efforts need to take into account the practical barriers which may impede parental involvement. Schools need to link the curriculum to home through learning activities and scaffolds. Parents need to feel and be empowered to be a part of the decision-making process. Families with special needs must be assisted through community services (e.g., sponsoring agencies, religious institutions, and key community leaders).
- Above all, it is important to establish a climate that makes each and every parent feel welcome. This may require some self-reflection on the part of schools, especially as it pertains to the parents of English language learners.

Question: How can professional development help teachers better address the needs of English language learners?

Concern: Lack of professional knowledge or skills.

Scaffolding Strategies

- Content for professional development should adhere to the following guidelines:
  - ❑ All teachers need to understand how to systematically plan the alignment of content and language objectives (what students should know and be able to do).
  - ❑ All teachers need to develop capacities to design standards-based assessments for collecting evidence of second language acquisition and academic achievement simultaneously.
  - ❑ All teachers need to become skillful at backward design (i.e., planning instructional experiences to help students complete the assessments successfully).
  - ❑ All teachers need to increase their repertoire of scaffolding strategies on an ongoing basis.
  - ❑ Content teachers need training in second language acquisition principles as well as the social, political, linguistic, and cultural dynamics of second language education.
  - ❑ ESL teachers need training in the dispositions and methods of content areas and in the teaching of multilevel proficiency groups.
  - ❑ All teachers need training on how to collaborate and coteach.
  - ❑ All teachers need modeling, guided practice, and feedback within a climate of trust and advocacy (the same learning process that students need).

Commentary

- Professional development is most effective as a part of a clear and consistent vision of learning that is shared schoolwide. Learning-centered classrooms benefit all students, albeit for different reasons. Adequate time and resources for ongoing and purposeful professional development need to be provided.
- School leaders and teachers would do well to review possible staff development options and to make informed decisions to target professional efforts to specific needs.
- Modeling for teachers what we want them to do with students seems the most effective way to design professional development experiences.
- School leaders need to identify specific expectations and clear criteria for performance and then support teachers through the improvement or solution process. Section three of this ASCD Action Tool provides a professional development rubric to increase teachers' capacities to work collaboratively for English language learners.

ASCD © 2007. All Rights Reserved.

- Parental involvement is multifaceted and reciprocal. Schools need to provide background sociocultural information and training to teachers and school staff so they can work effectively with parents and families (i.e., without being judgmental). Methods of two-way communication need to be institutionalized and not be dependent on the few persons who are bilingual. Outreach efforts need to take into account the practical barriers which may impede parental involvement. Schools need to link the curriculum to home through learning activities and scaffolds. Parents need to feel and be empowered to be a part of the decision-making process. Families with special needs must be assisted through community services (e.g., sponsoring agencies, religious institutions, and key community leaders).
- Above all, it is important to establish a climate that makes each and every parent feel welcome. This may require some self-reflection on the part of schools, especially as it pertains to the parents of English language learners.

 © 2007. All Rights Reserved.

Question: How can professional development help teachers better address the needs of English language learners?

Concern: Lack of professional knowledge or skills.

Scaffolding Strategies

- Content for professional development should adhere to the following guidelines:
  - All teachers need to understand how to systematically plan the alignment of content and language objectives (what students should know and be able to do).
  - All teachers need to develop capacities to design standards-based assessments for collecting evidence of second language acquisition and academic achievement simultaneously.
  - All teachers need to become skillful at backward design (i.e., planning instructional experiences to help students complete the assessments successfully).
  - All teachers need to increase their repertoire of scaffolding strategies on an ongoing basis.
  - Content teachers need training in second language acquisition principles as well as the social, political, linguistic, and cultural dynamics of second language education.
  - ESL teachers need training in the dispositions and methods of content areas and in the teaching of multilevel proficiency groups.
  - All teachers need training on how to collaborate and coteach.
  - All teachers need modeling, guided practice, and feedback within a climate of trust and advocacy (the same learning process that students need).

Commentary

- Professional development is most effective as a part of a clear and consistent vision of learning that is shared schoolwide. Learning-centered classrooms benefit all students, albeit for different reasons. Adequate time and resources for ongoing and purposeful professional development need to be provided.
- School leaders and teachers would do well to review possible staff development options and to make informed decisions to target professional efforts to specific needs.
- Modeling for teachers what we want them to do with students seems the most effective way to design professional development experiences.
- School leaders need to identify specific expectations and clear criteria for performance and then support teachers through the improvement or solution process. Section three of this ASCD Action Tool provides a professional development rubric to increase teachers' capacities to work collaboratively for English language learners.

ASCD © 2007. All Rights Reserved.

References and Additional Reading

Becker, H. (2001). *Teaching ESL K–12: Views from the classroom*. Boston: Heinle & Heinle.

Clegg, J. (Ed.). (1996). *Mainstreaming ESL: Case studies in integrating ESL into the mainstream curriculum*. Clevedon, United Kingdom: Multilingual Matters.

Cloud, N., Genesee, F., & Hamayan, E. (2000). *Dual language instruction: A handbook for enriched education*. Boston: Heinle & Heinle.

Echevarria, J., Vogt, M., & Short, D. (2004). *Making content comprehensible for English language learners: The SIOP model* (2nd ed.). Boston: Pearson Allyn & Bacon.

Fay, K., & Whaley, S. (2004). *Becoming one community: Reading & writing with English language learners*. Portland, ME: Stenhouse Publishers.

Freeman, Y. S., Freeman, D. E., & Mercuri, S. P. (2002). *Closing the achievement gap: How to reach limited-formal-schooling and long-term English learners*. Portsmouth, NH: Heinemann.

Garcia, G. (2003). *English language learners: Reaching the highest level of English literacy*. Newark, DE: International Reading Association.

Gibbons, P. (2002). *Scaffolding language, scaffolding learning: Teaching second language students in the mainstream classroom*. Portsmouth, NH: Heinemann.

Gottlieb, M. (2006). *Assessing English language learners: Bridges from language proficiency to academic achievement*. Thousand Oaks, CA: Corwin Press.

Houk, F. A. (2005). *Supporting English language learners: A guide for teachers and administrators*. Portsmouth, NH: Heinemann.

Krashen, S. (1981). *Second language acquisition and second language learning*. Oxford, United Kingdom: Pergamon Press.

Lachat, M. A. (2004). *Standards-based instruction and assessment for English language learners*. Thousand Oaks, CA: Corwin Press.

Lessow-Hurley, J. (2003). *Meeting the needs of second language learners: An educator's guide*. Alexandria, VA: Association for Supervision and Curriculum Development.

McNary, S. J., Glasgow, N. A., & Hicks, C. D. (2005). *What successful teachers do in inclusive classrooms*. Thousand Oaks, CA: Corwin Press.

Papatzikou Cochran, E. (2002). *Mainstreaming: Case studies in TESOL practice series*. Alexandria, VA: TESOL Publications.

Reiss, J. (2005). *Teaching content to English language learners: Strategies for Secondary school success*. White Plains, NY: Longman.

Richard-Amato, P. A,. & Snow, M. A. (Eds.). (2005). *Academic success for English language learners: Strategies for K–12 mainstream teachers*. White Plains, NY: Longman.

Sears, C. (1998). *Second language students in mainstream classrooms*. Clevedon, United Kingdom: Multilingual Matters.

Schecter, S. R., & Cummins, J. (2003). *Multilingual education in practice: Using diversity as a resource*. Portsmouth, NH: Heinemann.

Tomlinson, C. A. (1999). *The differentiated classroom: Responding to the needs of all learners*. Alexandria, VA: Association for Supervision and Curriculum Development.

Tse, L. (2001). *"Why don't they learn English?" Separating fact from fallacy in the U.S. language debate*. New York: Teachers College Press.

Walter, T. (2004). *Teaching English language learners: The how-to handbook*. White Plains, NY: Pearson Education.

Wiggins, G., & McTighe, J. (2005). *Understanding by design* (2nd ed.). Alexandria, VA: Association for Supervision and Curriculum Development.

Young, T. A., & Hadaway, N. L. (Eds.). (2006). *Supporting the literacy development of English language learners: Increasing success in all classrooms*. Newark, DE: International Reading Association.

Section Two

Literacy Strategies

Literacy Strategies

Literacy scaffolds consist of genre-based graphic organizers and strategies to develop vocabulary, reading, and writing skills. Each tool answers three questions—What is it? Why use it? How does it work?—to demonstrate declarative, conditional, and procedural knowledge (Mehigan, 2005). Sample standards-based performance indicators are used for the "Why use it?" discussion to show not only the conditions for use but also how instructional strategies need to be aligned with performance indicators so students practice the desired behaviors. Variations are provided for the needs of emergent (beginning) English language learners.

Section Two

ASCD   © 2007. All Rights Reserved.

Section Two

ASCD © 2007. All Rights Reserved.

ASCD © 2007. All Rights Reserved.

Section Two

Graphic Organizers

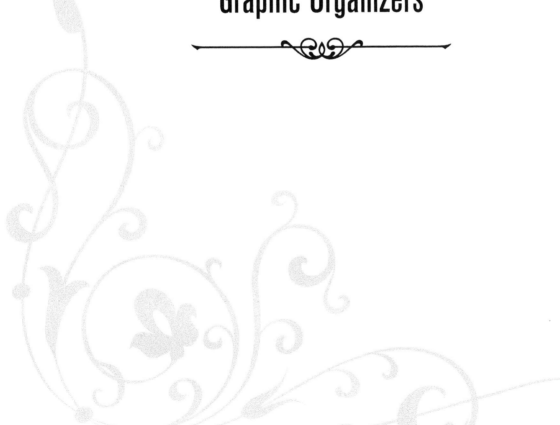

Graphic Organizers

Strategy	Language Acquisition for ELLs			Content Areas				Page
	Input (inter-pretive)	Intake (inter-personal)	Output (presenta-tional)	Language Arts	Science	Math	Social Studies	
Categorize/Classify Organizers	X	X	X	X	X	X	X	75
Compare/Contrast Organizers	X	X	X	X	X	X	X	79
Concept Development Organizers	X	X	X	X	X	X	X	83
Evaluation Organizers	X	X	X	X	X	X	X	87
Relational Organizers	X	X	X	X	X	X	X	91
Sequence Organizers	X	X	X	X	X	X	X	95

Strategies for
SUCCESS
with English Language Learners

SECTION: LITERACY STRATEGIES

GRAPHIC ORGANIZERS

Categorize/Classify Organizers

What are they?

Graphic organizers that categorize or classify ideas or information.

Why use them?

These graphic organizers can be used at any grade level and in any subject area. The examples below indicate what students may know or be able to do as a result of using graphic organizers to categorize or classify.

- *K–1 math: a right angle organizer.* Sort groups of objects by size and size order (increasing and decreasing).
- *Grade 3 science: a matrix organizer.* Organize observations of objects and events through classification and the preparation of simple charts and tables.
- *Grade 4 language arts: a categories organizer.* State a main idea and support it with details from the text.
- *Grade 5 language arts: a tree organizer.* Take notes to record and organize relevant data, facts, and ideas and use notes as part of prewriting activities.
- *Grade 5 mathematics: a plot organizer.* Plot points to form basic geometric shapes (identify and classify).
- *Grade 6 social studies: a grid organizer.* Use demographic information, mapping exercises, photographs, interviews, population graphs, church records, newspaper accounts, and other sources to conduct case studies of particular groups and classify information according to type of activity (social, political, economic, cultural, or religious).

- *Grade 7 language arts: a tree organizer.* Interpret data, facts, and ideas from informational texts by applying thinking skills such as classifying.
- *Grade 8 mathematics: a matrix organizer.* Represent numerical information in multiple ways: arithmetically, algebraically, and graphically.
- *Grade 8 science: a pyramid organizer.* Describe the flow of energy and matter through food chains or energy pyramids.
- *Grade 9 mathematics: a plot organizer.* Create a scatter plot of bivariate data.
- *Grade 10 social studies: a grid organizer.* Prepare essays and oral reports about the social, political, economic, scientific, technological, and cultural developments, issues, and events from various regions throughout history.
- *Grade 12 language arts: a right angle organizer.* Employ a range of postreading practices to think about new learning and to plan future learning.

How do they work?

Graphic organizers can be used in assessment to provide evidence of concept attainment (as in kindergarten sorting, science and mathematics examples). They can be used to support English language learners' during-reading or postreading experiences (as in social studies and language arts examples) or as prewriting tools (as in social studies and language arts examples). Students can complete these organizers through cooperative learning or as differentiation options (e.g., alternative assignments, choice boards, homework, tiered activities, writer's workshop).

Variations for Emergent English Language Learners

- Ask the ESL teacher to introduce words and phrases that signal meaning (for example; such as; to illustrate; for instance; in addition; and; again; moreover; also, too; furthermore; another; first of all; second; additionally; not only . . . but also).
- Pair ELLs with linguistic buddies or allow them to work in cooperative learning groups.
- Cue or provide some key content phrases or words with the organizers to help ELLs make meaning.

ASCD © 2007. All Rights Reserved.

Examples of Categorize/Classify Organizers

CATEGORIZE/CLASSIFY ORGANIZERS

Categories

Topic

| 1 | 2 | 3 |

Topic

1	
2	
3	

Matrix

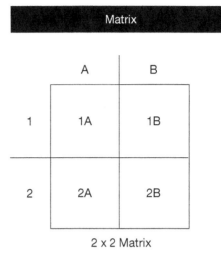

2 x 2 Matrix

Pyramid

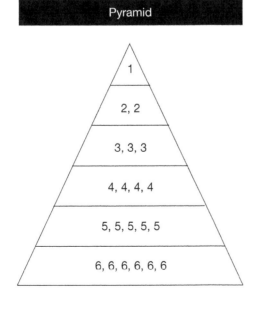

Plot

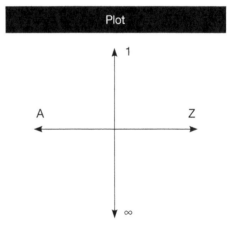

Tree

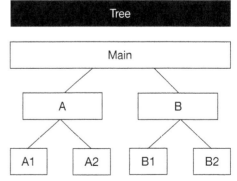

Section Two

Strategies for
SUCCESS
with English Language Learners

SECTION: LITERACY STRATEGIES

Compare/Contrast Organizers

What are they?

Graphic organizers that show how concepts or objects are alike or different.

Why use them?

These graphic organizers can be used at any grade level and in any subject area. The examples below indicate what students may know or be able to do as a result of using graphic organizers to compare or contrast.

- *K–1 language arts: a Venn diagram organizer.* Compare stories from personal experience with stories heard or read; compare characters, settings, or events in two or more stories; compare and contrast different versions of the same story.
- *K–1 mathematics: a same-different organizer.* Compare the similarities and differences of mathematical ideas.
- *Grade 2 language arts: a gathering grid organizer.* Study categories of words (e.g., transportation, sports) to learn new grade-level vocabulary.
- *Grade 4 social studies: a comparison chart organizer.* Identify and compare the physical, human, and cultural characteristics of different regions and people.
- *Grade 6 social studies: a compare/contrast information organizer.* Compare historical accounts of the same event in history; contrast the different facts included or omitted by each author; and determine the different authors' points of view.
- *Grade 6 mathematics: a Venn diagram organizer.* Construct Venn diagrams to sort data.

 © 2007. All Rights Reserved.

- *Grade 7 science: a compare/contrast chart organizer.* Compare and contrast the parts of plants, animals, and one-celled organisms.
- *Grade 7 social studies: a comparison chart organizer.* Explore the rights of citizens in other parts of the world and determine how they are similar to and different from the rights of U.S. citizens.
- *Grade 8 language arts: a compare/contrast organizer.* Compare a film, video, or stage version of a literary work with the written version.
- *Grade 10 social studies: a compare/contrast organizer.* Compare and contrast the experiences of different ethnic, national, and religious groups in the United States, explaining their contributions to U.S. society and culture.
- *Grade 11 mathematics: a Venn diagram organizer.* Use a Venn diagram to support a logical argument.

How do they work?

Compare/contrast organizers can be used as assessment tasks (as in kindergarten story comparisons or mathematical sorting), to build vocabulary (e.g., gathering grid for transportation), and to build background knowledge (as in social studies examples). The organizers can support postreading and prewriting understanding (e.g., comparing literary works with other media or comparing authors' points of view) or as visual supports for oral explanations (as in science and mathematics examples). Cooperative groups of students can complete compare/contrast organizers to provide evidence of concept attainment. The compare/contrast charts can be used as anchor activities or for homework assignments. (See the differentiation tools in the Instructional Practices area of this section of the manual.)

Variations for Emergent English Language Learners

- Ask the ESL teacher to introduce key words and phrases that signal comparison or contrast (however; but; as well as; on the other hand; while; although; different from; less than, fewer than; also, too; like; though; much as; yet; similarly; similar to; whereas; as opposed to). When appropriate, draw on the cultural backgrounds of the English language learners for comparison purposes (e.g., stories or information). Group students into trios and assign the roles of identifying "different," "different," and "same."

ASCD © 2007. All Rights Reserved.

COMPARE/CONTRAST ORGANIZERS

Section Two

Examples of Compare/Contrast Organizers

Venn Diagrams

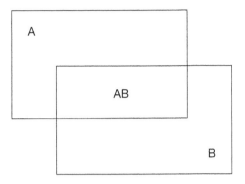

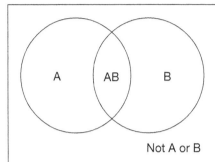

Comparison Charts

Same	Different

Item 1	Item 2	Item 1	Item 2
Compare			
Characteristic 1		Characteristic 1	
Characteristic 2		Characteristic 2	
Characteristic 3		Characteristic 3	

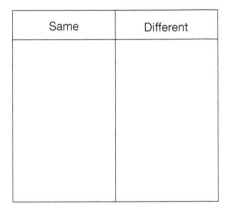

ASCD © 2007. All Rights Reserved.

COMPARE/CONTRAST ORGANIZERS

Section Two

The Gathering Grid

Category

Item 1	Item 2		Item 3	Item 4

ASCD © 2007. All Rights Reserved.

Strategies for
SUCCESS
with English Language Learners

GRAPHIC ORGANIZERS

Concept Development Organizers

What are they?

Graphic organizers that help build a knowledge base or expand on previously introduced ideas or information.

Why use them?

These graphic organizers can be used at any grade level and in any subject area. The examples below indicate what students may know or be able to do as a result of using graphic organizers to develop concepts.

- *K–1 language arts: a K-W-L chart organizer.* Engage learners in prereading and reading activities to identify what they know, want to know, and have learned about a specific story, theme, or topic.
- *K–1 mathematics: a 5W chart organizer.* Pose questions about learners and their surroundings to collect, organize, display, and analyze data.
- *Grade 3 language arts: a word web organizer.* Record significant details from informational texts.
- *Grade 4 social studies: a narrative text story mapping organizer.* Read and explore narrative accounts of important events from history to learn about different accounts of the past and begin to understand how interpretations and perspectives develop.
- *Grade 5 language arts: a narrative text story mapping organizer.* Identify literary elements such as setting, plot, and character in different genres.
- *Grade 5 social studies: an informative text thinking/writing pattern organizer.* Interpret the ideas, values, and beliefs contained in the Declaration of

Section Two

CONCEPT DEVELOPMENT ORGANIZERS

Section Two

Independence, the U.S. Constitution, the Bill of Rights, and other important historical documents.

- *Grade 6 science: a K-W-L chart organizer.* Formulate questions about natural phenomena; refine and clarify questions so that they are subject to scientific investigation.
- *Grade 7 language arts: a senses chart organizer.* Understand the purpose for writing when the purpose is to describe.
- *Grade 8 science: a mind-mapping organizer.* Explain the functioning of the major human organ systems and their interactions.
- *Grade 8 social studies: an informative text thinking/writing pattern organizer.* Define basic economic concepts such as scarcity, supply and demand, markets, opportunity costs, resources, productivity, economic growth, and systems.
- *Grade 9 science: an informative text thinking/writing pattern organizer.* Describe current theories about the origin of the universe and solar system.
- *Grade 10 mathematics: a variation of the K-W-L chart organizer (K-N-S, or know-need-solve).* Use a variety of problem-solving strategies to understand new mathematical content.
- *Grade 11 language arts: a mind-mapping organizer.* Interpret multiple levels of meaning and subtleties in text.

How do they work?

Concept development organizers can be used as a pre- during-, and postreading strategy (e.g., K-W-L chart, 5W chart, or K-N-S chart). The informative text thinking/writing pattern organizer and the narrative text story mapping are postreading and prewriting tools for informational and literary text, respectively. The word web and the mind-mapping examples can be used as assessment tasks, while the senses chart example would be a useful prewriting tool for students who need vocabulary development. Concept development organizers can be used at centers or as preparation for literature circles or Socratic seminars for students who need cues for oral participation (see the differentiation tools in the Instructional Practices area of this section of the manual).

Variations for Emergent English Language Learners

- Ask the ESL teacher to introduce words and phrases that signal meaning for concepts (for example; such as; to illustrate; in addition; again; and; moreover; also, too; another; not only . . . but also). Beginning English language learners can use a 5W chart or T-chart to show what they understand. A logical sequence would be to use concept maps, then word webs, and finally mind maps to further develop concepts. The prewriting concept tools of informative text thinking and narrative text story would be excellent alternative assignments or tiered activities until English language learners begin

ASCD © 2007. All Rights Reserved.

CONCEPT DEVELOPMENT ORGANIZERS

writing (see the differentiation tools in the Instructional Practices area of this section). Some English language learners could complete these organizers in their primary language as an interim step, and classroom or community resources could translate their work.

Examples of Concept Development Organizers

The Gathering Grid

Who
What
Where
When
Why

5W Chart

Looks
Tastes
Feels
Smells
Sounds

Senses Chart

Know	Wonder	Learned

Know-Wonder-Learned Chart

Word Web

Topic

Subtopic — detail

detail

Section Two

Section Two

CONCEPT DEVELOPMENT ORGANIZERS

Concept Map

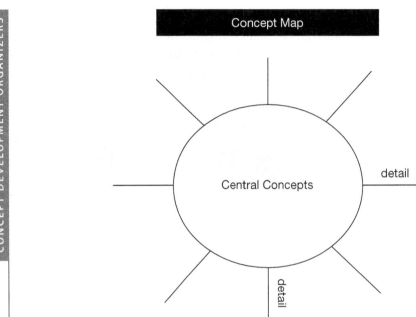

Central Concepts

detail

detail

Mind Map

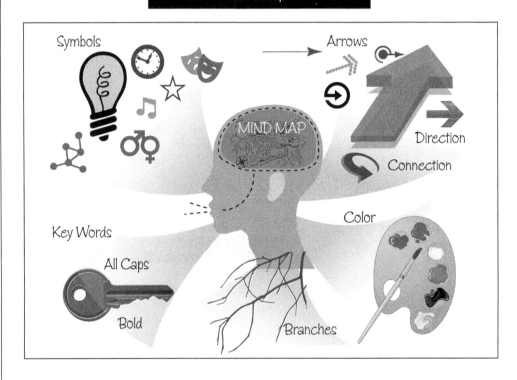

ASCD © 2007. All Rights Reserved.

Strategies for
SUCCESS
with English Language Learners

GRAPHIC ORGANIZERS

Evaluation Organizers

What are they?

Graphic organizers that help form and analyze opinions, solutions, and conclusions.

Why use them?

These graphic organizers can be used at any grade level and in any subject area. The examples below indicate what students may know or be able to do as a result of using graphic organizers to evaluate.

- *K–1 language arts: an agreement scale organizer.* Express an opinion or judgment about a story, poem, poster, or advertisement.
- *K–1 social studies: a plus/minus T-chart organizer.* Explain the probable consequences of the absence of government and rules (e.g., create a chart listing the reasons why all groups establish rules and laws).
- *Grade 2 language arts: a P-M-I organizer.* Form a personal opinion about the quality of texts read aloud on the basis of criteria such as characters and plot.
- *Grade 3 mathematics: a problem/solution organizer:* Determine whether a solution is reasonable in the context of the original problem.
- *Grade 5 social studies: a problem-solving chart organizer.* Develop conclusions about economic issues and problems by creating broad statements that summarize findings and solutions.
- *Grade 6 language arts: an agreement scale organizer.* Form an opinion on a subject on the basis of information, ideas, and themes expressed in presentations.

EVALUATION ORGANIZERS

- *Grade 6 science: a problem/solution chart organizer.* Interpret the organized data to answer the research questions or hypothesis and to gain insight into the problem.
- *Grade 7 mathematics: a decision-making flow chart organizer.* Provide a correct, complete, coherent, and clear rationale for the thought process used in problem solving.
- *Grade 7 social studies: a problem/solution organizer.* Participate in negotiation and compromise to resolve school and community disagreements and problems.
- *Grade 8 language arts: an agree/disagree chart organizer.* Evaluate the validity and accuracy of information, ideas, themes, opinions, and experiences in texts.
- *Grade 8 science: a problem-solving chart organizer.* Represent, present, and defend proposed explanations of everyday observations so others can understand and assess them.
- *Grade 10 language arts: an agree/disagree chart organizer.* Form opinions and make judgments about the validity of persuasive texts.
- *Grade 11 science: a decision-making flow chart organizer.* Carry out a research plan for testing explanations, including selecting and developing techniques, acquiring and building apparatus, and recording observations as necessary.
- *Grade 12 mathematics: a problem/solution organizer.* Determine information required to solve a problem, choose methods for obtaining the information, and define parameters for acceptable solutions.
- *Grade 12 social studies: a decision-making flow chart organizer.* Explain how economic decision making has become global as a result of an interdependent world economy.

How do they work?

Evaluation organizers engage students in higher-order thinking with the completion of open-ended tasks and are evidence of the gradual release of responsibility from teacher to students. They can be used to connect concepts to students' lives and to the lives of others in the world (see the language arts and social studies examples). They can be used to prepare students for literature circles and Socratic seminars (see the differentiation tools in the Instructional Practices area of this section) or to generate discussions (see the mathematics and science examples).

Variations for Emergent English Language Learners

- Ask the ESL teacher to introduce key words and phrases that signal problems or solutions (because; since; therefore; consequently; as a consequence; as a result; in order that; so that; then; if . . . then; thus; due to; accordingly; for this reason).
- Show ELLs how these organizers can help them express their feelings and opinions on issues that are as important to them as they are to other students.

ASCD © 2007. All Rights Reserved.

EVALUATION ORGANIZERS

Examples of Evaluation Organizers

Evaluation Charts

P	M	I
Plus	Minus	Interesting

+	−
Positive or Like or Agree	Negative or Dislike or Disagree

Scales

Agreement Scales

Agree   Disagree

Strongly Disgree	1	2	3	(4)	5	Strongly Agree

1   2   3   4   5   6   7   8   9   (10)

Needs Work   Satisfactory   Excellent

Evaluation Scale

Section Two

ASCD   © 2007. All Rights Reserved.

Strategies for
SUCCESS
with English Language Learners

GRAPHIC ORGANIZERS

Relational Organizers

What are they?

Graphic organizers that show how ideas, concepts, or various pieces of information are related to one another.

Why use them?

These graphic organizers can be used at any grade level and in any subject area. The examples below indicate what students may know or be able to do as a result of using graphic organizers to show relationships.

- *K–1 science: a fishbone organizer.* Describe the effects of common forces (pushes and pulls) of objects, such as those caused by gravity, magnetism, and mechanical forces.
- *Grade 3 mathematics: a pie chart organizer.* Represent problem situations in oral, written, concrete, pictorial, and graphical forms.
- *Grade 4 language arts: a cause/effect topic organizer.* Create a pattern to make expository writing clear and coherent.
- *Grade 5 social studies: a cause/effect organizational pattern.* Demonstrate how different experiences, beliefs, values, traditions, and motives cause individuals and groups to interpret historic events and issues from different perspectives.
- *Grade 6 mathematics: a pie chart organizer.* Determine and justify the most appropriate graph to display a given set of data (e.g., circle graph).
- *Grade 7 science: a cause/effect organizer.* Form and defend a logical argument about cause-and-effect relationships in an investigation.

 © 2007. All Rights Reserved.

Section Two

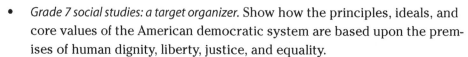

RELATIONAL ORGANIZERS

Section Two

- *Grade 7 social studies: a target organizer.* Show how the principles, ideals, and core values of the American democratic system are based upon the premises of human dignity, liberty, justice, and equality.
- *Grade 8 language arts: a cause/effect organizational pattern organizer.* Identify social and cultural contexts and other characteristics of a time period in order to enhance understanding and appreciation of text.
- *Grade 9 mathematics: a cause/effect organizational pattern organizer.* Construct various types of reasoning, arguments, justifications, and methods of proofs for problems.
- *Grade 10 science: a cause/effect organizer.* Develop and present proposals including formal hypotheses to test explanations—that is, predict what should be observed under specified conditions if an explanation is true.
- *Grade 11 social studies: a cause/effect organizational pattern organizer.* Investigate key events and developments and major turning points in world history to identify the factors that brought about change and the long-term effects of the changes.

How do they work?

The organizers can help students with concept formation (as in science, social studies, and language arts examples) or can be used as assessments of concept attainment (as in mathematics examples). They are useful as prewriting tools or as tools for preparation for oral presentations and explanations (as in language arts and social studies examples). They could also help prepare students for projects in social studies (see the differentiation tools in the Instructional Practices area of this section).

Variations for Emergent English Language Learners

- Ask the ESL teacher to introduce key words and phrases that signal cause and effect (because; since; therefore; consequently; as a consequence; as a result; in order that; so that; then; if … then; thus; due to; accordingly; for this reason).
- Show ELLs how visual representations of information can help them grasp concepts that verbal information alone might prevent.

ASCD © 2007. All Rights Reserved.

RELATIONAL ORGANIZERS

Examples of Relational Organizers

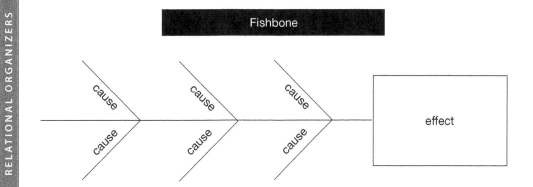

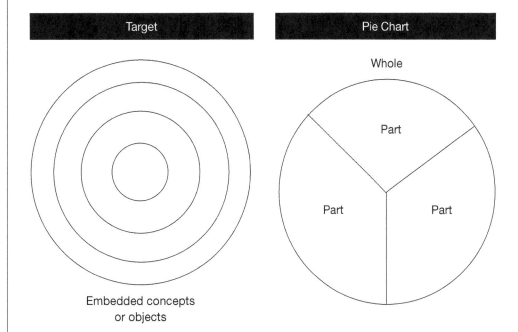

Section Two

Strategies for
SUCCESS
with English Language Learners

GRAPHIC ORGANIZERS

Sequence Organizers

What are they?

Graphic organizers that show chronological order.

Why use them?

These graphic organizers can be used at any grade level and in any subject area. The examples below indicate what students may know or be able to do as a result of using graphic organizers to show sequence.

- *K–1 language arts: a cartoon or picture strip organizer.* Draw or write a sequence of events in a story, or retell multiple pieces of information in sequence—for example, retell a story.
- *K–1 science: a cycle graph organizer.* Describe the major stages in the life cycles of selected plants and animals.
- *Grade 2 social studies: a time line organizer.* Develop time lines that display important events and eras from U.S. or world history.
- *Grade 5 science: a cycle graph organizer.* Explain how the atmosphere (air), hydrosphere (water), and lithosphere (land) interact, evolve, and change.
- *Grade 6 social studies: an events chain organizer.* Develop time lines by placing important events and developments in world history in their correct chronological order.
- *Grade 7 language arts: a cartoon or picture strip organizer.* Show how the author's use of language creates images or feelings.
- *Grade 8 social studies: an events chain organizer.* Trace some important historic events and developments of past civilizations.

 © 2007. All Rights Reserved.

SEQUENCE ORGANIZERS

Section Two

- *Grade 9 mathematics: a step chart organizer.* Prepare to communicate verbally and in writing a correct, complete, coherent, and clear design and explanation for the steps used in solving a problem.
- *Grade 12 social studies: an events chain organizer.* Distinguish between the past, present, and future by creating multiple-tier time lines that display important events and developments from world history across time and place.

How do they work?

Sequence organizers can be used as assessment tasks after reading (e.g., kindergarten retelling) or as a during-reading strategy (e.g., the grade 7 cartoon picture strip organizer). They can be used as tasks completed cooperatively to have evidence of concept formation (e.g., the social studies time lines and event chains or the science cycle graphs). Students can also use sequence organizers as prewriting tools or as visual displays for oral presentations (e.g., mathematics steps organizer). Sequence organizers can be used as a differentiation tool.

Variations for Emergent English Language Learners

- Ask the ESL teacher to introduce key words and phrases that signal the concept of sequence (first, second, third; in the first place; first of all; then; before; after; last; next; finally; meanwhile).
- Partner ELLs with linguistic buddies to complete the organizers.
- Use sequence organizers as a prereading strategy to build schema and background knowledge.

ASCD © 2007. All Rights Reserved.

SEQUENCE ORGANIZERS

Examples of Sequence Organizers

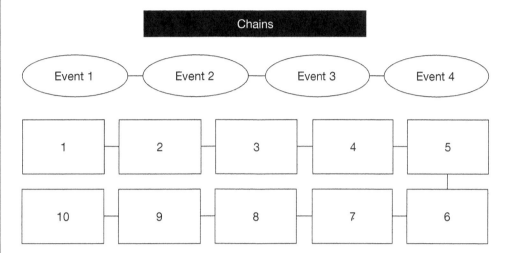

Chains

Event 1 — Event 2 — Event 3 — Event 4

| 1 | 2 | 3 | 4 | 5 |

| 10 | 9 | 8 | 7 | 6 |

Cartoon and Picture Strip

Picture 1	Picture 2	Picture 3	Picture 4	Picture 5

Step Chart

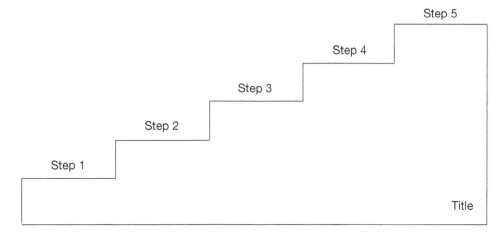

Step 5

Step 4

Step 3

Step 2

Step 1

Title

ASCD © 2007. All Rights Reserved.

Cycle Graph

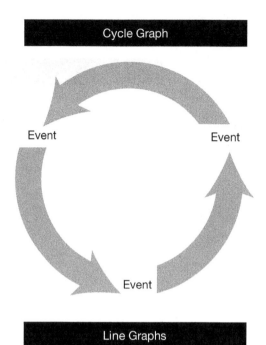

Event

Event

Event

Line Graphs

Time Line & Number Line

| 1910 | 1920 | 1930 | 1940 | 1950 | 1960 | 1970 | 1980 | 1990 | 2000 |

ASCD © 2007. All Rights Reserved.

Resources

Bellanca, J. (1990). *The cooperative think tank: Graphic organizers to teach thinking in the cooperative classroom.* Arlington Heights, IL: Skylight Training and Publishing.

Bellanca, J. (1992). *The cooperative think tank II: Graphic organizers to teach thinking in the cooperative classroom.* Arlington Heights, IL: Skylight Training and Publishing.

Billmeyer, R. (2003). *Strategies to engage the mind of the learner: Building strategic learners.* Omaha, NE: Dayspring Printing.

Kagan, S. (1998). *Smart card: Graphic organizers!* San Clemente, CA: Kagan Cooperative Learning.

Mehigan, K. (2005, March). The strategy tool box: A ladder to strategic teaching. *The Reading Teacher, 58*(6), 552–566.

Young, T. A., & Hadaway, N. L. (2006). *Supporting the literacy development of English language learners: Increasing success in all classrooms.* Newark, DE: International Reading Association.

Section Two

Vocabulary Strategies

Vocabulary Strategies

| Strategy | Language Acquisition for ELLs | | | Content Areas | | | | Grades | | Page |
	Input (Inter-pretive)	Intake (Inter personal)	Output (Presen-tational)	Lang-uage Arts	Science	Math	Social Studies	K–4	5–12	
Analogies		X	X	X	X	X	X		X	105
Character Trait Maps			X	X				X	X	107
Click and Clunk		X	X	X	X	X	X	X		109
Concept Definition Mapping		X	X	X	X	X	X		X	111
Connect Two		X	X	X	X	X	X	X		113
Contextual Redefinition	X	X		X	X	X	X	X		115
Find Someone Who		X		X	X	X	X	X	X	117
4-Square Vocabulary Approach	X			X	X	X	X	X	X	119

Strategy	Language Acquisition for ELLs			Content Areas				Grades		Page
	Input (Interpretive)	Intake (Interpersonal)	Output (Presentational)	Language Arts	Science	Math	Social Studies	K–4	5–12	
Frayer Model	X	X	X	X	X	X	X	X	X	121
Knowledge Rating Scale	X		X	X	X	X	X	X	X	123
Magnet Summaries		X	X	X	X		X	X	X	127
Missing Words	X	X		X	X		X	X		131
Open Word Sort		X		X	X	X	X	X		133
Semantic Feature Analysis	X			X	X	X	X	X	X	135
Semantic Gradient Scale		X		X	X		X	X	X	137
Simon Says, Science Says	X				X			X		139
Stephens Vocabulary Elaboration	X	X		X	X	X	X	X	X	141
10 Most Important Words	X	X		X	X	X	X	X		143
Verb Walls	X	X	X	X	X	X	X		X	145
Visual Structures	X			X	X		X	X		147
Vocab Alert!	X	X		X	X	X	X	X	X	149
Vocab Marks	X			X	X	X	X	X		151
Vocabulary Concept Chain		X	X		X		X	X	X	153
Vocabulary Graphics	X	X		X	X	X	X	X	X	155
Vocabulary Story Map	X	X		X				X	X	157
Vocabulary Writing in Math		X				X		X	X	159
Word Family Tree		X	X	X	X	X	X	X	X	161
Word of the Week			X	X	X	X	X	X		163

Section Two

ASCD © 2007. All Rights Reserved.

Strategies for SUCCESS with English Language Learners

VOCABULARY STRATEGIES

Analogies

Why use it?

Use of this strategy will help students to . . .

- Study categories of words to understand new vocabulary.
- Connect words and ideas to background knowledge.
- Recognize connections between words.
- Comprehend abstract words and phrases of grade-level content.
- Compare previously learned words by concept-based categories.
- Exchange information about academic topics.
- Understand cultural nuances of meaning.

How does it work?

The teacher selects a concept and, using a graphic organizer, models how it relates to a concept that the students recognize. Students are grouped and asked to identify categories they will compare and contrast (Stejnost & Thiese, 2006).

Variations for Emergent English Language Learners

- Ask the ESL teacher to preview or "frontload" the concepts beforehand so the students can come to class with a cue card, especially if the topic is culturally different.
- Allow a group of ELLs to do the same activity using their shared primary language.

ANALOGIES

Section Two

- Add pictures or rebuses to the two concepts so that ELLs (especially young students) have a visual context.
- Assign the role of recorder to the ELL students so they receive the "input" from their peers.
- Use a circle-seat-center strategy whereby some students are working with teacher assistance at the circle.
- Have some students work independently at their seats and others work in small-group centers so that either the classroom or ESL teacher can lead the circle as a coteaching strategy.

ASCD © 2007. All Rights Reserved.

Strategies for
SUCCESS
with English Language Learners

VOCABULARY STRATEGIES

Character Trait Maps

Why use it?

Use of this strategy will help students to . . .
- Comprehend and use descriptive vocabulary in literature.
- Participate in discussions using appropriate words and phrases.
- Rephrase ideas and thoughts to express meaning.
- Connect words and ideas in books to vocabulary usage.
- Use knowledge of key vocabulary to interpret stories.
- Use appropriate terms, vocabulary, and language for the language arts.
- Use resources to find words.

How does it work?

Words for labeling character traits are often missing in students' vocabularies. Even if the words are known, students are often unable to distinguish subtle differences in connotations. After reading a story, the class discusses the characters, and, in pairs, students try to visually verbalize the character traits. As a class again, the students compare their maps to select the words they think work best. See the example that follows (Burns, 1999).

Variations for Emergent English Language Learners

- Ask the ESL teacher to prepare students for this task by developing a sequence organizer of story events with students beforehand.
- Provide ELLs with a word bank of descriptive words to use for the character traits.

 © 2007. All Rights Reserved.

CHARACTER TRAIT MAPS

Section Two

- Use a cooperative learning strategy to build background knowledge before students complete the character trait map.
- Use the character trait map as an alternative assignment or assessment for ELLs after they observe a literature circle discussion (see the differentiation strategies in the Instructional Practices area of this section of the manual).
- Use the map as a prewriting tool to start the process of descriptive writing in a writing workshop (see the differentiation strategies in the Instructional Practices area of this section).

Example

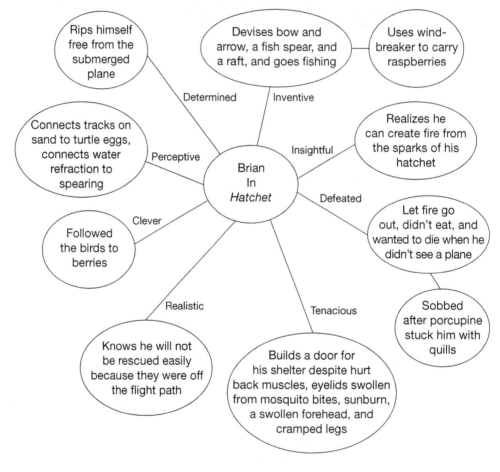

ASCD © 2007. All Rights Reserved.

Strategies for
SUCCESS
with English Language Learners

VOCABULARY STRATEGIES

Click and Clunk

Why use it?

Use of this strategy will help students to . . .

- Demonstrate comprehension of vocabulary essential for grade-level content meaning.
- Comprehend common and specific vocabulary in informational texts and literature.
- Classify previously learned words.
- Identify words in English that are similar to words found in primary language.
- Determine the meaning of unfamiliar words using context clues, dictionaries, and other classroom resources.
- Identify specific words causing comprehension difficulties.
- Use self-monitoring strategies to determine meaning of text.
- Acquire new vocabulary through reading.
- Learn the meaning of appropriate vocabulary and language for content areas.

How does it work?

Students create two columns on a paper and label them "click" and "clunk." They read a passage and then list words they understand ("click") or don't understand ("clunk") in the two columns. Direct instruction or student-led group discussions are used as follow-up to clarify meanings of the words (Sadler, 2001).

 © 2007. All Rights Reserved.

Section Two

Variations for Emergent English Language Learners

- Allow young or underprepared ELLs to use a picture dictionary.
- Have older ELLs use a bilingual dictionary.
- Point out the power of cognates (words that are similar between languages) if applicable.
- Jigsaw the material among groups of students so that each student is responsible for just a section. This will not only lessen the load of each student but will provide an information gap so that having whole-class discussion at the end will be engaging.
- Use a cooperative learning strategy as a rehearsal before the whole-class group discussion so ELLs have an opportunity to practice in small groups.

ASCD © 2007. All Rights Reserved.

Strategies for
SUCCESS
with English Language Learners

VOCABULARY STRATEGIES

Concept Definition Mapping

Why use it?

Use of this strategy will help students to . . .

*   Use and increase appropriate content-area terms, vocabulary, and language.
*   Determine the meaning of unfamiliar words by using dictionaries, glossaries, and other resources.
*   Classify words by concept-based categories.
*   Use self-monitoring strategies to clarify specific vocabulary essential to content-area comprehension.

How does it work?

This strategy teaches students the meaning of key concepts by helping them understand the essential attributes, qualities, or characteristics of a word's meaning. The teacher selects the content-obligatory words for the unit of study—that is, words that are essential to the concepts and understandings—and displays an example of a concept definition map. Another term is selected and the students brainstorm information for a map. In pairs, students work to complete a map with terms from the unit. Students write a complete definition, using the information from their maps (Schwartz, 1988).

Variations for Emergent English Language Learners

*   Allow ELLs to do concept maps in their primary language in the beginning, because first and foremost it is the concept that needs to be understood.

- Ask the ESL teacher to preteach the content-obligatory vocabulary with ELLs as part of their instructional time together.
- Have ELLs work together to complete concept maps as alternative assignments or modified assessments.
- Use the cooperative learning strategy of group-pair-individual: Students work in teams of four to brainstorm, then divide into pairs to complete the map, and finally work alone to write a complete definition.

ASCD © 2007. All Rights Reserved.

Strategies for
SUCCESS
with English Language Learners

SECTION: LITERACY STRATEGIES

VOCABULARY STRATEGIES

Connect Two

Why use it?

Use of this strategy will help students to . . .

- Study root words, prefixes, suffixes, and plural nouns to learn new vocabulary.
- Apply knowledge of word analysis to expand comprehension of vocabulary found in text.
- Comprehend and communicate using specific content-area terms, vocabulary, and language.
- Use word structure knowledge to determine meaning.
- Use self-monitoring strategies to attend to vocabulary.

How does it work?

This is a vocabulary tool that can be used as a before-, during-, or after-reading strategy. Given a list of words, students try to identify connections between any two words on the list and explain the rationale (Cloud, Genesee, & Hamayan, 2000).

Variations for Emergent English Language Learners

- Have ELLs focus on words that may look similar to words in their primary language, if applicable.
- Ask the ESL teacher to preteach the vocabulary as a prereading strategy and then have students revisit the terms as an after-reading strategy.
- Put students into pairs or trios and assign the role of "sorter" to the ELL while other students are the "explainers" or "definers."

Strategies for
SUCCESS
with English Language Learners

SECTION: LITERACY STRATEGIES

Contextual Redefinition

Why use it?

Use of this strategy will help students to . . .

- Use context to determine the meaning of words; apply knowledge of sentence and text structure to comprehend text.
- Determine the meaning of unfamiliar words using context clues, dictionaries, and other classroom resources.
- Distinguish between the dictionary meaning and the implied meaning of writers' words.
- Demonstrate comprehension and communicate essential vocabulary for grade-level content learning.
- Predict the meaning of words using background knowledge.
- Participate in discussions using appropriate words and phrases.
- Compare and contrast characteristics of words, phrases, and expressions.
- Use self-monitoring strategies to determine meaning of text.

How does it work?

This strategy provides a format for students to realize the importance of having the ability to use context clues to derive meaning. The teacher selects unfamiliar words from the text that are central to comprehending important concepts, and writes a sentence for each word on a transparency. Student groups meet to read through the sentences and try to guess a meaning for each word. The words in the original text are then provided so students can compare and verify in a dictionary if necessary. In essence, appropriate

Section Two

reading behavior is being modeled for the class (Moore, Moore, Cunningham, & Cunningham, 1998. Readence, Bean, & Baldwin, 1998).

Variations for Emergent English Language Learners

- Try to select some words that may be cognates (i.e., may be similar to words in a primary language) if applicable.
- Provide a rebus or pictures to give meaning visually.
- Provide a linguistic buddy for the group work.
- Ask the ESL teacher to preteach the words with the ELLs.
- Provide ELLs with a picture or bilingual dictionary.
- Distribute the learners' jobs so that the proficient speakers are the sentence readers or guessers and the ELLs are the verifiers.

ASCD © 2007. All Rights Reserved.

Strategies for
SUCCESS
with English Language Learners

VOCABULARY STRATEGIES

Find Someone Who

Why use it?

Use of this strategy will help students to . . .

- Demonstrate comprehension of everyday words and phrases; words that express personal, social, or school-related information; and vocabulary essential for grade-level content.
- Identify and use phrasal verbs and idiomatic expressions.
- Use appropriate vocabulary to exchange information about academic topics.
- Study categories of words to learn grade-level vocabulary; determine the meaning of words using classroom resources.
- Recognize words that are similar to words found in the primary language.
- Use self-monitoring strategies to acquire meaning of words.

How does it work?

This is an interactive tool to help students practice new vocabulary. Teachers prepare a "Find Someone Who . . ." form that looks similar to a Bingo card, putting a new vocabulary word or a defining phrase into each space. Each student is given a card to fill out as they roam around the room looking for a peer who can provide definitions or examples. Students write the name of the student and what he or she gives as the meaning of the word or the word itself, depending on the design of the card. The student who gets most of the spaces filled without using anyone twice wins (Kagan, 1992). See the example that follows.

 © 2007. All Rights Reserved.

Section Two

FIND SOMEONE WHO

Section Two

Variations for Emergent English Language Learners

- Provide visuals on the other side of the card to assist with meaning.
- Write the names of particular students so the ELLs can go directly to them.
- Ask the ESL teacher to preteach the vocabulary during their instructional time so the ELLs are prepared.

Example

Find Someone Who . . . can define and give examples of the following:			
Polygons	Quadrilaterals	Congruent triangles	Diameter
Sector of a circle	Central angle	Rhombi	Triangles

ASCD © 2007. All Rights Reserved.

Strategies for SUCCESS with English Language Learners

VOCABULARY STRATEGIES

4-Square Vocabulary Approach

Why use it?

Use of this strategy will help students to . . .

- Demonstrate comprehension of and employ vocabulary essential for grade-level content learning.
- Comprehend specific vocabulary found in informational texts and literature.
- Connect words and ideas in books to spoken language vocabulary and background knowledge.
- Use prior knowledge and experience to understand ideas and vocabulary.
- Identify multiple levels of meaning.

How does it work?

This strategy provides an interactive way to introduce key vocabulary words and helps students draw on their prior knowledge and personal experience. The strategy takes less time as students learn how to use it on their own. Students fold and number their papers into four squares. In square one, they write the key term as the teacher presents it in context and explains its definition. In square two, students write an example from personal experience that fits the term. In square three, they write a nonexample of the term. In square four, students write their own definition of the word (Stephens & Brown, 2005). See the example that follows.

4-SQUARE VOCABULARY APPROACH

Section Two

Variations for Emergent English Language Learners

- Pair up ELLs with a linguistic buddy (a student who shares the same language or a student who can assist).
- Allow ELLs to use their primary language and then have them translate later.
- Ask the ESL teacher to work with the ELLs either in class or out of class to practice the strategy.
- Use the cooperative learning strategy Circle-the-Sage so that some students are modeling for others in small groups.
- Jigsaw the vocabulary words or terms so that all students are responsible for some words and then, as a class, construct a 4-square word wall.

Example

(square 1) compromise compromised compromising	(square 2) Sometimes people have to settle things by giving up something they want. Some government delegates had to agree to give up some things they wanted to reach an agreement.
(square 3) The fighting couple could not settle their differences and so they divorced. An agreement between the two counties was not reached, and so a war was started.	(square 4) A compromise is an agreement between two or more people or groups where both must give up something.

Source: From *A Handbook of Content Literacy Strategies: 125 Practical Reading and Writing Ideas,* 2nd ed. (p. 96), by E. C. Stephens and J. E. Brown, 2005, Norwood, MA: Christopher-Gordon Publishers. Copyright 2005 by Christopher-Gordon Publishers. Reprinted with permission.

 © 2007. All Rights Reserved.

Strategies for
SUCCESS
with English Language Learners

VOCABULARY STRATEGIES

Frayer Model

Why use it?

Use of this strategy will help students to . . .

- Demonstrate comprehension and communicate specific and technical vocabulary for content-area learning.
- Classify words by content themes or concepts.
- Participate in discussions using appropriate words and phrases.
- Use appropriate vocabulary to exchange information about academic topics.
- Use resources (dictionaries, glossaries, word walls) to find meaning.
- Study categories of words to learn grade-level vocabulary.
- Work cooperatively with peers to comprehend text.
- Use prior knowledge and experience to understand ideas and vocabulary.

How does it work?

This is a word categorization tool that provides students with different ways to think about the meaning of word concepts and develop understanding of content-area vocabulary. Students form hierarchical word relationships by listing essentials, examples, nonessentials, and nonexamples of a particular word (knowing what a concept isn't can help define what it is). The teacher assigns concepts to groups and completes one with the class. Students then work in pairs to complete their concepts. They display their results so the concepts can be continuously used during the unit of study (Frayer, Frederick, & Klausmeier, 1969). See the example that follows.

Section Two

FRAYER MODEL

Section Two

Variations for Emergent English Language Learners

- Ask the ESL teacher to preteach the vocabulary words to be used.
- Pair each ELL with a linguistic buddy (a speaker of the same language or a friend).
- Provide ELLs with a picture or bilingual dictionary.
- Give ELLs terms that are culturally relevant to them.
- Use the circle (ELL with teacher) – seat (students working pairs) – center (students working in small groups) method to help students complete a task.
- Use a cooperative learning strategy for students to complete the task.

Example

Dinosaurs—Prehistoric Reptiles	
ESSENTIALS: prehistoric reptiles: backbone, lay eggs, straight legs, walk or run fast	NONESSENTIALS: cold-blooded (some may have been warm-blooded); eat meat (some eat plants): chew food, hunt in packs
EXAMPLES: brontosaurus, stegosaurus, diplodocus	NONEXAMPLES: snakes, crocodiles, turtles, lizards

ASCD © 2007. All Rights Reserved.

Strategies for
SUCCESS
with English Language Learners

VOCABULARY STRATEGIES

Knowledge Rating Scale

Why use it?

Use of this strategy will help students to . . .

- Demonstrate comprehension of and employ vocabulary essential for grade-level content learning.
- Comprehend specific vocabulary in informational texts and literature.
- Participate in discussions using appropriate vocabulary.
- Study categories of words to lean new grade-level vocabulary.
- Learn new words indirectly from reading books and other print sources.
- Learn grade-level vocabulary through a variety of means.
- Discuss the effect of vocabulary in evaluating ideas and information.
- Use appropriate terms, vocabulary, and language in content-areas.
- Identify words that determine meaning in text.
- Use self-monitoring strategies to identify vocabulary that causes comprehension difficulties.

How does it work?

The teacher prepares a matrix with the vocabulary terms listed on the vertical axis. Comments are written across the horizontal axis to elicit students' metacognitive awareness of their degree of familiarity with the words. Students place an x in the boxes that apply, share their responses in small groups, and then have a whole-class discussion. Students should revisit the terms during and after the unit to update their knowledge of the terms (Stejnost & Thiese, 2006). See the examples that follow.

ASCD © 2007. All Rights Reserved. 123

Section Two

Variations for Emergent English Language Learners

- Ask the ESL teacher to monitor ELL use of this strategy throughout the unit so that by the end of the unit students know all the words.
- Use a cooperative learning strategy to have student teams review their knowledge of the vocabulary.
- Have ELLs keep records of their knowledge rating in a journal. Hold conferences with them throughout the unit to monitor the transfer of the vocabulary from nonfamiliarity to usage.

Examples

	Knowledge Rating for Science					
Word	Have Seen or Heard	Can Say	Can Define	Can Spell	Can Use in a Sentence	Don't Know at All
diffusion	X					
permeable						X
glucose	X	X		X		
dialysis	X	X	X	X	X	
endocytosis						X
phagocytosis						X
impermeable						X
osmosis	X	X	X	X	X	

Source: From *Reading and Writing Across Content Areas,* 2nd ed. (p. 68), by R. L. Stejnost and S. M. Thiese, 2006, Thousand Oaks, CA: Corwin Press. Copyright 2006 by Sage Publications, Inc. Used by permission of Corwin Press.

ASCD © 2007. All Rights Reserved.

KNOWLEDGE RATING SCALE

Knowledge Rating for Social Studies						
Word	Have Seen or Heard	Can Say	Can Define	Can Spell	Can Use in a Sentence	Don't Know at All
oligarchy						X
anarchy	X	X	X	X	X	
democracy	X		X			
communism		X		X		
socialism						X
impeachment	X	X				
monarchy		X		X		
banishment	X					

Source: From *Reading and Writing Across Content Areas,* 2nd ed. (p. 69), by R. L. Stejnost and S. M. Thiese, 2006, Thousand Oaks, CA: Corwin Press. Copyright 2006 by Sage Publications, Inc. Used by permission of Corwin Press.

Section Two

Strategies for
SUCCESS
with English Language Learners

VOCABULARY STRATEGIES

Magnet Summaries

Why use it?

Use of this strategy will help students to . . .

- Comprehend specific vocabulary in informational text.
- Demonstrate comprehension and communicate specific, technical, and abstract words and phrases of grade-level content.
- Learn new words from books.
- Apply knowledge of basic parts of speech and sentence structure to comprehend texts.
- Connect words and ideas to spoken language and background knowledge.
- Determine the meaning of unfamiliar words and terms by using prior knowledge and context clues.
- Learn new words from reading books and other print sources.
- Work cooperatively with peers to comprehend text.
- Use effective and precise vocabulary in expository writing.
- Learn and extend new grade-level vocabulary through reading.

How does it work?

In this strategy, useful in prewriting, students identify key words—magnet words—from a reading and then use them to organize information into a summary. Students read a short portion of text, looking for key terms to which the details in the passage seem to connect. The teacher models how to write details connected to the magnet word. Students are given index cards for recording magnet words while they read the rest of the passage (younger students are instructed to identify a magnet word for each paragraph or

Section Two

MAGNET SUMMARIES

Section Two

heading). In groups, students share their words, decide on the best magnet words, and generate the details. The teacher can model for students how the information can be organized into a sentence. Students then construct sentences for their remaining cards (on scratch paper first and then on the back of the cards). Students arrange the cards in the order in which they want their summary to read (Buehl, 2001). See the example that follows.

Variations for Emergent English Language Learners

- Ask the ESL teacher to preteach the words so ELLs can have cue cards to use during group work.
- Have ELLs use their primary language to complete their magnet summaries and then work with a peer, sibling, or the ESL teacher to translate the summaries.
- Use a cooperative learning strategy that allows students to find and share words alone, decide on the best magnet words in pairs, and generate details as a team.
- Have students generate "collective" details.
- Use magnet summaries as an alternative assessment assignment or as an anchor activity.
- Use the student summaries as prewriting tools in a writing workshop (see the differentiation strategies in the Instructional Practices area of this section).

ASCD © 2007. All Rights Reserved.

Example

160 acres Farm for 5 years Congress **Homestead Act** 1862 Many went west	"Many people went west because of the **Homestead Act,** which gave 160 acres to people if they farmed them for five years."
Insects The Great Plains **Hardships** drought hot/cold weather crops failed	"In the Great Plains, people had **hardships** with the very hot and very cold weather, and their crops failed due to drought and insects."
way they plowed dug wells wheat **Dry Farming** irrigation windmills	"Farmers needed to do **dry farming,** so they dug wells, made windmills, and changed the way they plowed to grow wheat."
no trees far from each other loneliness **Homes on** dirt floors **the Prairie** sod houses "soddies"	"**Homes on the Prairie** were sod houses, called 'soddies' because they had no trees. People were lonely because the houses were far from each other."

Source: From *Classroom Strategies for Interactive Learning,* 2nd ed. (p. 81), by D. Buehl, 2001, Newark, DE: International Reading Association. Copyright 2001 by International Reading Association. Reproduced with permission.

ASCD © 2007. All Rights Reserved.

Strategies for SUCCESS with English Language Learners

SECTION: LITERACY STRATEGIES

VOCABULARY STRATEGIES

Missing Words

Why use it?

Use of this strategy will help students to . . .

- Predict the meaning of unknown words by using context.
- Use context to determine the meaning of words in text.
- Apply knowledge of sentence structure to comprehend text.
- Listen for unfamiliar words and learn their meaning.
- Identify words whose meanings are not readily understood by their context.
- Use self-monitoring strategies to determine meaning of text.
- Focus on key words or phrases that signal meaning.

How does it work?

This strategy engages students in reading a selection with certain words deleted, and then predicting in writing the missing words. It helps students learn to draw upon prior knowledge, use metacognitive skills, think inferentially, and understand relationships. The teacher selects a passage that the students haven't read and deletes certain words, leaving the beginning and ending sentences intact (the deleted words may be key vocabulary words; certain parts of speech; or words simply based on a numerical pattern, such as every seventh word). The teacher models how to skim a passage for an overview and how to read the material looking for clues. The teacher uses a think-aloud to model the metacognitive process of rereading the passage, monitoring the word choices and their effect upon the meaning of the passage (Stephens & Brown, 2005).

Section Two

MISSING WORDS

Section Two

Variations for Emergent English Language Learners

- Use only passages that ELLs have read before. Supply a word bank of the missing words.
- Have the ELLs paraphrase what other students say.
- Differentiate the reading selections and assign selections to ELLs according to level of difficulty.
- Provide picture cues in the missing spaces to give visual context.

ASCD © 2007. All Rights Reserved.

Strategies for
SUCCESS
with English Language Learners

SECTION: LITERACY STRATEGIES

VOCABULARY STRATEGIES

Open Word Sort

Why use it?

Use of this strategy will help students to . . .
- Classify previously learned words by content, themes, or concepts.
- Participate in discussions using appropriate words and phrases.
- Rephrase ideas and thoughts to express meaning.
- Study groups of words to learn new grade-level vocabulary.
- Apply knowledge of parts of speech and word structure to determine meaning of words.
- Connect words and ideas in books to spoken language vocabulary and background knowledge.
- Discuss the effect of vocabulary in explaining ideas, information, and experiences.
- Recognize multiple meanings of words and connections among words.
- Use specific vocabulary in writing.

How does it work?

This is a tool to use before, during, or after reading text. Student pairs are given words written on individual strips of paper. They collaborate to categorize the words by identifying and explaining relationships among them. Students then read and reorganize the words in a way that would be effective for teaching key information to others. Following the reading, they use their sorted words to explain the reading or answer questions (Cloud, Genesee, & Hamayan, 2000).

OPEN WORD SORT

Section Two

Variations for Emergent English Language Learners

- Assign the role of "sorter" to ELLs and the role of "explainer" to English-proficient students.
- Color-code vocabulary to give ELLs a visual cue for sorting.
- Provide picture cues or rebuses to assist ELLs with sorting.
- Ask the ESL teacher to help ELLs practice using the sorted words to explain or answer questions after reading.

ASCD © 2007. All Rights Reserved.

Strategies for
SUCCESS
with English Language Learners

SECTION: LITERACY STRATEGIES

VOCABULARY STRATEGIES

Semantic Feature Analysis

Why use it?

Use of this strategy will help students to . . .

- Classify previously learned words by content, themes, or concept-based categories.
- Demonstrate comprehension of specific terms, vocabulary, and language of grade-level content.
- Use prior knowledge and experience to understand ideas and vocabulary.
- Use self-monitoring strategies to develop vocabulary that causes comprehension difficulties.
- Identify words whose meanings are not readily understood in context.
- Focus on key words to generate and respond to questions.

How does it work?

This strategy develops vocabulary concepts and categorization skills when students find similarities and differences in related words. The teacher writes a category above a matrix, lists words or examples in the category vertically, and writes features horizontally on the matrix. Students study each feature and write a + if the word contains the feature and a – if it does not. The strategy helps students form broader vocabulary concepts and review information by comparing and contrasting words in the same category (Johnson & Pearson, 1984).

Variations for Emergent English Language Learners

- Ask the ESL teacher to preteach the vocabulary, and use the completed task as an alternative assessment for ELLs.
- Pair two ELLs together to complete the task and then have pairs switch so they can self-monitor their grid with another pair of students.
- Provide picture or bilingual dictionaries for ELL use.

ASCD   © 2007. All Rights Reserved.

Strategies for
SUCCESS
with English Language Learners

VOCABULARY STRATEGIES

Semantic Gradient Scale

Why use it?

Use of this strategy will help students to . . .

- Demonstrate comprehension and communicate using a range of vocabulary.
- Classify previously learned words by concept-based categories.
- Identify characteristics of English words and compare and contrast them with words of similar meaning in the primary language.
- Rephrase ideas and thoughts to express meaning.
- Learn how idiomatic words are used.
- Understand cultural nuances of meaning.
- Use vocabulary appropriate for different audiences and settings.
- Study antonyms and synonyms to learn new grade-level vocabulary.
- Discuss the effect of vocabulary.
- Recognize how authors use literary devices to create meaning.
- Use vocabulary to create a desired effect.

How does it work?

The scale helps students see how new words fit into patterns of words they already know. The teacher establishes the opposing terms of the semantic gradient scale. Students develop words that fit between the two poles. For example, developing words between *courageous* and *cowardly* might coordinate with a literature lesson, while a freedoms list might fit with a social studies unit (Blachowicz & Fisher, 2001). See the example that follows.

 © 2007. All Rights Reserved.

SEMANTIC GRADIENT SCALE

Section Two

Variations for Emergent English Language Learners

- Use this strategy in a vocabulary-building center (for younger learners) or as an alternative assignment or anchor activity (for older learners).
- Ask the ESL teacher to work with ELLs to complete scales.
- Provide bilingual dictionaries or English thesauruses to students.
- Use cooperative learning strategies as ways for students to share and build upon their scales.
- Construct semantic gradient scale word walls around the room.
- Have ELLs use the scales for revising written work (e.g., examining word choice in a writing workshop). See the differentiation strategies in the Instructional Practices area of this section.

Example

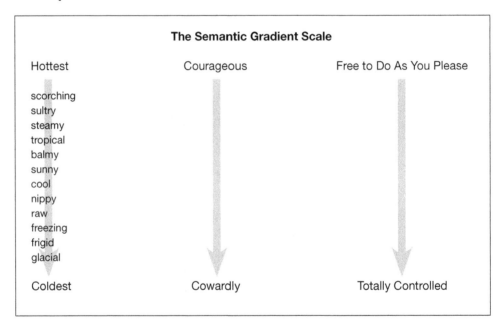

The Semantic Gradient Scale

Hottest	Courageous	Free to Do As You Please
scorching		
sultry		
steamy		
tropical		
balmy		
sunny		
cool		
nippy		
raw		
freezing		
frigid		
glacial		
Coldest	Cowardly	Totally Controlled

ASCD © 2007. All Rights Reserved.

Strategies for
SUCCESS
with English Language Learners

VOCABULARY STRATEGIES

Simon Says, Science Says

Why use it?

Use of this strategy will help students to . . .

- Demonstrate comprehension of and employ informal and formal vocabulary for content-area learning.
- Classify previously learned vocabulary by concept-based categories.
- Rephrase thoughts and ideas to express meaning.
- Use appropriate vocabulary to exchange information about academic topics.
- Learn the meaning of new words and use them in speech and writing.
- Match spoken words with physical actions.
- Use context to determine usage.
- Study categories of words to learn grade-level vocabulary.
- Use a dictionary to learn synonyms.
- Use playful language.
- Vary formality of language according to purpose.
- Use appropriate scientific terms, vocabulary, and language.

How does it work?

The teacher selects informal and formal ways of describing actions or events (e.g., "rises/floats," "falls/sinks"), then uses the game Simon Says to practice the actions with students. During science experiments, the teacher reminds the students that there is another way to describe similar events, which is how "science says" something. Words should be categorized on a word wall so

 © 2007. All Rights Reserved. 139

students can locate the formal vocabulary when they are recording data or writing lab reports.

Variations for Emergent English Language Learners

- Ask the ESL teacher to use the ESL strategy of Total Physical Response to preteach vocabulary for Simon Says.
- Provide ELLs with pictures or rebuses for the Science Says vocabulary.
- Use a cooperative learning strategy.

ASCD © 2007. All Rights Reserved.

Strategies for
SUCCESS
with English Language Learners

SECTION: LITERACY STRATEGIES

VOCABULARY STRATEGIES

Stephens Vocabulary Elaboration Strategy (SVES)

Why use it?

Use of this strategy will help students to . . .

- Demonstrate comprehension and communicate specific and technical vocabulary for content-area learning.
- Classify words by content themes or concepts.
- Participate in discussions using appropriate words and phrases.
- Use appropriate vocabulary to exchange information about academic topics.
- Use resources (dictionaries, glossaries) to find meaning.
- Study categories of words to learn grade-level vocabulary.
- Work cooperatively with peers to comprehend text.
- Use prior knowledge and experience to understand ideas and vocabulary.

How does it work?

In this strategy, students record a new word, the date they encountered it, and the context in which they found it. They propose a definition and check it against a dictionary or glossary and then provide examples and nonexamples based on their experiences. Students also record situational characteristics or elements to help them understand different meanings of the same words. They work in groups to complete a graphic organizer and share their work with other groups (Brown, Phillips, & Stephens, 1993).

 © 2007. All Rights Reserved.

Variations for Emergent English Language Learners

- Provide ESL teacher with vocabulary to preteach in preparation for group work.
- Provide picture or bilingual dictionaries to ELLs.
- Assign the role of dictionary checker to ELLs during group work.
- Use a completed graphic organizer as an alternative assignment or assessment for ELLs.

ASCD © 2007. All Rights Reserved.

Strategies for
SUCCESS
with English Language Learners

VOCABULARY STRATEGIES

10 Most Important Words

Why use it?

Use of this strategy will help students to . . .

- Demonstrate comprehension and employ vocabulary essential for grade-level content learning.
- Classify words by content or concept.
- Predict the meaning of words and ideas in informational text and literature.
- Determine the meaning of unknown words using context clues.
- Study categories of words to learn grade-level vocabulary.
- Connect words and ideas in books to spoken language vocabulary and background knowledge.
- Use appropriate terms, vocabulary, and language of grade-level content.
- Work cooperatively with peers to comprehend text.
- Use self-monitoring strategies to determine meaning of text.

How does it work?

This strategy is designed to help students become aware of the value of key concepts in developing content knowledge. It can be used as a pre- or post-unit activity. The teacher introduces a topic by helping students think about what they already know. Students are then asked to predict in pairs what they think the 10 most important words of the unit will be. Pairs share their lists with another pair, and they agree to a final list of 10. The lists are continually referred to and revised, and at the end of the unit the class reflects on which 10 were the most important after all (Stephens & Brown, 2005).

 © 2007. All Rights Reserved.

Section Two

Variations for Emergent English Language Learners

- Give ELLs a list of about 20 words beforehand that they can use in selecting their 10 most important.
- Provide pictures or rebuses with the words to give ELLs a context.
- Pair up each ELL with a linguistic buddy (a peer from the same language group or a helpful friend) for the first share.
- Hold conferences with ELLs throughout the unit to monitor their understanding of the 10 most important words.

ASCD © 2007. All Rights Reserved.

Strategies for SUCCESS with English Language Learners

VOCABULARY STRATEGIES

Verb Walls

Why use it?

Use of this strategy will help students to . . .

- Determine the meaning of unfamiliar words by using a classroom resource.
- Describe and explain phenomena using appropriate terms, vocabulary, and language from science, mathematics, technology, social studies, and literature.
- Use vocabulary to create a desired effect.
- Use precise vocabulary in writing analysis and evaluation.
- Use knowledge of structure, content, and vocabulary to understand text.
- Recognize multiple meanings of words and connections among words.
- Classify previously learned vocabulary by content.
- Rephrase ideas and thoughts to express meaning.
- Use appropriate vocabulary to exchange information about academic topics.

How does it work?

Understanding and using verbs helps students grasp the actions of a discipline. Teachers create a verb wall by posting a 50-verb list from their subject area on the wall. Teachers refer to specific verbs as they present concepts, and students use the verb wall for writing tasks in the specific subject areas.

VERB WALLS

Section Two

Variations for Emergent English Language Learners

- Ask the ESL teacher to preteach the verbs to be used for a concept.
- Provide ELLs with bilingual dictionaries.
- Have ELLs create a pictionary using the verbs as an alternative assignment or assessment.
- Have groups work together to create visual mind maps of the verbs to add to the verb wall.

ASCD © 2007. All Rights Reserved.

Strategies for
SUCCESS
with English Language Learners

SECTION: LITERACY STRATEGIES

Visual Structures

Why use it?

Use of this strategy will help students to . . .

- Comprehend common and specific vocabulary in informational texts and literature.
- Classify previously learned words by content, themes, or concepts.
- Participate in discussions using words and phrases.
- Use appropriate vocabulary to exchange information about academic topics.
- Use appropriate vocabulary for different audiences and settings.
- Apply knowledge of word analysis and text structure to expand comprehension of vocabulary found in text.
- Study categories of words to learn grade-level vocabulary.
- Learn grade-level vocabulary through a variety of means.
- Use grade-level vocabulary to communicate ideas, emotions, or experiences for different purposes.
- Learn and extend vocabulary through direct and indirect means.
- Acquire new vocabulary by reading across subjects and genres.

How does it work?

This strategy makes a clear connection between words and important concepts from a text through the use of visual structures that show the relationships explicitly. Examples include word webs or semantic mapping, word weave or matrixes, and vocabulary thermometers. Once the visual structure is created, teachers decide when to introduce it (before, during, or after reading)

VISUAL STRUCTURES

Section Two

and where to display it so students can revisit it during the unit. Later, students recategorize words into a new structure and retell the story using the structure for help, create a role-play using the vocabulary, or use the organizer for responding in writing. The organizer can also be used in a performance assessment that requires students to recreate the structure from memory (Barton, 2001).

Variations for Emergent English Language Learners

- Ask the ESL teacher to create visual structures with ELLs as a prereading strategy.
- Use cooperative learning strategies for the after-reading tasks.
- Use visual structures as alternative assignments or assessments.

ASCD © 2007. All Rights Reserved.

Strategies for SUCCESS with English Language Learners

VOCABULARY STRATEGIES

Vocab Alert!

Why use it?

Use of this strategy will help students to . . .

- Demonstrate comprehension of and employ vocabulary essential for grade-level content learning.
- Comprehend specific vocabulary in informational texts and literature.
- Participate in discussions using appropriate vocabulary.
- Study categories of words to learn new grade-level vocabulary.
- Learn new words indirectly from reading books and other print sources.
- Discuss the effect of vocabulary in evaluating ideas and information.
- Use appropriate terms, vocabulary, and language in content areas.
- Identify key words that determine meaning in text.
- Use self-monitoring strategies to identify vocabulary that causes comprehension difficulties.

How does it work?

This strategy helps make students aware of understanding important terms prior to reading or a lecture. It serves as a form of self-assessment as well. The teacher selects the most important words (about 5–10) from the text. Using a continuum, students self-assess their familiarity with each term. Then the teacher introduces the significance of the terms to the topic. As the students read or hear the text, they record information. Afterwards, the teacher engages the class in discussion to further clarify and develop understanding of the terms (Stephens & Brown, 2005). See the example that follows.

 © 2007. All Rights Reserved.

VOCAB ALERT!

Variations for Emergent English Language Learners

- Provide the ESL teacher with the list of words for use in helping ELLs record information.
- Use cooperative learning strategies to conduct the discussion.
- Have ELLs keep records of their knowledge ratings in a journal. Hold conferences with them throughout the unit to monitor their vocabulary understanding as it moves from nonfamiliarity to knowledge.

Example:

I know		It's sort of familiar		I don't know
1	2	3	4	5

List of Words:

1. embargo
    Notes: government restricts trade: see p. 356

2. treaty
    Notes: agreement between nations: see p. 359

3.

    _____

    Notes:

Source: From *A Handbook of Content Literacy Strategies: 125 Practical Reading and Writing Ideas,* 2nd ed. (p. 91), by E. C. Stephens and J. E. Brown, 2005, Norwood, MA: Christopher-Gordon Publishers. Copyright 2005 by Christopher-Gordon Publishers. Reprinted with permission.

ASCD © 2007. All Rights Reserved.

Strategies for SUCCESS with English Language Learners

VOCABULARY STRATEGIES

Vocab Marks

Why use it?

Use of this strategy will help students to . . .

- Demonstrate comprehension and communicate specific, technical, and abstract words and phrases of grade-level content.
- Use resources to find meaning of words.
- Identify specific words causing comprehension difficulties.
- Apply knowledge of context clues to determine meaning of words.
- Acquire new vocabulary by reading across subjects and genres.
- Use self-monitoring strategies to identify words that cause comprehension difficulties.

How does it work?

A vocab mark is a bookmark made from laminated paper with spaces for students to list unfamiliar words as they encounter them in their reading. The teacher models finding unfamiliar words while reading and how to record them on a vocab mark. Students make their own and begin to list new words, the page number, and a brief definition (using designated classroom resources). Some teachers structure the use of this strategy by specifying what students must look for—for example, three technical terms, two unfamiliar terms, and so on (Stephens & Brown, 2005).

© 2007. All Rights Reserved.

Section Two

VOCAB MARKS

Variations for Emergent English Language Learners

- Provide ELLs with picture or bilingual dictionaries.
- Ask the ESL teacher to locate cognates (words that are similar across languages) with ELLs as a starting point.
- Copy lists made by other students for ELLs to use.

Section Two

ASCD © 2007. All Rights Reserved.

Strategies for SUCCESS with English Language Learners

VOCABULARY STRATEGIES

Vocabulary Concept Chain

Why use it?

Use of this strategy will help students to . . .

- Demonstrate comprehension of specific technical and abstract words and phrases of grade-level academic content.
- Group previously learned words by concept-based relationships.
- Connect words and ideas to prior knowledge.
- Increase background knowledge by elaborating and integrating new vocabulary.
- Use appropriate content-area vocabulary, terms, and language.
- Work cooperatively with peers to determine meaning.
- Learn and extend grade-level vocabulary.
- Use precise vocabulary in writing.
- Analyze sentence structures that determine meaning of text in content areas.
- Identify words, phrases, and sentences that determine the meaning of text in content material.
- Focus on key words that signal the meaning of text.
- Use self-monitoring strategies to determine meaning.

How does it work?

Students study the vocabulary relating to the concept being studied. In pairs, they try to determine how the vocabulary words are related, and then organize the words into a concept chain (a circular set of words). After placing all the vocabulary words in the appropriate order, students write a relationship sentence to summarize how the chain of words expresses the meaning of the concept (Billmeyer, 2003). See the example that follows.

Variations for Emergent English Language Learners

- Give ELLs only words that have been pretaught by the ESL teacher.
- Use pictures or rebuses to provide visual clues.
- Provide ELLs with picture or bilingual dictionaries.
- Use cooperative learning strategies.
- Use the concept chain as a prewriting tool for a writing workshop (see the differentiation tools in the Instructional Practices area of this section).

Example:

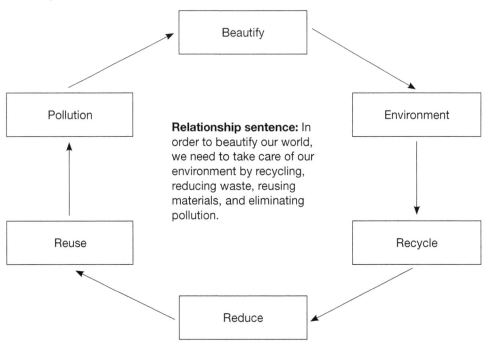

Relationship sentence: In order to beautify our world, we need to take care of our environment by recycling, reducing waste, reusing materials, and eliminating pollution.

Source: From *Strategies to Engage the Mind of the Learner: Building Strategic Learners* (p. 56), by R. Billmeyer, 2003, Omaha, NE: Rachel & Associates. Copyright 2003 by Rachel Billmeyer. Used by permission of Rachel & Associates.

ASCD © 2007. All Rights Reserved.

Strategies for
SUCCESS
with English Language Learners

VOCABULARY STRATEGIES

Vocabulary Graphics

Why use it?

Use of this strategy will help students to . . .

- Demonstrate comprehension and communicate specific, technical, and abstract words and phrases of grade-level academic content.
- Comprehend specific vocabulary in informational texts and literature.
- Rephrase thoughts and ideas to express meaning.
- Connect vocabulary and life experiences to ideas in books.
- Match pictures with words.
- Determine the meaning of unfamiliar words using context clues, dictionaries, thesauruses, and other classroom resources.
- Study antonyms and synonyms to learn new grade-level vocabulary.
- Use effective vocabulary in writing.
- Discuss the effect of vocabulary in evaluating ideas, information, and experiences.
- Apply knowledge of word analysis and sentence structures to determine meaning.
- Identify multiple levels of meaning.
- Use precise vocabulary in writing.
- Understand cultural nuances of meaning.
- Use self-monitoring strategies to determine meaning.

How does it work?

Students are given 5 x 7 index cards. As they encounter words in class, they write the teacher-given or book definition. At an appropriate point, they

 © 2007. All Rights Reserved.

Section Two

VOCABULARY GRAPHICS

Section Two

partner up to record the following information in each of the card's four corners: a sentence using the word, a synonym, an antonym, an illustration. Students build a vocabulary file with the cards to use for a designated purpose, such as writing (Stejnost & Thiese, 2006).

Variations for Emergent English Language Learners

- Allow ELLs to use the primary language as one of the options for the corners.
- Provide ELLs with a picture or bilingual dictionary.
- Use cooperative learning strategies so the ELLs are the receivers of information and their partners are the providers.
- Use the cards that students make in class in a vocabulary station. Send ELLs to that center to play the flashcard game together, in which students practice until all cards are in the "known" pile.

ASCD © 2007. All Rights Reserved.

Strategies for
SUCCESS
with English Language Learners

VOCABULARY STRATEGIES

Vocabulary Story Map

Why use it?

Use of this strategy will help students to . . .

- Comprehend specific vocabulary in literature.
- Classify words by concept-based categories.
- Participate in discussions using appropriate words and phrases.
- Rephrase ideas and thoughts to express meaning.
- Connect vocabulary and life experiences to ideas in books.
- Interpret words of characters in stories; learn new words from reading books.
- Recognize and use literary elements in speech and writing.
- Use knowledge of key vocabulary to interpret stories.
- Identify words, phrases, and sentences that determine meaning in literature.
- Acquire new vocabulary by reading literary genres.
- Recognize how authors use literary devices to create meaning.
- Distinguish between dictionary meaning and author's meaning.
- Understand cultural nuances of meaning.

How does it work?

Integrating new vocabulary with students' schema or prior experiences makes the words more accessible. For an upcoming story, the teacher maps out the story line, choosing vocabulary words that are critical to the story elements. Possible "big ideas" may not be in the story but are needed for effective discussion, and teachers and students should use the vocabulary for these ideas

 © 2007. All Rights Reserved.

Section Two

VOCABULARY STORY MAP

Section Two

multiple times in discussing, explaining, and summarizing (Beck & McKeown, 1981). See the following example.

Variations for Emergent English Language Learners

- Select stories that are universally known.
- Provide pictures or rebuses as visual clues.
- Ask the ESL teacher to preteach the strategy so ELLs can use it for a literature circle discussion.
- Have ELLs read the story in their primary language beforehand.
- Use cooperative learning strategies for students to complete story maps together.

Example:

"The Necklace" (Vocabulary Story Map)

Characters

Mathilde, who believes there is nothing more humiliating than to look poor among women who are rich.
M. Loisel, who gives his wife 400 francs for a ball gown.
She suffered ceaselessly from the ugliness of her curtains.

Setting

The vestibule of the palace
The ministerial ball
A tented garret

Problem

Mathilde loses a borrowed diamond necklace and is sick with chagrin and anguish.
M. Loisel borrows money and accepts ruinous obligations.
They are impoverished by the debt.

Possible Big Ideas

Putting on airs, humiliation, egotism, arrogance, conceit, vanity, disdain, haughtiness, destitute, indigent, irony, false pride, image, deprivation, poverty, calamity, compromised, luxuries

ASCD © 2007. All Rights Reserved.

Strategies for
SUCCESS
with English Language Learners

VOCABULARY STRATEGIES

Vocabulary Writing in Math

Why use it?

Use of this strategy will help students to . . .

- Define and use appropriate terminology related to mathematics.
- Demonstrate comprehension of and employ specific and technical vocabulary of grade-level mathematics.
- Identify words in English that are similar in meaning to words in the primary language.
- Use appropriate vocabulary to exchange information about mathematics.
- Use appropriate mathematical terms, vocabulary, and language.
- Use a picture dictionary to learn the meanings of new words.
- Match words with visual representations.
- Use classroom resources to determine meaning.
- Identify specific words causing difficulties in comprehension.
- Apply knowledge of context clues to determine meaning.
- Use prior knowledge and experience to understand ideas and vocabulary.
- Distinguish multiple meanings of words to understand mathematical usage.
- Use self-monitoring strategies to determine meaning.

How does it work?

Learning math is often equated to learning a new language due to the vocabulary-dense texts and conceptual context within which vocabulary is presented. One way to help students assimilate mathematical language is to have them create their own vocabulary journal using a structure that requires a visual representation of the meaning (Billmeyer, 2004).

Section Two

Variations for Emergent English Language Learners

- Provide students with a math glossary or a bilingual dictionary.
- Use the journal as an alternative assignment or assessment for ELLs.
- Use cooperative learning strategies to have students teach each other.
- Ask the ESL teacher to preteach the vocabulary.

ASCD © 2007. All Rights Reserved.

Strategies for
SUCCESS
with English Language Learners

VOCABULARY STRATEGIES

Word Family Tree

Why use it?

Use of this strategy will help students to . . .

- Demonstrate comprehension of and communicate specific, technical, and abstract words and phrases of grade-level academic content.
- Identify words in English that are similar to words in the primary language.
- Apply knowledge of word analysis, parts of speech, and sentence structures to determine meaning and comprehend text.
- Study root words, prefixes, suffixes, and plurals to learn new vocabulary.
- Study synonyms, antonyms, and homonyms to learn new grade-level vocabulary.
- Discuss the effect of vocabulary in evaluating ideas, information, and experiences.
- Determine the meaning of unfamiliar words by using context clues, as well as dictionaries and other classroom resources.
- Use prior knowledge and experience to understand ideas and vocabulary.
- Distinguish between dictionary meaning and implied meaning.
- Interpret multiple levels of meaning.
- Use self-monitoring strategies to determine meaning.

How does it work?

This strategy involves students in connecting a key term to its origins, to related words or words that serve a similar function, and to situations in which one might expect the word to be used. Select a group of target words for students to investigate (e.g., pivotal words in a story or unit of study, or

 © 2007. All Rights Reserved.

general high-utility vocabulary). Students work with partners or in cooperative groups to complete the organizer using appropriate resources (Buehl, 1999). See the example that follows.

Variations for Emergent English Language Learners

- Ask the ESL teacher to preteach the vocabulary.
- Provide bilingual dictionaries to ELLs.
- Assign roles to each student (e.g., ELLs could look words up in the dictionary).
- Use the trees as alternative assignments or assessments for ELLs.

Example:

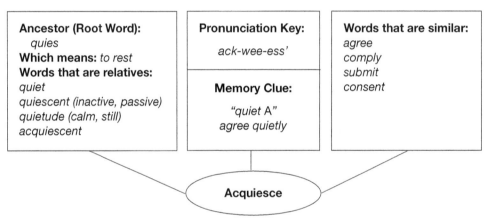

Ancestor (Root Word):
   quies
Which means: *to rest*
Words that are relatives:
quiet
quiescent (inactive, passive)
quietude (calm, still)
acquiescent

Pronunciation Key:
   ack-wee-ess'

Memory Clue:
   "quiet A"
agree quietly

Words that are similar:
agree
comply
submit
consent

Acquiesce

Definition: *to go along reluctantly, to give in maybe even if you really don't want to*

A sentence where you found this word:
*Eventually the Native Americans **acquiesced** to the treaty, even though they felt betrayed by the government.*

Who would say it? Pick three kinds of people who might say this word and write a sentence showing how they might use it:

Politician

*After a few changes to the bill, the senator **acquiesced** to vote for it.*

Judge

*The judge told the jury that every member had to **acquiesce** to reach the verdict.*

Business Person

*I will **acquiesce** to buy your computers if you guarantee that they will work for my company.*

Source: From "Word Family Trees: Heritage Sheds Insight into Words' Meaning and Use," by D. Buehl, 1999, *WEAC News & Views,* 35(2), p. 14. Copyright 1999 by Wisconsin Education Association Council. Reprinted with permission.

ASCD © 2007. All Rights Reserved.

Strategies for
SUCCESS
with English Language Learners

SECTION: LITERACY STRATEGIES

VOCABULARY STRATEGIES

Word of the Week

Why use it?

Use of this strategy will help students to . . .

- Demonstrate comprehension of and employ vocabulary that expresses personal information, school-related information, or grade-level content learning.
- Participate in discussions using appropriate words and phrases.
- Demonstrate how idiomatic expressions are used in English.
- Identify the meaning of phrasal verbs.
- Use new vocabulary to talk about life experiences.
- Determine the meaning of unfamiliar words by using dictionaries and other classroom resources.
- Apply knowledge of sentence structure to comprehend texts.
- Use descriptive, vivid, and playful language.
- Identify specific words causing comprehension difficulties.
- Discuss the effect of vocabulary in evaluating ideas, information, and experiences.
- Identify multiple levels of meaning.

How does it work?

The process of choosing new words on their own helps students to construct an ever-widening vocabulary. Students identify a new word (or idiom) that they are interested in adding to their vocabulary. They list the word, the part of speech, the definitions, and a sentence. Students use "their" word in class all week. They share their words with partners, then small groups, then the class (Stephens & Brown, 2005).

Variations for Emergent English Language Learners

- Ask the ESL teacher to select a word of the week for each ELL (a cognate if possible).
- Provide a picture or bilingual dictionary.
- Use cooperative learning strategies to share the words.

© 2007. All Rights Reserved.

References

Barton, J. (2001). *Teaching with children's literature.* Norwood, MA: Christopher-Gordon Publishers.

Beck, I., & McKeown, M. (1981). Developing questions that promote comprehension: The story map. *Language Arts, 58,* 913–918.

Billmeyer, R. (2003). *Strategies to engage the mind of the learner: Building strategic learners.* Omaha, NE: Rachel & Associates.

Billmeyer, R. (2004). *Strategic reading in the content areas: Practical applications for creating a thinking environment.* Omaha, NE: Rachel & Associates.

Blachowicz, C., & Fisher, P. (2001). *Teaching vocabulary in all classrooms* (2nd ed.). Englewood Cliffs, NJ: Prentice-Hall.

Brown, A. L., Phillips, L. B., & Stephens, E. C. (1993). *Toward literacy: Theory and applications for teaching writing in the content areas.* Belmont, CA: Wadsworth.

Buehl, D. (1999). Word family trees: Heritage sheds insight into words' meaning and use. *WEAC News & Views, 35*(2), 14.

Buehl, D. (2001). *Classroom strategies for interactive learning* (2nd ed.). Newark, DE: International Reading Association.

Burns, B. (1999). *How to teach balanced reading and writing.* Thousand Oaks, CA: Corwin Press.

Cloud, N., Genesee, F., & Hamayan, E. (2000). *Dual language instruction: A handbook for enriched education.* Boston: Heinle & Heinle.

Frayer, D. A., Frederick, W. C., & Klausmeier, H. G. (1969). *A schema for testing the level of concept mastery* (Working Paper No. 16). Madison, WI: Wisconsin Research and Development Center.

Johnson, D. D., & Pearson, P. D. (1984). *Teaching reading vocabulary* (2nd ed.). New York: Holt, Rinehart & Winston.

Kagan, S. (1992). *Cooperative learning resources for teachers.* San Juan Capistrano, CA: Resources for Teachers.

Moore, D. W., Moore, S. A., Cunningham, P. M., & Cunningham, J. W. (1998). *Developing readers and writers in the content areas, K–12* (3rd ed.). New York: Longman.

Readence, J. E., Bean, T. W., & Baldwin, R. S. (1998). *Content area literacy: An integrated approach* (6th ed.). Dubuque, IA: Kendall/ Hunt.

Sadler, C. R., (2001). *Comprehension strategies for middle grade learners: A handbook for content teachers.* Newark DE: International Reading Association.

Schwartz, R. (1988, November). Learning to learn vocabulary in content area textbooks. *Journal of Reading, 32,* 108–117.

Stejnost, R. L., & Thiese, S. M. (2006). *Reading and writing across content areas* (2nd ed.). Thousand Oaks, CA: Corwin Press.

Stephens, E. C., & Brown, J. E. (2005). *A handbook of content literacy strategies: 125 practical reading and writing ideas* (2nd ed.). Norwood, MA: Christopher-Gordon Publishers.

Wormeli, R. (2005). *Summarization in any subject.* Alexandria, VA: Association for Supervision and Curriculum Development.

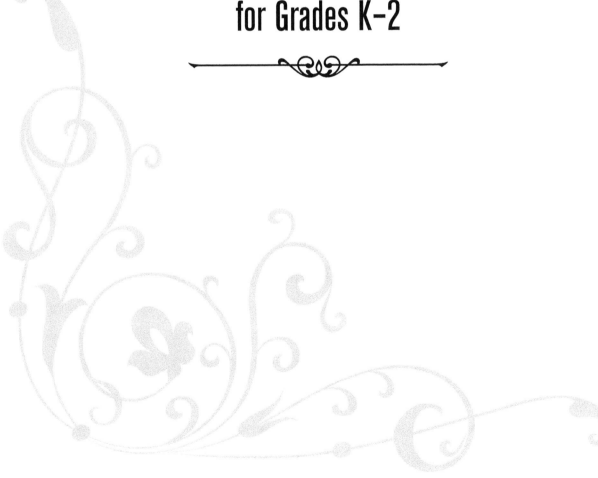

Reading and Writing Strategies
for Grades K–2

Reading and Writing Strategies
for Grades K–2

| Strategy | Language Acquisition for ELLs | | | Reading Process | | | Text Type | | Page |
	Input (Inter-pretive)	Intake (Inter-personal)	Output (Presen-tational)	Pre-reading	During Reading	After Reading	Fiction	Non-fiction	
Character Home Pages			X			X	X		171
Choral Reading		X			X		X		173
Comprehension Game			X			X	X	X	175
Creating Content-Related Picture Books			X			X		X	177
Do You Hear What I Hear?		X			X			X	179
Echo Reading		X			X		X		181
Experience-Text Relationships		X			X		X		183
Independent Reading		X			X		X	X	185

ASCD © 2007. All Rights Reserved.

Section Two

Strategy	Language Acquisition for ELLs			Reading Process			Text Type		Page
	Input (Inter-pretive)	Intake (Inter-personal)	Output (Presen-tational)	Pre-reading	During Reading	After Reading	Fiction	Non-fiction	
Language Experience Approach	X	X		X	X		X		187
Literacy Work Centers	X	X	X	X	X	X	X	X	189
Memory Box	X			X			X	X	191
Patterned Reading		X			X		X		193
PREP	X		X	X		X		X	195
Reader-Generated Questions	X	X	X	X	X	X	X	X	197
Recorded Books	X			X	X		X		199
Say Something		X			X		X		201
Sketch to Stretch			X			X	X	X	203
Split Screen	X	X	X	X	X	X		X	205
Sticky Notes		X			X		X	X	207
Story Hats		X	X		X	X	X		209
Story Impression	X	X	X	X	X	X	X		211
Talking Drawings	X		X	X		X		X	213
The Instant Storyteller			X			X	X		215
Writer's Workshop			X			X	X		217

ASCD © 2007. All Rights Reserved.

Strategies for
SUCCESS
with English Language Learners

SECTION: LITERACY STRATEGIES

Character Home Pages

Why use it?

Use of this strategy will help students to . . .

- Interpret words of characters in story.
- Describe a character from a story.
- Dramatize differences and similarities in characters.
- Compare characters from two or more stories.
- Explain why two different characters view an event differently.
- Make connections between personal experiences and stories read.
- Identify and explain ideas and experiences from texts.
- Identify what they know and have learned from a text.
- Comprehend and respond to literary texts.
- Label drawings with letters or words.

How does it work?

This strategy capitalizes on students' interest in technology and the Internet. Students create a home page for a character they select from a reading. The teacher models how to develop a home page; then students identify a character, assume the point of view of that character, and design the home page using information categories such as "What I look like," "What I am like as a person," and so on. Some teachers use this strategy to have students explore other aspects of the book also—for example, setting or author of the book (Stephens & Brown, 2005).

 © 2007. All Rights Reserved.

CHARACTER HOME PAGES

Section Two

Variations for Emergent English Language Learners

- Use a buddy system so students can create their home page in their primary language or with a student who can translate or model.
- Have parents or siblings help students beforehand with a story book that comes in the primary language if necessary.
- Use a cooperative learning strategy so that a proficient student talks while the emergent English language learner draws, and then have them switch roles.
- Ask the ESL teacher to preview the story and focus on characterization before the story is read in class.
- Ask the ESL teacher to come into class and use parallel or alternative coteaching models to split the class into two groups.

ASCD © 2007. All Rights Reserved.

Strategies for
SUCCESS
with English Language Learners

READING AND WRITING STRATEGIES FOR GRADES K–2

Choral Reading

Why use it?

Use of this strategy will help students to . . .

- Show familiarity with title and author of texts.
- Listen attentively to spoken language.
- Listen attentively for different purposes.
- Listen respectively without interrupting others.
- Attend to a listening activity for a specified time period.
- Listen to literary text to appreciate.
- Identify and produce spoken words that rhyme.
- Enjoy and respond to vivid language (e.g., rhymes).
- Work cooperatively with peers to comprehend text.
- Recognize vocabulary from picture texts.
- Retell or dramatize parts of stories.
- Role-play characters or events from stories.
- Share reading experiences to establish, maintain, and enhance personal relationships.
- Participate in small- or large-group storytelling for social interaction.

How does it work?

Two or more students read a passage in unison. Less-fluent readers try to follow the reading model provided by those who are more fluent. Group members may be teachers, parents, older students, or peer students (Carbo, 1997).

 © 2007. All Rights Reserved.

Section Two

CHORAL READING

Section Two

Variations for Emergent English Language Learners

- Ask the ESL teacher to conduct a picture walk of the book beforehand so emerging ELLs will have a general idea of story structure.
- Ask the ESL teacher to preview pronunciation and meaning of essential words or phrases.
- As a prereading activity, do a word rhyme activity for the whole class or at a specific center.
- Have parents work on the concept of rhyme in the primary language with an appropriate story.
- Select books that have universal appeal (e.g., folk tales) for the choral reading.

ASCD © 2007. All Rights Reserved.

Strategies for
SUCCESS
with English Language Learners

READING AND WRITING STRATEGIES FOR GRADES K–2

Comprehension Game

Why use it?

Use of this strategy will help students to . . .

- Read and follow directions.
- Use resources such as picture dictionaries to find word meanings.
- Learn new words from books.
- Connect vocabulary and life experiences to ideas in texts.
- Determine the meaning of unfamiliar words.
- Use grade-level vocabulary.
- Use decoding strategies.
- Use complete sentences with correct forms.
- Recall sequence of events from stories.
- Identify character and setting.
- Answer questions in response to texts.
- Comprehend and respond to literary texts.
- Identify and explain ideas from texts.
- Interpret words of characters from stories.
- Form opinions about stories.
- Summarize main ideas from informational texts.
- State the main idea.
- Work cooperatively with peers.
- Answer literal, inferential, and critical/application questions.
- Support point of view with examples from text.

COMPREHENSION GAME

Section Two

How does it work?

The teacher makes a game board with red, blue, or white squares and cut-out cards of red, blue, and white construction paper. On the set of red cards, the teacher writes story questions pertaining to *who, what, where, when, why*, and *how*. On the blue set, vocabulary words are written. On the white cards (synonym cards), the teacher writes a sentence with a word underlined. Players roll the dice (or use a spinner), go to the numbered square, and select a card that represents that color. If it is red, students answer a story question; blue, a vocabulary question; or white, a synonym for the underlined word. If students are correct, they stay on the square. If they are incorrect, they go back to *Start* (Mercer & Mercer, 1998).

Variations for Emergent English Language Learners

- Have English language learners look up the vocabulary in a picture dictionary as an activity before playing the game.
- Use picture cues or icons wherever possible on the cards.
- Have similar-language students play together so those who are more proficient can translate when needed.
- While other students are engaged in independent reading, play (or ask an assistant or a parent volunteer to play) with the English language learners as practice sessions before they play with peers.
- Ask the ESL teacher to practice playing the game with emerging English language learners as part of the pull-out class time.
- Differentiate the questions with additional colored cards as needed for ELL levels.

ASCD © 2007. All Rights Reserved.

Strategies for
SUCCESS
with English Language Learners

READING AND WRITING STRATEGIES FOR GRADES K–2

Creating Content-Related Picture Books

Why use it?

Use of this strategy will help students to . . .

- Study categories of words to learn new grade-level vocabulary.
- Distinguish between texts with stories and texts with information.
- Read informational texts to collect data, facts, and ideas.
- Acquire information from nonfiction text.
- Use illustrations to assist understanding.
- Use comprehension strategies to clarify meaning (e.g., fill out graphic organizer, take notes to record facts).
- Work cooperatively with peers to comprehend text.
- Use classroom resources to support the writing process.
- Write text that establishes a topic and use words that can be understood by others.
- Learn and use the writing process.
- Write sentences in logical order and create paragraphs to develop ideas.
- Write to express opinions and judgments.
- Give and seek constructive feedback to improve writing.
- Begin to convey personal voice in writing.
- Use word processing.
- Maintain a portfolio of informational writings and drawings.
- Share writing with others.

CREATING CONTENT-RELATED PICTURE BOOKS

Section Two

How does it work?

The teacher shares a number of content-related picture books (picture walks, read-alouds, shared reading, guided reading). Students select a topic, brainstorm information, and conduct additional research as needed. Then students complete the writing process as follows: create a storyboard, draft the text, create or obtain pictures and illustrations, revise and edit the text, and present the completed text (Stephens & Brown, 2005).

Variations for Emergent English Language Learners

- Begin with topics students might be familiar with or spend time building background knowledge before reading books (e.g., use demonstrations, videos, field trips, and experiential activities).
- Differentiate with multiple materials and references; include some with supporting visuals and illustrations or in the students' primary languages.
- Differentiate through flexible groupings and assign the job of illustrator to beginning-level English language learners.
- Have students write the draft in their primary languages and then ask the ESL teacher or a parent to help put the drafts into English.
- Ask the ESL teacher to work on the book during pull-out time or to come into the classroom to assist with centers.

ASCD © 2007. All Rights Reserved.

Strategies for
SUCCESS
with English Language Learners

READING AND WRITING STRATEGIES FOR GRADES K–2

Do You Hear What I Hear?

Why use it?

Use of this strategy will help students to . . .

- Attend to a listening activity for an extended period of time.
- Respond appropriately to what is heard.
- Identify purpose for reading.
- Show interest in reading a range of informational text.
- Ask questions when listening to text.
- Acquire information from nonfiction text.
- Interpret information presented.
- Identify what they know and have learned about a specific topic.
- Draw pictures to record facts or ideas gathered.
- Organize text information in drawings or graphic organizers.
- Connect information from personal experiences to information from nonfiction texts.
- Summarize main ideas and supporting details (with assistance) from informational text.
- Form an opinion about a book read.
- Report information gathered to peers.
- Share information about what they have learned using appropriate visual aids.

How does it work?

The teacher reads aloud brief, challenging informational texts that are centered on one higher-order thinking question. Students draw, take notes, or complete a graphic organizer during the reading, focusing on the text in order to answer the question. They then discuss their product with each other, using a cooperative learning strategy. Students add ideas they have gathered from others to their drawings as an introduction to the concept of revising after peer conferences (Silver, Strong, & Perini, 2000. Strong & Silver, 1998).

Variations for Emergent English Language Learners

- Differentiate the question.
- Ask the ESL teacher to preview text and the question during pull-out time.
- Divide the class into two groups (either homogeneous or heterogeneous) and ask the ESL teacher to read with one group.
- Use a cooperative learning strategy to support students who can not draw ideas independently.
- Pair similar-language students when appropriate.

ASCD © 2007. All Rights Reserved.

Strategies for SUCCESS with English Language Learners

READING AND WRITING STRATEGIES FOR GRADES K–2

Echo Reading

Why use it?

Use of this strategy will help students to . . .

- Listen attentively to spoken language to appreciate literary texts.
- Participate in small- or large-group storytelling to interact with peers.
- Identify and produce spoken words that rhyme.
- Count or tap the number of syllables in spoken words.
- Identify the same sounds in different spoken words.
- Understand that the purpose of print is to communicate.
- Follow left-to-right and top-to-bottom direction when reading.
- Distinguish between letters and words, and print and pictures.
- Track print by pointing to written words when texts are read aloud.
- Check accuracy of decoding using context to monitor and self-correct.
- Sight-read common, high-frequency words.
- Identify the parts of a book.
- Match spoken words with pictures.
- Respond to vivid language.
- Identify the author's use of repetition and rhyme.
- Learn new words indirectly.
- Notice when sentences do not make sense.
- Respond orally to questions and directions.
- Show interest in reading a range of texts (stories, poems, and plays).
- Retell or dramatize.
- Recite poems or nursery rhymes.
- Use computer software to support reading.

 © 2007. All Rights Reserved.

ECHO READING

Section Two

- Share reading experiences to establish, maintain, and enhance personal relationships.

How does it work?

The teacher reads and discusses a story with the children, then reads a sentence or two and the students repeat it using the same intonations. A big book or multiple copies of a storybook can be used. Pointing to the words as they are read helps the children focus on print instead of simply relying on auditory memory. For very young readers, this strategy helps establish the concept of print and allows them to "read" an entire text with assistance. Mature readers may incorporate some words into their sight vocabulary. English language learners can "echo-read" with more experienced children, especially following a modeling session (Carbo, 1997).

Variations for Emergent English Language Learners

- Ask the ESL teacher to preview text to work on pronunciation and key vocabulary. Echo-reading is an inherently scaffolded reading experience for English language learners and offers a natural model for students to follow.

ASCD © 2007. All Rights Reserved.

Strategies for
SUCCESS
with English Language Learners

READING AND WRITING STRATEGIES FOR GRADES K–2

Experience-Text Relationships

Why use it?

Use of this strategy will help students to . . .

- Connect new vocabulary and life experiences to ideas in texts.
- Answer questions about text.
- Draw on prior experiences to understand new data, facts, and ideas.
- Make connections between personal experiences and stories read.
- Form opinions about the differences between events in a story and events in own life.
- Recall a sequence of events from a personal experience.
- Dictate information from personal experience.
- Compare stories from personal experiences with stories heard or read.
- Connect or relate information from personal experience to nonfiction texts.
- Share what they know and have learned about a topic.
- Use own perspectives and opinions to comprehend text.
- Read for different purposes.
- Use self-monitoring strategies such as rereading and cross-checking.
- Apply corrective strategies.
- Engage in independent silent reading.
- Answer literal, inferential, and critical/application questions after listening or reading.
- Participate in discussions about grade-level texts.
- Support point of view with text information.
- Maintain a personal reading list to reflect goals and accomplishments.

 © 2007. All Rights Reserved.

Section Two

EXPERIENCE-TEXT RELATIONSHIPS

Section Two

How does it work?

This strategy is a variation of K-W-L and is inherently scaffolded as a pre-, during-, or after-reading experience. It uses discussion to link what children already know to what they will be reading about. It consists of three steps: (1) the teacher has the children explain the experiences they have had or knowledge they have that relates to the story; (2) the teacher has the children read short parts of the story, usually a page or two, answering the teacher's questions after each section; and (3) the teacher attempts to draw relationships for the children between the content of the story and their outside experience and knowledge (Opitz & Rasinski, 1998).

Variations for Emergent English Language Learners

- Ask the ESL teacher to practice the strategy during pull-out time or to come into class and conduct the strategy with one group while you do the same with the other.
- Add icons to the questions to give visual support.
- Select a text that is culturally familiar to English language learners so they have their moment of "knowing" in front of their peers.

ASCD © 2007. All Rights Reserved.

Strategies for
SUCCESS
with English Language Learners

READING AND WRITING STRATEGIES FOR GRADES K–2

Independent Reading

Why use it?

Use of this strategy will help students to . . .
- Engage in independent silent reading.
- Read voluntarily for their own purposes.
- Learn new words from books.
- Read familiar texts independently.
- Show interest in reading a range of texts for a variety of purposes.
- Show familiarity with some books and authors.
- Read with increasing fluency and confidence from a variety of texts.
- Evaluate and select books, tapes, and poems on the basis of personal choice or teacher-selected criteria.
- Respond to text to express feelings, opinions, and judgments.
- Maintain a personal reading list to reflect goals and accomplishments.

How does it work?

Popular forms of independent reading include Sustained Silent Reading (SSR), Drop Everything and Read (DEAR), Buddy Reading, and Reader's Workshop. These forms allow children to have free choice of their reading, to meet on a regular basis with peers and teachers to share what they are reading, and to have the option of creating a personal response to what they read (Fountas & Pinnell, 1996).

INDEPENDENT READING

Section Two

Variations for Emergent English Language Learners

- Use picture or pattern books so the language requirements of the text do not preclude English language learners from participating in independent reading.
- Use buddy reading for some students.
- Use this opportunity to spend some time alone with English language learners.

ASCD © 2007. All Rights Reserved.

Strategies for
SUCCESS
with English Language Learners

Language Experience Approach

Why use it?

Use of this strategy will help students to . . .

- Use personal experience to stimulate own writing with assistance.
- Engage in conversations with adults and peers regarding experiences.
- Share favorite anecdotes with peers and adults.
- Dictate stories with a beginning, middle, and end.
- Express the mood of a story by using a variety of words with assistance.
- Develop original literary text using words that can be understood by others.
- Track print by pointing to written words when texts are being read.
- Write voluntarily to communicate with others.
- Write for different purposes (e.g., tell stories, communicate feelings, provide information).
- Use word processing.
- Share reading experiences with peers and adults.
- Share writing with others.
- Participate in small- or large-group storytelling.
- Engage in purposeful oral reading.
- Listen respectively and attentively.
- Evaluate the content of stories by identifying whether information is realistic.
- Maintain a portfolio of writings with assistance.

LANGUAGE EXPERIENCE APPROACH

Section Two

How does it work?

This strategy helps develop reading and writing through the use of the student's own language, thoughts, and ideas. Students are able to read the stories with minimal cueing because they already know the meaning. The following steps can be done with the entire class, small groups, or individuals: (1) engage the students in a conversation about an experience they have had; (2) as they speak, write on the board, on chart paper, on an overhead projector, or at the computer; (3) read the story to the students, pointing precisely to each word; and (4) reread a sentence, pointing to the words, and then have the students read the sentence while pointing to the words.

Note: The original approach recommended writing exactly what the students say, but these authors suggest using the opportunities to teach correct language through the explicit paraphrase technique. The teacher models correct language form, both orally and in writing (Brisk & Harrington, 2000).

Variations for Emergent English Language Learners

- Send a tape recorder home and teach parents or an older sibling how to do this strategy in the home language.
- Ask the ESL teacher to begin to work with the students to transform their stories into English and to use the explicit paraphrase technique.

ASCD © 2007. All Rights Reserved.

Strategies for
SUCCESS
with English Language Learners

READING AND WRITING STRATEGIES FOR GRADES K–2

Literacy Work Centers

Why use it?

Use of this strategy will help students to . . .

- Follow simple directions.
- Identify and produce spoken words that rhyme.
- Form words in rhyming word families.
- Categorize, blend, segment, add, delete, and substitute phonemes to make or change words.
- Use a picture dictionary to learn meanings of words in books.
- Use classroom resources to acquire information.
- Interpret information represented in simple charts and webs.
- Engage in prereading and reading activities to select books, make connections between personal experiences and stories read, predict what might happen next, identify what they know and have learned, and answer questions.
- Use graphic or semantic organizers.
- Use comprehension strategies.
- Change the sequence of events.
- Distinguish between real and imaginary texts.
- Retell or dramatize stories.
- Share reading and writing experiences and work cooperatively with others.
- Show interest in reading a range of texts from a variety of genres.
- Copy letters and words.
- Draw or write facts and ideas.
- Use graphics to communicate ideas or information.

LITERACY WORK CENTERS

Section Two

- Listen to literary texts to appreciate and enjoy or respond to vivid language.
- Maintain a reading log with goals and accomplishments.
- Maintain a portfolio of writings with assistance.

How does it work?

A literacy work station is an area within the classroom where students work alone or interact with one another, using instructional materials to explore and expand their literacy. It is a place where a variety of activities reinforces and extends learning, often without the assistance of the teacher. Children practice reading, writing, speaking, listening, and working with letters and words. Some sample work stations might include a big book work station, writing work station, drama work station, ABC/word study work station, poetry work station, computer work station, buddy reading work station, creation work station, science/social studies work station, and handwriting work station (Diller, 2003).

Variations for Emergent English Language Learners

- Have English language learners work their way through the centers starting with those that offer more context and less language (e.g., drama) and progressing to those that offer less context and more language (e.g., writing).
- Ask the ESL teacher to come into class during centers for coteaching.

ASCD © 2007. All Rights Reserved.

Strategies for
SUCCESS
with English Language Learners

SECTION: LITERACY STRATEGIES

READING AND WRITING STRATEGIES FOR GRADES K–2

Memory Box

Why use it?

Use of this strategy will help students to . . .
- Participate in small- or large-group storytelling.
- Learn the meaning of new words and use them in own speech.
- Connect vocabulary and life experiences to ideas in books.
- Make predictions about story events.
- Retell or dramatize stories or parts of stories.
- Show interest in reading a wide range of texts from different genres.
- Engage in prereading and reading activities to make connections and predictions and to draw conclusions.
- Listen to literary texts to match spoken words with objects or pictures, and to identify specific people, places, and events.
- Identify characters in a story and explain what each contributes to the story's events.
- Use own perspectives and opinions to comprehend texts.
- Share information using appropriate visual aids.
- Answer literal, inferential, or critical/application questions after reading.

How does it work?

This strategy is used best with fiction or biographies. The teacher puts together a memory box, a collection of objects that represent events in a story, then shows each object to the class, talking about its significance to the story. Next, the teacher reads the story. A variation is to have students put together a

MEMORY BOX

Section Two

memory box with objects they think the story will be about (Stephens & Brown, 2005).

Variations for Emergent English Language Learners

- Ask the ESL teacher to put together a memory box with English language learners during pull-out time or to come into class and work with one of two groups.

ASCD © 2007. All Rights Reserved.

Strategies for **SUCCESS** with English Language Learners

READING AND WRITING STRATEGIES FOR GRADES K–2

Patterned Reading

Why use it?

Use of this strategy will help students to . . .

*   Identify and produce spoken words that rhyme.
*   Follow left-to-right and top-to-bottom direction.
*   Track print by pointing to written words.
*   Identify parts of a book and their functions.
*   Recognize that written words represent spoken words.
*   Learn new words from books and use them in own speech.
*   Connect vocabulary and life experiences.
*   Sight-read grade-level high-frequency words automatically.
*   Notice when sentences do not make sense.
*   Retell or dramatize parts of books.
*   Show interest in reading a range of books.
*   Share reading experiences with peers and adults.
*   Listen attentively to spoken language; appreciate and enjoy literary texts.
*   Match spoken words with pictures.
*   Answer simple questions in response to texts.
*   Develop fluency and confidence as readers.

How does it work?

This strategy is excellent for enhancing the second language acquisition process and is also inherently scaffolded for English language learners. Children are able to "read" predictable books with the teacher right away. The teacher uses a story with a simple pattern, such as "Brown Bear, Brown Bear,

What Do You See?" Although children "read" books like these from memory of the patterns, from nursery rhymes, and from picture cues, they are able to sound like adult readers. They feel accomplished and gain confidence while developing word and print awareness, a sense of sentence and story, increased vocabularies, and their first ideas about fluency (Burns, 1999).

Variations for Emergent English Language Learners

• Always have a center full of pattern books for students.

ASCD © 2007. All Rights Reserved.

Strategies for
SUCCESS
with English Language Learners

READING AND WRITING STRATEGIES FOR GRADES K–2

PREP (Preview, Read, Examine, Prompt)

Why use it?

Use of this strategy will help students to . . .

- Engage in prereading and reading activities to identify what they know, want to know, and have learned about a specific story or topic.
- Read grade-level texts with comprehension and for different purposes.
- Use comprehension strategies (e.g., reread and self-correct) to clarify meaning of text.
- Use self-monitoring strategies such as rereading and cross-checking.
- Use graphic organizers to organize information.
- Write data, ideas, and facts gathered.
- Take notes to record information with assistance.
- Describe the connections between experiences and ideas and information in texts.
- Answer literal, inferential, and critical/application questions about texts read.
- Lead or participate in discussion about grade-level books, integrating multiple strategies (e.g., ask questions, clarify misunderstandings, support points of view, summarize information).

How does it work?

As a variation of K-W-L, this strategy is inherently scaffolded. The teacher instructs the students to construct questions before reading. Questions engage the minds of the readers and focus their thinking during reading. The teacher uses PREP as a change from K-W-L. Ideas and vocabulary that are recorded can be used later in a writing experience. Students enjoy creating a class book about the topic (Langer, 1981). See the math example that follows.

Variations for Emergent English Language Learners

- Ask the ESL teacher to practice with students during pull-out time.
- Keep class books in a specific place and have English language learners read them during independent reading or as an anchor activity.

Example:

Sarah's mom made a bird house for the back yard. First Sarah saw 9 birds fly into the house. Then 5 more flew into the house. How many birds are there in all?

Before Reading What I already know . . .	During Reading Questions to focus my learning . . .	After Reading What I have learned . . .
It's a story problem. There are numbers in it. There is a question mark.	What kind of problem is it? Will I add or subtract? What words tell me what to do?	It is a plus problem because it says, "How many in all?" There are two numbers to add.

Source: From *Strategic Reading in the Content Areas: Practical Applications for Creating a Thinking Environment* (p. 200), by R. Billmeyer, 2004, Omaha, NE: Rachel & Associates. Copyright 2004 by Rachel Billmeyer. Used by permission of Rachel & Associates.

ASCD © 2007. All Rights Reserved.

Strategies for
SUCCESS
with English Language Learners

READING AND WRITING STRATEGIES FOR GRADES K–2

Reader-Generated Questions

Why use it?

Use of this strategy will help students to . . .

- Connect words and ideas in books to prior knowledge.
- Read grade-level texts for different purposes.
- Use comprehension strategies (e.g., predict/confirm, reread) to clarify meaning.
- Work cooperatively with peers to comprehend text.
- Identify purpose for reading.
- Ask and answer literal, inferential, and critical/application questions.
- Use graphic organizers to organize information.
- Summarize main ideas from informational texts.
- Use own perspectives and opinions to comprehend text.
- Read grade-level informational texts to collect data, ideas, and facts.
- Distinguish between texts with stories and texts with information.
- Engage in prereading and reading activities to predict what might happen, draw conclusions, identify, explain and evaluate ideas from texts.
- Identify what they know, want to know, and have learned about a topic.
- Use self-monitoring strategies such as cross-checking.
- Read with increasing fluency and confidence from a variety of texts.
- Maintain a personal reading list to reflect reading goals and accomplishments.

Section Two

READER-GENERATED QUESTIONS

Section Two

How does it work?

This strategy walks students through the steps of the reading process: stimulate background knowledge, predict, read, and synthesize. The teacher (1) introduces the topic of the reading through pictures, maps, time lines, and real objects, and has students relate the topic to their own experiences; (2) asks the students to generate 1–10 questions about the topic; (3) has the students guess responses to the questions in small groups; (4) reads the story aloud or has the students read the text alone or in pairs; (5) asks the students to answer the questions or to check on their guesses; and (6) has the students respond to the reading by writing a summary, completing a graph, drawing a picture, outlining the content, or completing some other activity (Brisk & Harrington, 2000).

Variations for Emergent English Language Learners

- Ask the ESL teacher to practice the strategy during pull-out time.
- Provide cue questions to the English language learner so they can participate.
- Pair up English language learners with similar-language or nurturing peers.
- Have English language learners progress through response options, starting with pictures and moving to graphs, outlines, and summaries.

ASCD © 2007. All Rights Reserved.

Strategies for
SUCCESS
with English Language Learners

READING AND WRITING STRATEGIES FOR GRADES K–2

Recorded Books

Why use it?

Use of this strategy will help students to . . .

- Listen attentively to spoken language for different purposes.
- Follow left-to-right and top-to-bottom direction.
- Track print by pointing to written words when texts are read aloud.
- Learn new words from books.
- Read familiar texts at the emergent level with assistance.
- Locate and use classroom resources to acquire information.
- Engage in prereading and reading activities to select books and tapes on the basis of interest or teacher-selected criteria.
- Predict what could happen next, form an opinion about text events compared to own life.
- Listen to literary texts to appreciate and enjoy, match spoken words with pictures, identify character and setting, and respond to vivid language.
- Answer questions in response to texts.
- Read with increasing fluency and confidence.
- Express feelings about literary works.
- Show interest in reading a range of texts.
- Keep a log of books read to track accomplishments.

How does it work?

Recorded reading is an excellent strategy to enhance the second language acquisition process and is inherently scaffolded. Children listen one or more times to a word-for-word recording while following along in the text, and then

Section Two

read it aloud. Less-fluent readers can listen one or more times to segments of 2–5 minutes recorded at a slower-than-usual pace, and then read the passage aloud (Carbo, 1989).

Variations for Emergent English Language Learners

* Send recorded books home for practice.
* Select stories that are culturally universal.
* Always keep a center of recorded books so English language learners can participate in independent reading activities.

ASCD © 2007. All Rights Reserved.

Strategies for
SUCCESS
with **English Language Learners**

READING AND WRITING STRATEGIES FOR GRADES K–2

Say Something

Why use it?

Use of this strategy will help students to . . .

- Listen attentively to spoken language, including grade-level books read aloud.
- Listen to literary texts to appreciate and enjoy.
- Identify characters, setting, and plot.
- Converse with adults and peers regarding books.
- Role-play characters and events from stories.
- Express feelings about works of fiction.
- Compare stories from personal experiences with stories heard.
- Express the mood of a story by using a variety of words.
- Retell stories in logical order.
- Ask for clarification.
- Express an opinion or judgment about a story.
- Explain personal criteria for liking a book.
- Compare and contrast events or characters in a story with own lives.
- Participate in small- or large-group storytelling.
- Answer literal, inferential or critical/application questions after reading text.
- Use previous reading and life experiences to understand literature.
- Connect literary texts to previous life experiences to enhance understanding.
- Show interest in a range of texts.

SAY SOMETHING

Section Two

How does it work?

Students are invited to take turns saying something at intervals during the reading of a story in order to respond personally to an engaging piece of literature. The focus is on reading to say something rather than reading to decode individual words (Cloud, Genesee, & Hamayan, 2000).

Variations for Emergent English Language Learners

- Ask the ESL teacher to preview text during pull-out time, or divide the class into two groups and ask the ESL teacher to come in for parallel or alternative coteaching.
- Give cue cards with icons to English language learners to select something to say.
- Select stories with culturally universal appeal.

ASCD © 2007. All Rights Reserved.

Strategies for
SUCCESS
with English Language Learners

READING AND WRITING STRATEGIES FOR GRADES K–2

Sketch to Stretch

Why use it?

Use of this strategy will help students to . . .
- Increase background knowledge by elaborating ideas from texts.
- Connect life experiences to ideas in texts.
- Use comprehension strategy of visualizing to clarify meaning of texts.
- Explain ideas from texts.
- Engage in reading activities to show what they have learned from text.
- Use illustrations to assist in understanding the content of a text.
- Draw to express opinions and judgments to share what they know, depict an opinion about events in texts, compare characters and settings within or between stories, or describe the difference between real and imaginary texts.
- Maintain a portfolio of drawings.

How does it work?

This strategy helps students learn to visualize what they read. Individually, with a partner or a team, students draw and share the mental images conveyed in a reading. They may also sketch the personal meaning of a reading. Students share their drawings with peers (Short, Harste, & Burke, 1996).

Variations for Emergent English Language Learners

- Use the cooperative learning strategy of pairing students and having the receiver draw what the sender describes; if necessary, describers could use their primary language first.

Strategies for
SUCCESS
with English Language Learners

READING AND WRITING STRATEGIES FOR GRADES K–2

Split Screen

Why use it?

Use of this strategy will help students to . . .

- Identify purpose for reading.
- Determine the meaning of unfamiliar words by using context clues.
- Attend to a listening activity for a specific purpose.
- Use the strategy of visualizing to comprehend text.
- Ask questions when listening to text read.
- Summarize main ideas and supporting details, both orally and in writing.
- Lead or participate in discussion.
- Demonstrate comprehension of grade-level text.
- Recognize the value of illustration to the reading process.
- Make judgments about relevant and irrelevant information.
- Take notes to record facts; organize the notes in a prewriting activity.
- Share writing with others.

How does it work?

This strategy, a note-making strategy, builds listening and visualizing skills that are necessary for effective reading. The teacher reads a book or passage aloud and along the way discusses difficult vocabulary words with students. The teacher then reads the book or passage again, this time a bit more slowly and with emphasized emotion. During this reading, students sketch their ideas on one side of the paper and write words or phrases on the other side. The teacher needs to pause during this rereading to give students time to create their visualizations on the organizer. At key points, the teacher stops reading

 © 2007. All Rights Reserved.

and asks students to explain their pictures to each other. After the second reading, students work in groups to create posters (Silver, Strong, & Perini, 1999). See the example that follows.

Variations for Emergent English Language Learners

- Cue the split screen of the English language learner by writing the words (they then draw).
- Ask the ESL teacher to practice during pull-out time, or divide the class and ask the ESL teacher to come in for parallel or alternative coteaching.

Example:

Words (Ideas and Details)	Pictures (Sketches and Doodles—No Words)
butterflies bees drink nectar bring pollen help flower	

ASCD © 2007. All Rights Reserved.

Strategies for SUCCESS with English Language Learners

SECTION: LITERACY STRATEGIES

Sticky Notes

Why use it?

Use of this strategy will help students to . . .

- Identify purpose for reading; use decoding strategies.
- Connect words and ideas in texts to prior knowledge.
- Learn new words indirectly from texts.
- Read grade-level texts for different purposes.
- Use comprehension strategies (reread, self-correct, connect self to text) to clarify meaning in texts.
- Ask and answer questions in response to texts.
- Use own perspectives and opinions to comprehend text.
- Interact with and respond to text.
- Engage in reading activities to identify, explain, and evaluate ideas.
- Read with increasing fluency and confidence.
- Show interest in reading a range of grade-level texts.
- Share reading experiences with peers and adults.

How does it work?

Students write on their sticky notes why they chose passages they want to discuss with others. The teacher models the strategy using passages students learned from, loved, couldn't stop reading, felt connected to, questioned, thought were funny, or were puzzled by (Peterson & Eeds, 1990).

STICKY NOTES

Section Two

Variations for Emergent English Language Learners

- Model the strategy first.
- Add icons to the sticky notes English language learners will use, to support them as they look for specific passages.
- Ask the ESL teacher to practice the strategy during pull-out time.
- Pair students with similar language backgrounds or pair English language learners with nurturing classmates.

ASCD © 2007. All Rights Reserved.

Strategies for
SUCCESS
with English Language Learners

READING AND WRITING STRATEGIES FOR GRADES K–2

Story Hats

Why use it?

Use of this strategy will help students to . . .

- Listen attentively to literary texts, appreciate and enjoy texts, and respond to vivid language.
- Use a picture dictionary as a resource for vocabulary development.
- Identify character and setting, match spoken words with pictures, and recall events.
- Learn new words from books.
- Connect life experiences to ideas in texts.
- Retell parts of stories.
- Comprehend, respond to, or interpret literary text.
- Form an opinion about events in own life related to events in a story.
- Express the mood of a story.
- Express an opinion about the color, form, and style of illustrations.
- Show interest in reading a range of grade-level texts.
- Share reading experiences with peers and adults.
- Participate in small- or large-group storytelling experiences.
- Show familiarity with title and author of grade-level texts.
- Maintain a portfolio of drawings.

How does it work?

Students draw scenes from a story on 11 x 14 sheets of construction paper while the story is read aloud. They share the pictures with one another and then fold the paper into a hat to wear home (Schlick Noe & Johnson, 1999).

ASCD © 2007. All Rights Reserved.

STORY HATS

Section Two

Variations for Emergent English Language Learners

- Use icons on the sheet to remind students of the "who, where, what, why, and how" story elements.
- Have students share their hats with one another.
- Have students use their hats at home with their families to retell the story in their primary language.

ASCD © 2007. All Rights Reserved.

Strategies for
SUCCESS
with English Language Learners

READING AND WRITING STRATEGIES FOR GRADES K–2

Story Impression

Why use it?

Use of this strategy will help students to . . .

- Decode grade-level texts using a variety of strategies.
- Sight-read common, high-frequency words.
- Identify purpose for reading.
- Connect words and ideas in books to prior knowledge.
- Use comprehension strategies (predict/confirm, reread) to comprehend text.
- Sequence events in retelling stories.
- Use own perspectives and opinions to comprehend text.
- Engage in prereading and reading activities to predict what might happen; draw conclusions; identify characters, setting, and events; change the sequence of events in a story; or recognize different plots in books.
- Develop an original literary text; create a story with a beginning, middle, and end.
- Listen to literary texts to identify specific story elements and to compare stories.
- Show interest in reading literary genres.
- Read with increasing fluency and confidence.
- Share the process of writing with peers and adults.
- Begin to develop a voice in writing.

STORY IMPRESSION

Section Two

How does it work?

The strategy is inherently scaffolded in that it follows the instructional process of gradual release of responsibility (i.e., teacher models, guided practice, compare with exemplar, independent practice). Students are prompted to creatively predict the plot of a story. The teacher lists clue words or important phrases (in drawings or print); the words should convey the main character, the setting, and the problem in the story. Students read the clues together, brainstorm how they link together, and dictate a story to the teacher. After reading, the class compares their story impression with the actual story. Once they are familiar with this strategy, students can do it on their own or in small groups (Cloud, Genesee, & Hamayan, 2000).

Variations for Emergent English Language Learners

- Ask the ESL teacher to practice the strategy during pull-out time, or split the class into two groups and ask the ESL teacher to come and do alternative coteaching.
- Provide English language learners with some brainstorming icons beforehand.

ASCD © 2007. All Rights Reserved.

Strategies for
SUCCESS
with English Language Learners

READING AND WRITING STRATEGIES FOR GRADES K–2

Talking Drawings

Why use it?

Use of this strategy will help students to . . .

- Create a drawing to represent a concept.
- Draw to express opinions and judgments, to share what they know and have learned about a topic, or to respond in pictures to an experience shared by classmates.
- Take turns speaking in a group.
- Stay on topic.
- Speak audibly.
- Report information briefly to peers.
- Attend to a listening activity for a specified period of time.
- Listen attentively for a specified purpose.
- Respond with expression appropriate to what is heard.
- Interpret information represented in charts and webs.
- Begin to collect data, facts, and ideas.
- Engage in prereading and reading activities to connect life experiences to ideas in texts, ask and answer questions about texts, retell information or stories, and match words with pictures.
- Use the comprehension strategy of visualizing to clarify texts.
- Work cooperatively with peers to comprehend texts.
- Show interest in reading a range of texts.
- Maintain a portfolio of drawings that express opinions and judgments.

Section Two

How does it work?

This strategy is a visual version of K-W-L and is inherently scaffolded for English language learners. It uses simple student drawings as a bridge between background knowledge and new information to be studied in the text. The teacher asks students to make a drawing showing what they already know about a topic. Students then get into small groups and share their drawings, discussing the similarities and differences among the drawings. A whole-class follow-up discussion takes place, and then the class organizes their thoughts into a single concept map. Students either read or are read to and then modify their drawing, add to their drawing, or begin a new drawing based on what they have just learned. Students then get into small groups again to compare their first and second drawings with one another (Readence, Moore, & Rickelman, 2000).

Variations for Emergent English Language Learners

*   Ask the ESL teacher to prepare students with ideas or to preread the texts during pull-out time.
*   Use cooperative learning strategy of Think-Pair-Share for the small-group sharing to provide peer models.
*   Ask the ESL teacher to come into class to team-teach for the whole-class discussion and concept map development.

ASCD © 2007. All Rights Reserved.

Strategies for
SUCCESS
with English Language Learners

READING AND WRITING STRATEGIES FOR GRADES K–2

The Instant Storyteller

Why use it?

Use of this strategy will help students to . . .

- Converse with peers and adults regarding pictures, books, and experiences.
- Role-play characters and events from stories; express feelings about stories.
- Compare stories from personal experience with stories read or heard.
- Express the mood or emotion of a story by using a variety of words.
- Retell stories using a logical sequence.
- Ask for clarification of events in a story.
- Participate in small-group storytelling.
- Speak with speed and expression appropriate to the purpose and audience.
- Respond appropriately to what others are saying.
- Listen attentively to spoken language.
- Develop original literary text; create a story with a beginning, middle, and end.
- Write to describe characters, settings, or events.
- Identify the problem and solution in a story.
- Work cooperatively with peers for literacy activities.
- Share the process of writing with peers in a cooperative group.

 © 2007. All Rights Reserved.

How does it work?

This strategy has five steps: (1) the teacher identifies groups with roles (storyteller, timer, recorder, responder); (2) the teacher provides each group with visual images (e.g., photos, artworks, CD covers); (3) the storyteller selects a visual and spends two minutes planning a story; (4) the storyteller relates the story for three minutes while the recorder writes notes; and (5) the responder gives feedback on the story. Roles are switched and eventually the group selects one of the stories to retell to the class (Stephens & Brown, 2005).

Variations for Emergent English Language Learners

- Have English language learners progress in the roles they are assigned: timer for newcomers; responder for somewhat proficient students; recorder for more proficient students; and, finally, storyteller.
- Ask the ESL teacher to prepare students during pull-out time or to come into the classroom for coteaching.
- Send visuals home with English language learners so parents can tell stories in primary languages. Be sure to select pictures with culturally universal appeal.

 © 2007. All Rights Reserved.

Strategies for
SUCCESS
with English Language Learners

READING AND WRITING STRATEGIES FOR GRADES K–2

Writer's Workshop

Why use it?

Use of this strategy will help students to . . .

- Draw and write to express opinions and judgments and to share what they know and have learned.
- Compare characters and settings within and between stories.
- Develop original literary text; create a sequenced story or poem.
- Write to respond to text, expressing feelings about characters or events.
- Describe characters, settings, or events.
- Retell a story using own words.
- Identify the problem and solution in a story.
- Respond in words to an experience.
- Describe the differences between real and imaginary events.
- Write original text using the writing process.
- Write a variety of compositions with assistance using different organizational patterns.
- Make judgments about relevant and irrelevant information to include in writing.
- Write sentences in logical order and use paragraphs to organize ideas.
- Use capitalization, punctuation, and spelling rules in final products.
- Participate in writing conferences with teachers and peers to improve own and others' writing.
- Write voluntarily for different purposes.
- Maintain a portfolio of writings (drawings).

Section Two

 © 2007. All Rights Reserved.

WRITER'S WORKSHOP

How does it work?

Writer's workshop is inherently scaffolded because it is process-oriented and allows for differentiation of process and product. During a block of time, children learn the processes involved in reading and writing. The teacher structures the time to ensure that children have an opportunity to plan, organize, and carry out writing projects in response to stories they have read or listened to. Students learn how to select their own topics and develop their ideas through multiple drafts, thus acquiring an understanding of the writing process. The block of time for writers' workshop in kindergarten is approximately 30–40 minutes—in 1st and 2nd grade, about 45–60 minutes. Components can include a shared writing event, independent writing time, conferences, sharing, minilessons, and keeping notebooks and reading logs (Dorn & Soffos, 2001).

Variations for Emergent English Language Learners

- Ask the ESL teacher to have English language learners complete some stages during ESL pull-out time, or ask the ESL teacher to come to the classroom to team-teach.
- Allow English language learners to use the primary language as needed to participate in the writing process.

Section Two

ASCD © 2007. All Rights Reserved.

References

Brisk, M. E., & Harrington, M. M. (2000). *Literacy and bilingualism: A handbook for all teachers.* Mahwah, NJ: Lawrence Erlbaum Associates.

Billmeyer, R. (2004). *Strategic reading in the content areas: Practical applications for creating a thinking environment.* Omaha, NE: Rachel & Associates.

Burns, B. (1999). *How to teach balanced reading and writing.* Thousand Oaks, CA: Corwin Press.

Carbo, M. (1989). *How to record books for maximum reading gains.* Syosset, NY: National Reading Styles Institute.

Carbo, M. (1997). *What every principal should know about teaching reading: How to raise test scores and nurture a love of reading.* Syosset, NY: National Reading Styles Institute.

Cloud, N., Genesee, F., & Hamayan, E. (2000). *Dual language instruction: A handbook for enriched education.* Boston: Heinle & Heinle.

Diller, D. (2003). *Literacy work stations: Making centers work.* Portland, ME: Stenhouse Publishers.

Dorn, L. J., & Soffos, C. (2001). *Scaffolding young writers: A writer's workshop approach.* Portland, ME: Stenhouse Publishers.

Fountas, I. C., & Pinnell, G. S. (1996). *Guided reading: Good first teaching for all children.* Portsmouth, NH: Heinemann.

Langer, L. A. (1981). From theory to practice: A prereading plan. *Journal of Reading, 25,* 152–156.

Mercer, C. D., & Mercer A. R. (1998). *Teaching students with learning problems* (5th ed.). Upper Saddle River, NJ: Prentice Hall.

Opitz, M. F., & Rasinski, T. (1998). *Good-bye round robin: 25 effective oral reading strategies.* Portsmouth, NH: Heinemann.

Peterson, R,. & Eeds, M. (1990). *Grand conversations: Literature groups in action.* New York: Scholastic.

Readence, J. E., Moore, D. W., & Rickelman, R. J. (2000). *Prereading activities for content area reading and learning* (3rd ed.). Newark, DE: International Reading Association.

Schlick Noe, K. L., & Johnson, N. J. (1999). *Getting started with literature circles.* Norwood, MA: Christopher-Gordon.

Short, K. G., Harste, J. C., & Burke, C. L. (1996). *Creating classrooms for authors and inquirers* (2nd ed.). Portsmouth, NH: Heinemann.

Silver, H. F., Strong, R. W., & Perini, M. (1999). *Discovering nonfiction: 25 powerful teaching strategies.* Santa Monica, CA: Canter & Associates.

Silver, H. F., Strong, R. W., & Perini, M. J. (2000). *Reading for meaning: The teaching strategies library.* Trenton, NJ: Thoughtful Education Press.

Strong, R. W., & Silver, H. F. (1998). [Simple and deep: Factors affecting classroom implementation and student performance]. Unpublished research.

Strong, R. W., Silver, H. F., Perini, M. J., & Tuculescu, G. M. (2002). *Reading for academic success: Powerful strategies for struggling, average, and advanced readers, grades 7–12.* Thousand Oaks, CA: Corwin Press.

Stephens, E. C., & Brown, J. B. (2005). *A handbook of content literacy strategies: 125 practical reading and writing ideas* (2nd ed.). Norwood, MA: Christopher-Gordon Publishers.

Section Two

Reading Strategies
for Grades 3-12

Reading Strategies
for Grades 3-12

Strategy	Language Acquisition for ELLs			Reading Process			Best Content Area				Page
	Input (Inter-pretive)	Intake (Inter-personal)	Output (Presen-tational)	Pre-reading	During Reading	After Reading	LA	Sc	Math	SS	Page
Anticipation/ Prediction Guide	X	X		X	X		X	X		X	227
Check Those Facts!		X	X		X	X	X	X		X	229
Circle-Seat-Center			X			X	X	X	X	X	231
Coding		X	X		X	X	X	X	X	X	233
Collaborative Strategic Reading	X	X	X	X	X	X	X	X	X	X	235
Concept Collection	X	X	X	X	X	X					237
Cornell Method of Note Taking	X	X	X	X	X	X	X	X	X	X	239
Directed Reading and Thinking Activity (DRTA)		X	X		X	X	X			X	241

ASCD © 2007. All Rights Reserved.

Section Two

Strategy	Language Acquisition for ELLs			Reading Process			Best Content Area				Page
	Input (Inter-pretive)	Intake (Inter-personal)	Output (Presen-tational)	Pre-reading	During Reading	After Reading	LA	Sc	Math	SS	
Elaborative Interrogation	X	X	X	X	X	X	X	X	X	X	243
Ethical Choices	X	X	X	X	X	X	X	X		X	245
Four-Way Reporting & Recording		X	X		X	X	X	X		X	247
Group Summarizing	X	X	X	X	X	X	X	X		X	249
Inductive Learning	X	X	X	X	X	X	X	X		X	251
Infofiction		X	X		X	X	X			X	253
Interactive Reading Guide	X	X	X	X	X	X	X	X	X	X	255
Investigative Teams		X			X		X			X	259
Key Concept			X			X			X		261
Kindling	X	X		X	X		X	X		X	263
K-N-W-S	X	X	X	X	X	X			X		265
Learning Logs		X			X		X	X	X	X	267
L.E.T.S. Connect	X	X	X	X	X	X	X			X	269
Listservers, Message Boards, DVD-ROMs/CD-ROMs			X			X	X	X	X	X	271
Math Notes		X	X		X	X			X		273
Math Reading Keys	X	X	X	X	X	X			X		275
Narrow Reading		X			X		X			X	279
Opinion Guide		X	X		X	X	X	X		X	281
Paired Guided Reading		X	X		X	X	X	X	X	X	283

ASCD © 2007. All Rights Reserved.

Strategy	Language Acquisition for ELLs			Reading Process			Best Content Area				Page
	Input (Inter-pretive)	Intake (Inter-personal)	Output (Presen-tational)	Pre-reading	During Reading	After Reading	LA	Sc	Math	SS	
Peer Reading		X	X		X	X	X	X	X	X	285
Pen in Hand		X			X		X	X	X	X	287
Proposition Support Outlines	X	X	X	X	X	X	X	X	X	X	289
QAR		X	X		X	X	X			X	291
Q-Space			X			X	X	X	X	X	293
Question Menu	X	X	X	X	X	X	X	X		X	295
Questioning the Author		X	X		X	X	X			X	299
RAFT			X			X	X	X	X	X	301
Read Three Times		X			X				X		305
Reading for Meaning		X	X		X	X	X	X	X	X	307
Reading-and-Writing-to-Learn Journals			X			X	X	X	X	X	309
REAP		X	X		X	X	X	X		X	311
Reciprocal Teaching	X	X	X		X	X	X	X	X	X	313
ReQuest		X			X		X	X	X	X	315
ROW		X	X		X	X	X	X		X	317
Save the Last Word for Me		X	X		X	X	X			X	319
Science Connection Overview	X	X		X	X			X			321
Scintillating Sentences and Quizzical Quotes		X	X		X	X	X			X	325
Scored Discussion			X			X	X	X		X	327

ASCD © 2007. All Rights Reserved.

Section Two

| Strategy | Language Acquisition for ELLs | | | Reading Process | | | Best Content Area | | | | Page |
	Input (Inter-pretive)	Intake (Inter-personal)	Output (Presen-tational)	Pre-reading	During Reading	After Reading	LA	Sc	Math	SS	
Skimming & Scanning		X			X	X	X	X	X	X	331
SMART	X	X			X	X	X	X	X	X	333
SPAWN			X			X	X	X	X	X	335
SQ3R	X	X	X	X	X	X	X	X	X	X	337
Story Grammars and Maps		X	X		X	X	X				339
Task Rotation			X			X	X	X	X	X	343
Think-Aloud Self-Assessment		X			X		X	X	X	X	345
T-Notes		X	X		X	X	X	X	X	X	347
Two-Minute Preview	X				X		X	X	X	X	349
Visual Reading Guide	X	X		X	X			X	X	X	351
X Marks the Spot		X			X		X	X	X	X	353

ASCD © 2007. All Rights Reserved.

Strategies for
SUCCESS
with English Language Learners

READING STRATEGIES FOR GRADES 3–12

Anticipation/Prediction Guide

Why use it?

Use of this strategy will help students to . . .

- Identify purpose for reading.
- Adjust reading rate according to purpose for reading.
- Use self-monitoring strategies, such as rereading, attending to vocabulary, and cross-checking.
- Use comprehension strategies to monitor own reading (predict/confirm).
- Relate data and facts from informational texts to prior information and experience.
- Use prior knowledge and experience to understand ideas and vocabulary found in books.
- Use prior knowledge in concert with text information to support comprehension, from forming predictions to drawing conclusions.
- Skim material to locate specific information.
- Use knowledge of structure, content, and vocabulary to understand informational text.
- Identify missing, conflicting, or unclear information.
- Select, reject, and reconcile ideas and information in light of beliefs.

How does it work?

Anticipation guides have two columns, labeled "Me" and "Text." Before reading the text, students place a check in the "Me" column next to any statement with which they agree. After reading the text, students compare their opinions with information contained in the text (Herber, 1978). See the examples that follow.

ANTICIPATION/PREDICTION GUIDE

Section Two

Variations for Emergent English Language Learners

- Ask the ESL teacher to guide the ELLs through the prereading activity to expose them to the concepts beforehand.
- Highlight or provide specific page numbers for each of the statements to be found in the text.
- Pair ELLs with linguistic buddies so the buddy can translate or explain the material.
- Provide ELLs a bilingual dictionary to assist with key words.
- Use coteaching strategies.

Examples:

An example for a math anticipation guide on statistics might look like the following:

Me	Text	
_____	_____	1. There are several kinds of averages for a set of data.
_____	_____	2. The mode is the middle number in a set of data.
_____	_____	3. Range tells how far apart numbers in a data set can be.
_____	_____	4. Outliers are always ignored.
_____	_____	5. Averages are always given as percentages.

An example for a science anticipation guide on matter might look like the following:

Me	Text	
_____	_____	1. Matter is made up of elements.
_____	_____	2. An element is made up of many different atoms.
_____	_____	3. An element is the same thing as a compound.
_____	_____	4. Most compounds are made up of molecules.
_____	_____	5. Elements are represented by chemical symbols.

Source: From *Teaching Reading in Mathematics* (p. 43), by M. L. Barton and Heidema, 2002, Aurora, CO: McREL. Copyright 2002 by Mid-continent Research for Education and Learning. Adapted with permission.

ASCD © 2007. All Rights Reserved.

Strategies for
SUCCESS
with English Language Learners

READING STRATEGIES FOR GRADES 3–12

Check Those Facts!

Why use it?

Use of this strategy will help students to . . .

- Locate and use media resources to acquire information.
- Find, combine, and evaluate information from print and electronic sources for inquiries.
- Preview informational texts to assess content and organization and select texts useful for the task.
- Skim texts to gain an overall impression and scan texts for particular information.
- Read unfamiliar texts to collect data, facts, and ideas.
- Combine multiple strategies to enhance comprehension and response.
- Recognize when comprehension has been disrupted and initiate self-correction strategies, such as rereading and adjusting reading rate.
- Compare and contrast information on one topic from two or more sources.
- Make inferences and draw conclusions on the basis of information from the text.
- Judge accuracy and validity of content and information.
- Identify different perspectives on an issue presented in more than one text.
- Interpret and evaluate data, facts, and ideas in informational texts, online and electronic databases, and Web sites.
- Participate collaboratively in group discussions of texts.

How does it work?

This strategy serves a dual purpose: to help students become better judges of information found on the Internet and to allow students to explore an area of interest related to the content. Each student selects a topic of research; students are directed to use a search engine such as Google or Ask Jeeves, to locate information about their topic. Students print the articles they locate, making sure they have the URLs, and seek corroborating articles from two additional Internet sources. They compare and contrast the information and draw conclusions about the validity of their sources. Through panel or roundtable discussions, they share the information (Stephens & Brown, 2005).

Variations for Emergent English Language Learners

- Have ELLs locate information in their primary languages as well as English so they can shadow-read for information (i.e., read in primary language first).
- Identify specific Web sites for ELLs to search to ensure material that is comprehensible—for example, the material may have illustrations or an adjusted reading level.
- Ask the ESL teacher to coteach.

ASCD © 2007. All Rights Reserved.

Strategies for
SUCCESS
with English Language Learners

SECTION: LITERACY STRATEGIES

READING STRATEGIES FOR GRADES 3–12

Circle-Seat-Center

Why use it?

Use of this strategy will help students to . . .

- Engage in independent silent reading.
- Use comprehension strategies, such as rereading and discussing with teacher to clarify meaning of text, summarizing, and answering questions.
- Identify main ideas and supporting details in informational texts.
- Use graphic organizers to record details.
- Ask questions to clarify understanding and to focus reading of text.
- Identify unclear information with assistance.
- Use opinions and reactions of teachers to evaluate personal interpretation of ideas and information.
- Combine multiple strategies to enhance comprehension and responses.
- Use strategies such as discussing with others and reading guides to assist in comprehension.
- Work collaboratively with peers to respond to texts.
- Demonstrate comprehension of texts through a variety of responses.

How does it work?

Have students read the text. Divide the class into three groups: Circle, Seat, and Center. The circle group reviews the text with your assistance. The seat group members work alone using study guides. The center group works on a project related to the text. Students rotate to all three groups (Sadler, 2001).

 © 2007. All Rights Reserved.

231

Variations for Emergent English Language Learners

- Assign weakest readers to the circle as their first stop.
- Ask the ESL teacher to prepare study guides for the seat station for ELLs.
- Ask the ESL teacher to coteach.
- Design the group projects so all students have a role in showing what they know and can do.

ASCD © 2007. All Rights Reserved.

Strategies for
SUCCESS
with English Language Learners

SECTION: LITERACY STRATEGIES

READING STRATEGIES FOR GRADES 3–12

Coding

Why use it?

Use of this strategy will help students to . . .
- Work cooperatively with peers to comprehend text.
- Identify main ideas and supporting details.
- Identify specific words causing comprehension difficulties.
- Organize and categorize text information by using knowledge of a variety of structures (e.g., sequence, cause/effect).
- Use knowledge of story structure, story elements and key vocabulary to interpret stories.
- Recognize a range of literary techniques.
- Employ self-monitoring strategies and engage in self-correcting behaviors when comprehension has been disrupted.
- Use text features such as headings, captions, and titles to understand and interpret informational texts.
- Identify unclear information.
- Interpret multiple levels of meaning and subtleties in text.
- Formulate questions to be answered when reading.
- Participate in discussions about text.

How does it work?

Using a complex reading selection, students take notes on the text while reading alone or in pairs. The note-taking system consists of colored markers for main ideas, circles for new terms, numbers for sequential events, arrows for related concepts, and question marks for unclear issues. Pairs share with others when finished (Devine, 1988).

Variations for Emergent English Language Learners

- Ask the ESL teacher to code a text for the ELLs in advance according to their linguistic levels, and then have the ELLs read the text to comprehend the coding.
- Allow ELLs to work together as pairs and then share with another pair of students who are English-proficient.
- Have the ELLs reread the same text a few weeks later so they can metacognitively monitor their strategies and progress.

ASCD © 2007. All Rights Reserved.

Strategies for
SUCCESS
with English Language Learners

READING STRATEGIES FOR GRADES 3–12

Collaborative Strategic Reading

Why use it?

Use of this strategy will help students to . . .

- Work collaboratively with peers to comprehend text.
- Participate in discussion by integrating multiple strategies (e.g., predict, summarize, clarify).
- Engage in purposeful oral reading in small groups.
- Make, confirm, or revise predictions.
- Use self-monitoring strategies such as rereading, attending to vocabulary, and cross-checking to determine meaning of text.
- Identify the themes or message of a text.
- Distinguish between relevant and irrelevant information.
- Identify a conclusion that summarizes the main idea.
- Summarize main ideas of informational text and details from literary text orally and in writing. Generate literal, inferential, and evaluative questions.
- Employ a range of postreading responses to think about new learning.

How does it work?

Students of various reading and achievement levels work in small groups to assist one another in applying four reading strategies to facilitate their comprehension of content-area text:

1. *Preview:* Prior to reading, students recall what they already know about the topic and predict what the passage might be about.

 © 2007. All Rights Reserved.

235

Section Two

2. *Click and clunk:* During reading, students monitor comprehension by identifying *clunks,* or difficult words and concepts in a passage, and using fix-up strategies when the text does not make sense.

3. *Get the gist:* During reading, students restate the most important idea in a paragraph or section.

4. *Wrap up:* After reading, students summarize what has been learned and generate questions that a teacher might ask on a test.

Initially, the teacher presents the strategies to the whole class using modeling, role-playing, and teacher think-alouds. Students record their ideas in learning logs and complete response activities (Klingner & Vaughn, 2000).

Variations for Emergent English Language Learners

- Assign the task of wrap-up to ELLs so they are summarizing what the group has discussed.
- Provide ELLs with "question spinners" that provide cue words to help them generate questions.
- Try a coteaching model with the ESL teacher.

ASCD © 2007. All Rights Reserved.

Strategies for
SUCCESS
with English Language Learners

READING STRATEGIES FOR GRADES 3–12

Concept Collection

Why use it?

Use of this strategy will help students to . . .

- Identify purposes for reading.
- Use self-monitoring strategies such as rereading, cross-checking, and attending to vocabulary.
- Connect words and ideas in books to spoken language vocabulary and background knowledge.
- Read unfamiliar text to collect ideas and concepts.
- Use graphic organizers to record significant details from informational texts.
- Analyze information on the basis of new or prior knowledge and personal experience.
- Identify information that is implied rather than stated.
- Evaluate concepts in texts by identifying a central idea and supporting details.
- Recognize how new information is related to prior knowledge or experiences.
- Identify multiple layers of meaning.
- Draw conclusions and make inferences on the basis of explicit and implied information.

How does it work?

This strategy is a variation of K-W-L for older students. Students divide their paper into four columns and label them Familiar Concepts, Evidence, New

CONCEPT COLLECTION

Section Two

Concepts, and Evidence. Before reading, students fill out the first column by listing major concepts they already know about the topic. They read the selection, recording evidence that supports concepts in the first column. After reading, they identify new concepts they've developed as a result of reading. They then look for evidence to support these concepts. Developing concepts as opposed to listing facts requires teacher modeling and substantial guided practice over time (Brown, Phillips, & Stephens, 1993). See the example that follows.

Variations for Emergent English Language Learners

- Allow ELLs to complete the Familiar Concepts column in their primary language, with the ESL teacher, or through the use of illustrations.
- Provide reading guides to assist ELLs with the New Concepts column.
- Provide the option of shadow-reading (primary language first) to support ELLs who are literate in their primary language so they can read about new concepts in the primary language before doing so in English.
- Pair students up to complete the tasks.
- Be sure to model as a prereading strategy so students can practice as the during-reading strategy.

Sample Template:

Familiar Concepts	Evidence	New Concepts	Evidence

ASCD © 2007. All Rights Reserved.

Strategies for
SUCCESS
with English Language Learners

READING STRATEGIES FOR GRADES 3–12

Cornell Method of Note Taking

Why use it?

Use of this strategy will help students to . . .

- Formulate questions to be answered by reading.
- Focus on key words and phrases to generate questions.
- Ask questions to self-monitor comprehension, to clarify understanding, and to focus reading.
- Locate and summarize main ideas and supporting details from text.
- Recognize and use text features (headings and subheadings) from informational texts to understand content.
- Participate in discussion about texts by integrating multiple strategies (ask questions, take notes).
- Identify a conclusion that summarizes the main idea.
- Draw conclusions and make inferences on the basis of explicit and implied information.
- Use graphic organizers to record significant details from informational texts.
- Answer questions with accurate and complete responses.

How does it work?

Students use this strategy to summarize main ideas and details from their reading. The teacher guides students in a survey of the text to identify topics and subtopics and has students convert the topics and subtopics into questions. As students read, they stop periodically to fill in details and main ideas (some will need this process modeled). Upon completion of the reading,

CORNELL METHOD OF NOTE TAKING

Section Two

students take time to review and refine their notes (Strong, Silver, Perini, & Tuculescu, 2002).

Variations for Emergent English Language Learners

- Ask the ESL teacher to survey the text with ELLs either before class or in class through parallel coteaching.
- Provide ELLs with "question spinners" that provide cue words to help them generate questions (available from www.kaganonline.com in English and Spanish).
- Model the process and then differentiate the materials (e.g., use the jigsaw strategy).
- Allow ELLs to illustrate their notes.
- Provide half-completed notes to assist ELLs to find the material.

Example:

Questions	Details	Main Idea

ASCD © 2007. All Rights Reserved.

Strategies for
SUCCESS
with English Language Learners

READING STRATEGIES FOR GRADES 3–12

Directed Reading and Thinking Activity (DRTA)

Why use it?

Use of this strategy will help students to . . .

- Identify the purpose for reading.
- Use comprehension strategies to monitor own reading (e.g., predict/confirm, reread, self-correct) to clarify meaning of text.
- Use knowledge of structure to identify and interpret plot, character, and events; make predictions; draw conclusions; and make inferences about events and characters.
- Use specific evidence from stories to identify themes; to describe characters, their actions, and their motivations; and to relate a sequence of events.
- Define characteristics and identify literary elements of different genres.
- Determine how the use and meaning of literary devices (symbolism, flashback, foreshadowing) convey an author's message or intent.
- Identify social and cultural context to enhance understanding.
- Use word recognition skills and strategies accurately and automatically to understand text.
- Determine the meaning of unfamiliar words by using context clues.
- Recognize how the author's use of language creates images or feelings.
- Engage in oral readings and discussions of text.

How does it work?

This strategy consists of (1) directing the reading-thinking process and (2) fundamental skills training. The first element entails setting purposes for

ASCD © 2007. All Rights Reserved.

DIRECTED READING AND THINKING ACTIVITY (DRTA)

Section Two

reading, reading to verify those purposes, pausing to evaluate understanding, and then reading again. Three essential questions guide this strategy: *What do you think will happen next? Why do you think so? How can you prove it?* The teacher selects predetermined reading points (e.g., points where there is a major shift in the action, a new character is introduced, or a conflict is resolved). After they read, students complete the three questions that are designed to encourage thoughtful contemplation, reflective discussion, and individual purposes for reading. The second element of the tool consists of students' reexamining the text to learn to effectively use the skills of word recognition, contextual analysis, and concept development (Stauffer, 1969).

Variations for Emergent English Language Learners

- Try using alternative coteaching for this strategy, whereby the ESL teacher models the skills of word recognition, contextual analysis, and concept development, and the classroom teacher models answering the three essential questions; students switch between the two lessons.
- Ask the ESL teacher to prepare ELLs beforehand with a first reading so they come to class prepared.
- Divide the predetermined reading points for pairs of students to share the load, and then have students share their sections.

ASCD © 2007. All Rights Reserved.

Strategies for
SUCCESS
with English Language Learners

READING STRATEGIES FOR GRADES 3–12

Elaborative Interrogation

Why use it?

Use of this strategy will help students to . . .

- Ask questions to focus on reading.
- Make connections between text being read and own lives.
- Use prior knowledge in concert with text information to support comprehension.
- Organize and categorize text information by using text structures (cause/effect).
- Locate information in text needed to answer questions or solve problems.
- Identify signal words to aid in comprehension of ideas (cause/effect).
- Use knowledge of text structures to recognize and discriminate differences among a variety of texts and to support understanding.
- Use established criteria to analyze the quality of information in text.
- Draw conclusions and make inferences on explicit and implied information from text.
- Recognize how one's own point of view contributes to forming ideas.
- Select, reject, and reconcile ideas and information in light of prior knowledge and experiences.
- Participate in discussion by integrating multiple strategies (e.g., ask questions, clarify relationships).
- Work cooperatively with peers to comprehend text.
- Generate and answer literal, inferential, and evaluative questions.

 © 2007. All Rights Reserved.

Section Two

ELABORATIVE INTERROGATION

Section Two

How does it work?

This strategy aims to rekindle an inquisitive attitude toward learning by teaching students to ask appropriate *why* questions. The teacher select a series of factual statements from the reading, presents them to the students, and models appropriate *why* questions to focus their attention on implied cause/effect relationships. Next the teacher presents students with the formula for asking *why* questions (see the example that follows). Students work with partners to generate *why* questions and to brainstorm possible answers; they create a series of questions to exchange with another pair (using different reading sections). Students learn that relationships between information are important (Pressley, Symons, McDaniel, Snyder, & Turnure 1988).

Variations for Emergent English Language Learners

- Ask the ESL teacher to prepare ELLs with questions beforehand.
- Partner ELLs with linguistic buddies who can translate possible answers during the brainstorming sessions.
- Differentiate the reading sections for ELLs.

Example:
Formula for Answering Why Questions

Why What I Am Learning Now What I Already Know About Possible Relationship

ASCD © 2007. All Rights Reserved.

Strategies for
SUCCESS
with English Language Learners

READING STRATEGIES FOR GRADES 3–12

Ethical Choices

Why use it?

Use of this strategy will help students to . . .

- Use prior knowledge and experience to understand ideas and vocabulary found in books.
- Use self-monitoring strategies such as self-questioning to construct meaning.
- Compare and contrast information on one topic from two different sources.
- Find, evaluate, and combine information from different sources for teacher-selected or student-generated inquiries.
- Identify missing, conflicting, or unclear information.
- Make inferences and draw conclusions from texts.
- Identify information that is implied rather than stated.
- Use graphic organizers to record ideas from texts.
- Evaluate the validity and accuracy of information, ideas, themes, opinions, and experiences in texts (identify conflicting information; consider the background or qualification of writers' questions, assumptions, beliefs, intentions, and biases; evaluate examples, details, or reasons used to support ideas; identify fallacies of logic that lead to unsupported conclusions; discriminate between messages and hidden agendas; identify techniques used to persuade).
- Use established criteria to analyze the quality of information in text.
- Judge accuracy of content to gather facts.
- Identify different perspectives such as social, cultural, ethnic, and historical on an issue presented in one or more than one text.

 © 2007. All Rights Reserved.

ETHICAL CHOICES

Section Two

- Use opinions of teachers and classmates to evaluate personal interpretation of ideas and information.
- Participate in discussion about texts by integrating multiple strategies (support point of view, work cooperatively with peers).

How does it work?

This strategy helps students take a position after exploring difficult issues. The teacher introduces an issue with opposing positions, and students discuss a position based on what they know. The teacher then provides a packet of reading materials (balanced accounts). Students complete an issues map, listing pro and con arguments, and compare their original stand with the issue map to determine whether they have changed their opinions (Stephens & Brown, 2005).

Variations for Emergent English Language Learners

- Gather information on issues in primary languages of ELLs.
- Ask the ESL teacher to build background knowledge on issues.
- Differentiate reading material (e.g., multiple materials and references) for ELLs.
- Pair ELLs with linguistic buddies to complete the issues map.
- Use complementary or support coteaching models with the ESL teacher.

ASCD © 2007. All Rights Reserved.

Strategies for
SUCCESS
with English Language Learners

READING STRATEGIES FOR GRADES 3–12

Four-Way Reporting and Recording

Why use it?

Use of this strategy will help students to . . .

- Identify purpose for reading.
- Use self-monitoring strategies such as rereading, cross-checking text features, and attending to unfamiliar vocabulary.
- Compare and contrast information from more than one source.
- Make inferences and draw conclusions.
- Evaluate information by identifying central ideas and primary details.
- Use a variety of strategies to support understanding of texts.
- Condense, combine, or categorize information from more than one source.
- Recognize how different authors treat similar themes.
- Identify different perspectives on an issue, such as social, cultural, ethnic, and historical.
- Take notes to record and organize ideas and use notes as part of prewriting activities.
- Employ a range of postreading practice.
- Work cooperatively with others to determine meaning.
- Demonstrate comprehension through a variety of responses.

How does it work?

This strategy is intended to help students develop a repertoire of note-making strategies so they can make decisions to follow their style or the features of a text. The teacher arranges students into groups of four, in which each group

FOUR-WAY REPORTING AND RECORDING

Section Two

member becomes responsible for a different reading related to the topic. Students read the text and select a method of note making. They then share notes with a partner; while one shares the other takes notes using a different method of note making (adapted as needed by grade level). The groups of four continue to share all their information until each student has all four quadrants of the sample organizer completed. The groups then complete a synthesis task—for example, students develop criteria for an oral presentation or a speech (Strong, Silver, Perini, & Tuculescu, 2002).

Variations for Emergent English Language Learners

- Differentiate reading material by level of understanding.
- Use a note-making strategy that is more visual than linguistic (e.g., mapping).
- Provide reading guides and partially completed notes for ELLs.
- Use parallel or peer coteaching models to prepare for oral presentation or speeches.

Example:

Concept Mapping	Power Notes
Cornell Method	Listing

ASCD © 2007. All Rights Reserved.

Strategies for
SUCCESS
with English Language Learners

READING STRATEGIES FOR GRADES 3–12

Group Summarizing

Why use it?

Use of this strategy will help students to . . .
- Identify purpose for reading.
- Preview informational text to assess content and organization and to build schemas.
- Categorize text information using knowledge of text structures.
- Recognize and use organizational features such as headings and subheadings to locate information.
- State or summarize a main idea and support or elaborate on it with relevant details.
- Collect and interpret data, facts, and ideas from unfamiliar texts.
- Use text features such as captions, tables, charts, graphs, maps, notes, and other visuals to interpret texts.
- Combine multiple strategies to enhance comprehension and response (predict/confirm, summarize).
- Distinguish between relevant and irrelevant information.
- Take notes to record data, facts, and ideas with teacher direction and independently.

How does it work?

Class summaries help learners review and remember information while also helping students practice the skill of distinguishing between key and subordinate ideas. The teacher instructs students to survey the text passage to identify major topics for focus, then divides the board or chart paper into

Section Two

GROUP SUMMARIZING

Section Two

parts and labels the sections based on major topics (establishing a purpose for reading). After students have read the text, volunteers provide information for each of the categories. The critical information is then transferred to the appropriate labeled sections of the chart or board. For example, the sections for a science unit on electricity might include description, kinds of electricity, electric circuits, producing electricity, using electricity, and measuring electricity (Brown, Day, & Jones, 1983).

Variations for Emergent English Language Learners

- Ask the ESL teacher to survey the text beforehand with ELLs.
- Provide reading guides for the during-reading stage.
- Pair students up with linguistic buddies.
- Use a "smart board" to record information and give printed notes to ELLs to review with the ESL teacher afterwards.

ASCD © 2007. All Rights Reserved.

Strategies for
SUCCESS
with English Language Learners

READING STRATEGIES FOR GRADES 3–12

Inductive Learning

Why use it?

Use of this strategy will help students to . . .
- Connect words and ideas in books to spoken language vocabulary and background knowledge.
- Identify a purpose for reading.
- Use comprehension strategies to monitor own reading (predict/verify or refute).
- Collect data, facts, and ideas from unfamiliar texts.
- Relate ideas to prior information and knowledge.
- Use knowledge of text structure to recognize and discriminate among a variety of texts.
- Make predictions, draw conclusions, and make inferences about ideas or events.
- Identify information or ideas that are implied rather than stated.
- Make, confirm, or revise predictions.
- Condense, combine, or categorize new information or ideas.
- Generate a list of significant questions or concepts to assist with text analysis.
- Engage in purposeful oral reading in groups or pairs.
- Use graphic organizers to record main ideas and details.

How does it work?

Teachers select approximately 30 words and phrases from the reading that support the generalizations they expect students to make. In small groups,

© 2007. All Rights Reserved.

Section Two

INDUCTIVE LEARNING

students group the words into categories based on common attributes. Then they must devise a descriptive label for each group that succinctly identifies the common relationship among words. Students use their groupings to make three hypotheses or predictions about the reading. They then read the selection to find out whether their hypotheses or predictions were correct or mistaken. Using an organizer, they jot down evidence from the reading that supports or refutes each hypothesis or prediction (Silver, Strong, & Perini, 2000).

Variations for Emergent English Language Learners

- Try to select some words that are cognates (similar across languages) as a part of the list.
- Group students into trios and have ELLs sit in the middle with the responsibility of recording the sorted words, the second student with the responsibility of reading, and the third student with the responsibility of making the hypothesis or prediction.
- Provide the words beforehand to the ESL teacher.

ASCD © 2007. All Rights Reserved.

Strategies for
SUCCESS
with English Language Learners

READING STRATEGIES FOR GRADES 3–12

Infofiction

Why use it?

Use of this strategy will help students to . . .

- Show interest in a wide range of grade-level texts including fiction and nonfiction.
- Select literature on the basis of interest from a variety of genres and by different authors.
- Compare and contrast information on one topic from multiple sources.
- Locate and use media resources to acquire information.
- Read print-based and electronic texts for specific purposes.
- Find, evaluate, and combine information from print and electronic sources for inquiries.
- Use knowledge of text structures to discriminate among texts and to support understanding.
- Explain statements of fact and fiction.
- Make inferences and draw conclusions.
- Analyze, contrast, support, and critique points of view in a wide range of genres.
- Evaluate the validity and accuracy of information, ideas, themes, opinions, and experiences by identifying conflicting information, questioning assumptions and intentions of writers, identifying fallacies of logic that lead to unsupported conclusions, and discriminating between apparent messages and hidden agendas.
- Use established criteria to analyze the quality of information in text.
- Judge accuracy of content to gather facts and information.

 © 2007. All Rights Reserved.

INFOFICTION

- Identify different perspectives on issues, such as social, cultural, ethnic, and historical.

How does it work?

Students read novels that have a significant informational dimension (novels that combine fact and fiction). While reading the novel, students identify the informational content in the book by checking facts in reference books or through reliable sources on the Internet. The teacher and students plan further investigation of the information (Stephens & Brown, 2005).

Variations for Emergent English Language Learners

- Use the time-honored ESL strategy of shadow-reading (reading in primary language and English to increase comprehension).
- Use coteaching models to complete tasks.

Example:

Book Title and Author

Factual Information	Page #	Verification Source

ASCD © 2007. All Rights Reserved.

Strategies for
SUCCESS
with English Language Learners

READING STRATEGIES FOR GRADES 3–12

Interactive Reading Guide

Why use it?
Use of this strategy will help students to . . .
- Learn grade-level vocabulary through a variety of means.
- Identify purpose for reading.
- Use self-monitoring strategies such as rereading, adjusting rate of reading, and cross-checking to determine meaning.
- Apply corrective strategies with peers and reference tools.
- Use text structure to recognize differences among texts.
- Understand written directions and procedures.
- Collect and interpret data and ideas from unfamiliar texts.
- Recognize and use organizational features to locate information.
- Skim material to gain an overview of content or to locate information or ideas.
- Combine multiple strategies to enhance comprehension and response.
- Evaluate information, ideas, opinions, and themes in texts by identifying, with assistance, main ideas, details that are primary, and details that are less important.
- Identify literary elements such as setting, plot, and character in different genres.
- Identify the ways in which characters and events develop throughout a story.
- Identify different perspectives on issues, such as social, cultural, ethnic, and historical.
- Engage in purposeful oral reading in groups or pairs.
- Participate cooperatively in group discussions of texts.

INTERACTIVE READING GUIDE

Section Two

How does it work?

This strategy is a treasure hunt that helps students learn to locate information in textbooks, especially when the texts are too difficult for independent reading. The teacher (1) previews reading assignments to determine major information to be learned and to locate possible pitfalls for understanding; (2) constructs an interactive reading guide for students to complete with a partner or in cooperative groups; (3) divides the passage into segments—those to be read orally by individuals to their groups, those to be read silently by each student, and those less important to be skimmed; and (4) has each group use the guide to report the information (Wood, 1988). See the examples that follow.

Variations for Emergent English Language Learners

- Try alternative coteaching to preview the text (ESL teacher previews vocabulary and builds background knowledge, and classroom teacher previews ideas and use of text features).
- If possible, provide a bilingual interactive reading guide.
- Place ELLs with linguistic buddies for the reading task.

ASCD © 2007. All Rights Reserved.

Example:

Interactive Reading Guide for Biology	Interactive Reading Guide for History

Water Clarity and Sediments (pages 11–12)
1. Look at the drawing of the fish at the top of the page. Two things are mentioned as "stream trouble-makers." What are these two things?
2. A key word in your reading is *clarity*. **Student A:** Read aloud paragraph 1 to your group. **Group:** Decide what *water clarity* means and write it below: If you were a fish, what would be the best type of water, according to paragraph 1?
3. Paragraph 2 talks about the color of a stream. **Group:** Silently skim this paragraph and find two things that can change the color of water in a stream.
4. Paragraph 3 is the main point of your article. **Student B:** Read paragraph 3 aloud to your group. **Group:** Decide what effects algae and sediments have on water.
5. Paragraph 4 describes algae. **Group:** Silently read the paragraph and look for the following information on algae:
  • What kinds of streams are most likely to have algae?
  • What exactly are algae?
  • What color is water that has a lot of algae?
6. **Student C:** Read paragraph 5 aloud to your group. **Group:** Tell what kinds of things could be sediment in a stream.
7. **Group:** Read paragraph 6 silently and look for ways sediment gets into streams. Discuss what these ways are and write them here.
8. **Group:** Silently skim paragraphs 7, 8, and 9. If you were a fish, which source of sediment sounds the worst to you?
9. Sediment and algae make water cloudy, which cause trouble for fish. The next paragraphs tell five reasons why. **Student A:** Silently read paragraphs 10 and 11. **Student B:** Silently read paragraphs 12 and 13. **Student C:** Silently read paragraph 14. Share the five reasons why cloudy water is bad for fish and write them below in your own words.
 	
Source: Developed by D. Buehl & S. Krauskopf, 1998, Madison East High School. Madison. WI.
	Section A: Introduction to Ellis Island (pages 1–2)
	1. **Class:** Listen and follow along in the article as I read this passage to you. Then based on what you remember, respond to the questions below. If you need to, you can locate information from the article:
	  • Ellis Island is located in what city?
	  • What famous national landmark can be seen from Ellis Island?
	  • List four reasons that were mentioned about why immigrants came to the United States.
	Section B: Early Immigration to the United States (pages 2-3)
	1. **Partners:** Read paragraph 1 silently and decide on an answer to the following question:
	  • Who were the first immigrants to the United States?
	2. **Partner X:** Read aloud paragraph 2. **Partner Y:** Listen and decide how to answer the following questions:
	  • Were the early immigrants to the United States regarded as a good thing?
	  • Why or why not?
	3. **Partner Y:** Read aloud paragraph 3. **Partner X:** Listen and decide how to answer the following questions:
	  • Did the government keep very close track of immigrants in the early days?
	  • What clues in the article helped you figure this out?
	4. **Partners:** Read paragraphs 4, 5, and 6 silently. List four things that attracted people to the United States.
	5. **Partner X:** Read paragraphs 7 and 8 out loud. **Partner Y:** Listen and decide how to answer this question:
	  • What were some of the nationalities of the new immigrants?
	  • What was the attitude of many Americans to the new immigrants?
	
	Source: Developed by D. Buehl & P. McDonald, 1999, Madison East High School, Madison, WI.

Source: From *Classroom Strategies for Interactive Learning* (2nd ed.) (p. 71), by D. Buehl, 2001, Newark, DE: International Reading Association. Copyright 2001 by International Reading Association. Reproduced with permission.

INTERACTIVE READING GUIDE

Section Two

Strategies for
SUCCESS
with English Language Learners

READING STRATEGIES FOR GRADES 3–12

Investigative Teams

Why use it?

Use of this strategy will help students to . . .

- Discriminate among a variety of texts.
- Read with increasing fluency and confidence from a variety of texts.
- Select books independently to meet informational needs.
- Maintain a personal reading list to reflect goals and accomplishments.
- Lead and participate in group discussions about grade-level texts by integrating multiple strategies (e.g., ask questions, clarify misunderstandings, support point of view, summarize ideas).
- State main ideas and support or elaborate with relevant details in texts.
- Compare and contrast information.
- Use established criteria to analyze the quality of information.
- Analyze information from different sources by making connections and showing relationships to other texts.
- Evaluate the validity and accuracy of information, ideas, opinions, and themes in texts by identifying conflicting information, multiple levels of meaning, apparent messages and hidden agendas, propaganda, and persuasive techniques.
- Identify different perspectives on issues—such as social, cultural, ethnic, and historical—presented in multiple texts.
- Judge a text by using evaluative criteria from a variety of perspectives, such as literary, political, and personal.

Section Two

INVESTIGATIVE TEAMS

How does it work?

This strategy resembles literature circles but is used for nonfiction or infofiction. Groups of students are given a different book on a particular topic or theme. The teacher assigns roles such that each student is always an investigative reporter and then any of the following: headline writer, graphic artist, editorial consultant, critic, travel reporter, ad designer, researcher, social columnist. The teacher and class establish a calendar for reading and responding, for meeting in groups for discussion, and for rotating roles (Stephens & Brown, 2005).

Variations for Emergent English Language Learners

- Differentiate reading material based on primary language or on level of English proficiency.
- Assign roles of graphic artist or ad designer to ELLs in the beginning.
- Use coteaching models to implement the strategy.

ASCD © 2007. All Rights Reserved.

Section Two

Strategies for
SUCCESS
with English Language Learners

READING STRATEGIES FOR GRADES 3–12

Key Concept

Why use it?

Use of this strategy will help students to . . .

- Learn words and concepts directly and indirectly through reading.
- Use comprehension strategies such as attending to vocabulary to clarify meaning of text.
- Locate information in a text that is needed to solve a problem.
- Read and follow multistep directions or procedures to solve problems or complete assignments.
- Identify a conclusion that summarizes a main idea.
- Distinguish relevant and irrelevant information.
- Interpret facts taken from graphs, charts, and other visuals.
- Use self-monitoring strategies such as attending to key words to enhance understanding.
- Apply corrective strategies such as discussing with others to assist in comprehension.
- Take notes to record data, facts, and ideas by following teacher direction and by writing independently.
- Develop an idea within a brief text.
- Understand the purpose for reading and writing.

How does it work?

This strategy helps students understand key concepts in mathematics and improve their comprehension of mathematics texts. The teacher records a phrase identifying the lesson focus and describes or explains the key concept

KEY CONCEPT

Section Two

(or students do so after reading a section of the text). Students write a concise summary of the key concept in the grid and summarize any properties, rules, or processes essential for understanding the key concept. The teacher helps the students complete the examples/nonexamples section, and students complete a practice problem (Stephens & Brown, 2005).

Variations for Emergent English Language Learners

- Ask the ESL teacher to preview the key words and phrases beforehand.
- Provide nonlinguistic representations of the key words or phrases.
- Provide a graphic organizer with linguistic cues to assist with summary writing.
- Provide ELLs with linguistic buddies to assist with translations or problem solving.

Example:

Lesson Focus

Key Concept	Properties, Rules, Processes
Examples/Nonexamples	**Practice Problem**

ASCD © 2007. All Rights Reserved.

Strategies for SUCCESS with English Language Learners

READING STRATEGIES FOR GRADES 3–12

Kindling

Why use it?

Use of this strategy will help students to . . .

- Connect words and ideas in books to background knowledge.
- Use comprehension strategies such as connecting background knowledge to new ideas, visualizing, and collaborating with others to clarify meaning.
- Use prior knowledge in concert with text to support comprehension, from forming predictions to making inferences and drawing conclusions.
- Infer underlying message or theme from written text.
- Engage in purposeful oral reading in small groups.
- Recognize how information is related to prior knowledge and experience.
- Read grade-level texts and answer literal, inferential, and evaluative questions.
- Use previous reading and life experiences to understand literature.
- Make connections between texts being read and own lives and lives of others.
- Participate in group discussions about ideas and texts.
- Demonstrate comprehension of and response to text through a range of responses such as writing and discussing.
- Write voluntarily to communicate ideas.
- Understand the purpose for writing.
- Vary the formality of writing depending on the audience and purpose.

Section Two

KINDLING

Section Two

How does it work?

This strategy uses provocative questions to help students generate informal ideas and activate prior knowledge. The ideas are fleshed out through writing and peer collaboration to become the foundation for active reading. The teacher poses an open-ended question before students read, encourages students to think about what they might already know and what they will need to know to answer the question, and refers students to their journals to sketch their thoughts. Students meet in pairs or small groups to share their thoughts, record them on chart paper, and then read the given text (Strong, Silver, Perini, & Tuculescu, 2002).

Variations for Emergent English Language Learners

- Ask the ESL teacher to preview the open-ended question with ELLs beforehand to help them generate ideas and acquire key vocabulary to discuss sketches.
- Differentiate the material to be read but not the topic.
- Use coteaching models to implement this strategy.

ASCD © 2007. All Rights Reserved.

Strategies for
SUCCESS
with English Language Learners

READING STRATEGIES FOR GRADES 3–12

K-N-W-S

Why use it?

Use of this strategy will help students to . . .

- Identify a purpose for reading.
- Use self-monitoring strategies such as rereading, adjusting rate of reading, and cross-checking.
- Connect words and ideas in texts to background knowledge.
- Recognize specialized vocabulary.
- Relate data and facts from informational text to prior information and experience.
- Read unfamiliar texts to collect data, facts, and ideas.
- Locate information in a text that is needed to solve a problem.
- Use text features such as tables, charts, graphs, notes, and other visuals to understand text.
- Distinguish between relevant and irrelevant information.
- Identify missing, conflicting, unclear, or irrelevant information.
- Draw conclusions and make inferences on the basis of explicit and implied information.
- Read and follow written directions and procedures to solve problems and accomplish tasks.
- Engage in self-correcting behaviors when comprehension is disrupted.
- Use graphic organizers to record significant details from informational text.

 © 2007. All Rights Reserved.

K-N-W-S

Section Two

How does it work?

Students use a graphic organizer similar to the K-W-L chart (what I **K**now, **W**ant to know, and **L**earned). The columns for math reading are K for facts I **K**now from the information in the problem, N for information I do **N**ot need from the problem, W for **W**hat the problem is asking me to find, and S for the strategy, operation, or tools I need to use to **S**olve the problem (Barton & Heidema, 2002).

Variations for Emergent English Language Learners

- Ask the ESL teacher to preview essential vocabulary.
- Try using the complementary or support coteaching models for this strategy.

Example:

What I *Know*	Information I do *Not* need	*What* I need to find	Strategy I will use to *Solve*

ASCD © 2007. All Rights Reserved.

Strategies for SUCCESS with English Language Learners

READING STRATEGIES FOR GRADES 3–12

Learning Logs

Why use it?

Use of this strategy will help students to . . .

- Use comprehension strategies to self-monitor comprehension.
- Use self-monitoring strategies such as identifying specific vocabulary causing comprehension difficulties, rereading, and cross-checking to determine meaning.
- Identify specific words causing comprehension difficulties in written language.
- Ask questions to clarify understanding and to focus on meaning.
- Summarize main ideas.
- Infer underlying themes or messages from text.
- Identify missing or unclear information.
- Take notes to record data, facts, and ideas.

How does it work?

This strategy involves structured content journals based on reading assignments from the textbook (Reiss, 2005).

Variations for Emergent English Language Learners

- Use learning logs as an excellent anchor activity or alternative assignment for ELLs or as a bridge between the ESL and mainstream classrooms.
- Try using a cooperative learning strategy afterwards to assist students to answer questions they may have.

Section Two

 © 2007. All Rights Reserved.   267

LEARNING LOGS

Section Two

Example:

Text Pages	What I Understood	Difficult Vocabulary	Questions I Have

ASCD © 2007. All Rights Reserved.

Strategies for
SUCCESS
with English Language Learners

READING STRATEGIES FOR GRADES 3–12

L.E.T.S. Connect

Why use it?

Use of this strategy will help students to . . .

- Engage in a variety of shared reading experiences.
- Listen to or read grade-level text and ask questions to clarify understand-ing or answer literal, inferential, or critical/application questions.
- Participate in grade-level discussion about text by integrating multiple strategies (e.g., ask questions, clarify misunderstandings, support point of view, summarize).
- Use knowledge of organizational features of genres to enhance understanding.
- Use specific evidence to identify themes and describe characters, their actions, and their motivations.
- Use knowledge of story structure, story elements, and key vocabulary to interpret stories.
- Present a point of view or interpretation of a text.
- Make connections between texts being read and own lives, the lives of others, other texts read in the past, and the world at large.
- Work cooperatively with peers to comprehend text.
- Suspend judgment until all perspectives have been presented.

How does it work?

The teacher (1) selects a text to read aloud; (2) reviews with students the importance of thinking about what they are learning before, during, and after reading; (3) explains what the acronym L.E.T.S. stands for (L = listen to the

Section Two

selection, E = engage with the content, T = think about the characteristics of the genre, S = say something to your partner about your thoughts); (4) organizes students into pairs or trios; and (5) reads the selection aloud to the students and at various predetermined times stops reading and announces, "L.E.T.S. connect." As a final connection, students create a summary statement about the entire selection (Cutts, 2002).

Variations for Emergent English Language Learners

- Ask the ESL teacher to preview the text beforehand.
- Provide visual clues to enhance understanding (e.g., pictures, a film) beforehand.
- Provide linguistic buddies for ELLs who can translate.
- Try complementary or support coteaching models to implement the strategy.

ASCD © 2007. All Rights Reserved.

Strategies for SUCCESS with English Language Learners

READING STRATEGIES FOR GRADES 3–12

Listservers, Message Boards, DVD-ROMs/CD-ROMs

Why use it?

Use of this strategy will help students to . . .

- Maintain a personal reading list to reflect reading goals and accomplishments.
- Show interest in a wide range of print and nonprint materials.
- Locate and use library media resources to share information and ideas.
- Read print-based and electronic library texts silently on a daily basis for enjoyment.
- Read grade-level texts from a variety of genres in varying text formats for a variety of purposes.
- Use a variety of strategies to support understanding, such as adjust reading rate.
- Use opinions and reactions of participants to evaluate personal interpretation of ideas, information, and experience.
- Participate cooperatively and collaboratively in group discussions of texts.
- Skim material to gain an overview of content or to locate specific information.
- Compare and contrast information from multiple sources.
- Use computer software to support the reading and writing processes.

How does it work?

Listservers are electronic discussion groups organized around a common interest of the members. Students participate through e-mail. For example, Book Report is a listserver for students to share their reactions to books they

 © 2007. All Rights Reserved.

have read. Other listservers are for content areas such as math, science, and social studies, so students can verify the information they might read in their books. Message boards are Web based and usually hosted by a third party. Participants must go to the message board rather than having messages arrive in their e-mail boxes. Membership is interest driven so the discussions are focused on specific topics. Content teachers can supplement their classroom resources with content-appropriate DVD-ROMs or CD-ROMs (the former can hold as much information as an entire library, while the latter can replace entire books). Both can be resources focused on particular topics and presented in multimedia fashion. An original text may be narrated and include still photos, background music, film clips, audio clips, graphics, and automated cartoons. One of the benefits of these resources is that they provide interactive reading and writing opportunities (Stephens & Brown, 2005).

Variations for Emergent English Language Learners

*   Collaborate with the ESL teacher (and ELLs themselves) to locate the most beneficial materials and sites.

ASCD © 2007. All Rights Reserved.

Strategies for
SUCCESS
with English Language Learners

READING STRATEGIES FOR GRADES 3–12

Math Notes

Why use it?

Use of this strategy will help students to . . .

- Use self-monitoring strategies such as rereading, adjusting rate of reading, and cross-checking.
- Recognize specialized vocabulary.
- Relate data and facts from informational text to prior information and experience.
- Read unfamiliar texts to collect data, facts, and ideas.
- Locate information in a text that is needed to solve a problem.
- Read and follow multistep directions or procedures to solve problems or complete assignments.
- Ask questions to clarify understanding.
- Draw conclusions and make inferences on the basis of explicit and implied information.
- Take notes to record data, facts, and ideas.
- Use graphic organizers to record significant details from informational text.

How does it work?

The teacher presents a word problem that students must solve. Students use the "window" to help them take notes and deepen their understanding. They break down the problem in this sequence:

- In the "Facts" box, they identify the facts of the problem and what is missing.

Section Two

MATH NOTES

Section Two

    – In the "Question" box, they isolate the main question that the problem is asking, and they search for hidden questions and assumptions.

    – In the "Diagram" box, they visualize and draw the problem as they see it.

    – In the "Steps" box, they determine what steps will solve the problem (Silver, Strong, & Perini, 2000).

Variations for Emergent English Language Learners

- Use the complementary or support coteaching models.
- Pair ELLs with linguistic buddies—the student who speaks more English is responsible for completing the "Facts" and "Questions" boxes and the ELL is responsible for the "Diagram" and "Steps" boxes.

Example:

Math Notes	
The Facts What are the facts? What is missing?	**The Steps** What steps can we take to solve the problem?
The Question What question(s) need to be answered? Are there any hidden questions that need to be answered? Now use the back of this page to solve the problems.	**The Diagram** How can we represent the problem visually?

Source: From *Tools for Promoting Active, In-Depth Learning,* 2nd ed. (pp. 66–67), by H. F. Silver, R. W. Strong, and M. J. Perini, 2001, Ho Ho Kus, NJ: Thoughtful Education Press. Copyright 2001 by Thoughtful Education Press. Adapted with permission.

 © 2007. All Rights Reserved.

Strategies for SUCCESS with English Language Learners

READING STRATEGIES FOR GRADES 3–12

Math Reading Keys

Why use it?

Use of this strategy will help students to . . .

- Adjust reading rate according to purpose for reading.
- Use self-monitoring strategies such as rereading, attending to vocabulary and sentence structure, summarizing, using classroom resources, and cross-checking.
- Learn new vocabulary and concepts directly and indirectly.
- Distinguish between dictionary and implied meanings.
- Read unfamiliar text to collect data, facts, and ideas.
- Read and understand written directions.
- Identify and interpret facts taken from visuals (charts, graphs).
- Answer literal, referential, and evaluative questions.
- Locate information in a text that is needed to solve a problem.
- Identify information that is implied rather than stated or information that is missing or unclear.
- Make inferences and draw conclusions.
- Distinguish between relevant and irrelevant information.
- Read the steps of a procedure in order to solve a problem or complete a task.
- Take notes to record data, facts, and ideas.
- Work cooperatively with peers to comprehend text.

Section Two

MATH READING KEYS

Section Two

How does it work?

Students must learn that reading math texts is different from reading other kinds of textbooks; math language is conceptually laden but precise and compact, and students often glide over the text thinking about or looking for the problems to solve. In this strategy, the teacher (1) models how to read a challenging section of text on an overhead by thinking aloud and highlighting *knowledge gaps*—spots where the author thinks readers have sufficient knowledge and therefore need no further explanation; (2) points out how the think aloud followed certain steps (see the example that follows); (3) pairs students to read portions of the text during class time and encourages students to compile their own definitions of key terms in a notebook; and (4) has students create a classroom dictionary of key math terms (Buehl, 2001).

Variations for Emergent English Language Learners

* Use the support or complementary coteaching strategies for modeling the process.
* Pair ELLs with linguistic buddies who can explain or translate in primary languages.
* Have ELLs keep bilingual or nonlinguistic (pictorial) dictionaries.

Example:

Math Reading Keys Bookmark

1. Read carefully to make sure each sentence makes sense.
2. Summarize what you read in your own words.
3. When you encounter tough words think of easier words that mean the same thing and substitute.
4. Discuss with a partner what you read.
   a. Make sure you understand.
   b. Clear up things you don't understand.
5. Look for things the author assumes you already know, and things you have learned in math before.
6. Read with a pencil.
   a. Work any examples provided.
   b. Reread each section after working the examples.
7. Write and store your own definitions for key terms in a notebook.

Source: From "Making Math Make Sense: Tactics Help Kids Understand Math Language," by D. Buehl, 1998, *WEAC News and Views*, 34(3), p. 17. Copyright 1998 by Wisconsin Education Association Council. Reprinted with permission.

ASCD © 2007. All Rights Reserved.

MATH READING KEYS

Translating Math Terms into English

Decimal Notation

The way we write numbers, using 0, 1, 2, 3, 4, 5, 6, 7, 8, 9.
Each place in the number is a power of ten.

hundred thousands	ten thousands	thousands	hundreds	tens	ones
Example: 7	0	9 ,	8	7	3

Source: From *Classroom Strategies for Interactive Learning,* 2nd ed. (p. 84), by D. Buehl, 2001, Newark, DE: International Reading Association. Copyright 2001 by International Reading Association. Reproduced with permission.

Section Two

 © 2007. All Rights Reserved.

Strategies for
SUCCESS
with English Language Learners

READING STRATEGIES FOR GRADES 3–12

Narrow Reading

Why use it?

Use of this strategy will help students to . . .

- Maintain a personal reading list to reflect reading goals and accomplishments.
- Engage in independent silent reading for extended periods of time.
- Use a variety of strategies to support understanding of texts.
- Read with increasing fluency and confidence from a variety of texts.
- Read with comprehension and for different purposes.
- Adjust reading rate according to purpose for reading.
- Discriminate among a variety of texts and define characteristics of different genres.
- Use technology to support reading.
- Demonstrate comprehension of grade-level texts.
- Show interest in reading a wide range of grade-level texts, topics, genres, and authors.
- Select literature on the basis of need and interest from a variety of genres and by different authors.
- Read, view, and interpret literary texts from a variety of genres.
- Recognize differences among genres.
- Be familiar with titles and authors of a wide range of literature.
- Learn vocabulary through a variety of means.
- Identify opportunities for improvement of reading comprehension skills.

NARROW READING

Section Two

How does it work?

Narrow reading is reading on the same topic over a number of texts. Teachers can collect stories on an engaging topic or theme, reading in a single genre (e.g., a series with recurring characters and situations, or texts from a single author). The Internet also provides a vast amount of authentic text on almost any topic. From a reading perspective, focusing on texts on a recurrent topic gives learners the chance to practice reading more fluently and quickly. From a vocabulary perspective, multiple exposures to recurrent words facilitate vocabulary learning (Krashen, 1981).

Variations for Emergent English Language Learners

- Collaborate with the ESL teacher or with ELLs to select appropriate reading materials.
- Use narrow reading as a way of sustaining primary language development by allowing the selection of materials accordingly.

ASCD © 2007. All Rights Reserved.

Strategies for
SUCCESS
with English Language Learners

READING STRATEGIES FOR GRADES 3–12

Opinion Guide

Why use it?

Use of this strategy will help students to . . .

*   Identify purpose for reading.
*   Connect ideas in books to background knowledge.
*   Use comprehension strategies to monitor own reading (predict/confirm, compare/contrast opinions) and clarify meaning.
*   Summarize main ideas.
*   Support point of view with details from the text.
*   Relate data and facts from informational texts to prior knowledge and experience.
*   Compare and contrast information on one topic.
*   Use prior knowledge in concert with text information to support comprehension, from making predictions to making inferences and drawing conclusions.
*   Present a point of view or interpretation of a text, such as its theme, and support it with significant details.
*   Note and describe aspects of the writer's craft.
*   Identify information that is implied rather than stated.
*   Judge accuracy of content.
*   Use opinions of peers to evaluate personal interpretation of ideas and information.
*   Evaluate the content by identifying the author's purpose and statements of fact, opinion, and exaggeration.
*   Identify different perspectives on an issue, such as social, cultural, ethnic, and historical.

Section Two

- Work cooperatively with peers to comprehend and respond to text.
- Participate in discussions by integrating multiple strategies.

How does it work?

This strategy provides students with a series of statements to respond to from two different perspectives: their own and the author's. The teacher creates an opinion guide by writing 3–7 statements from the reading material. Each statement is preceded by two columns: one labeled "you" and the other "author." The students read and mark whether they agree or not. While they read the text, they search for ideas to help them understand the author's opinions and then, after reading, mark whether they think the author agreed or disagreed with the statements. In small groups or as a whole class, students discuss each statement, comparing the opinions of all (Stephens & Brown, 2005).

Variations for Emergent English Language Learners

- Ask the ESL teacher to survey ELLs for their opinions beforehand so they come to class with background knowledge.
- Pair ELLs with linguistic reading buddies.

ASCD © 2007. All Rights Reserved.

Strategies for
SUCCESS
with English Language Learners

READING STRATEGIES FOR GRADES 3–12

Paired Guided Reading

Why use it?

Use of this strategy will help students to . . .
- Identify purpose for reading.
- Use self-monitoring strategies such as rereading and cross-checking to assist comprehension.
- Read unfamiliar text to collect data, facts, and ideas.
- Compare and contrast information.
- Read text and ask questions to clarify understanding and to focus reading.
- Read text and answer literal, referential, or critical/application questions.
- Organize and categorize text information by using knowledge of text structures (cause and effect, fact and opinion).
- Make inferences and draw conclusions.
- Identify information that is stated rather than implied.
- Take notes to record data, facts, and ideas.
- Work cooperatively with peers to comprehend text.
- Participate in discussion about text by integrating multiple strategies (e.g., ask questions, clarify information, summarize information).
- Use opinions of peers to evaluate personal interpretation of ideas.
- Use graphic organizers to record main ideas and significant details.

How does it work?

The teacher directs the students to read a certain amount of text with a specific purpose (e.g., the first four paragraphs to find three major causes of pollution). When they have finished reading, students record on sticky notes

 © 2007. All Rights Reserved. 283

Section Two

what they remember. In pairs, they compare and discuss their notes, grouping the ones that are similar. They monitor themselves by asking, "Did we leave out anything important? Was there anything we didn't understand?" Then they reread the material as they check, add to, or change their notes. Students repeat the process until they finish reading and finally arrange their notes into a graphic organizer that demonstrates the relationship of the notes (Stephens & Brown, 2005).

Variations for Emergent English Language Learners

- Provide partially completed or visually supported sticky notes and graphic organizers to direct ELLs' attention.
- Pair ELLs with linguistic buddies to share notes.
- Try coteaching with the ESL teacher.

ASCD © 2007. All Rights Reserved.

Strategies for
SUCCESS
with English Language Learners

READING STRATEGIES FOR GRADES 3–12

Peer Reading

Why use it?

Use of this strategy will help students to . . .

- Read grade-level texts with comprehension and for different purposes.
- Use self-monitoring strategies such as cross-checking, summarizing, and self-questioning to construct meaning of text.
- Ask questions to clarify understanding and to focus reading.
- Summarize main ideas of informational texts and details from imaginative text orally and in writing.
- Identify a conclusion that summarizes a main idea.
- Read grade-level text and answer literal, referential, and critical/application questions.
- Use specific evidence from stories to identify themes, describe characters, and relate a sequence of events.
- Identify missing, conflicting, unclear, and irrelevant information.
- Draw conclusions and make inferences on the basis of explicit and implied information.
- Take notes to record data, facts, and ideas.
- Work cooperatively with peers to comprehend and respond to text.
- Participate in discussion about text by integrating multiple strategies (e.g., ask questions, summarize information).
- Use opinions and reactions of peers to evaluate personal interpretations of text.

How does it work?

The teacher selects a reading, breaks it up into manageable sections, and creates a question or a set of questions that will require students to summarize the section. Students work in pairs to read the first section, mark their text, and engage in coaching partnerships (reader A puts the reading aside while the coach asks the summarizing questions and coaches reader A to a more complete answer using her marked copy). Then students reverse roles for each of the remaining sections of the text. When they are finished, the students use the summarizing questions and notes to create a summary collaboratively. Over time, the teacher models and coaches students through the process of identifying their own summarizing questions and using their skills to summarize readings and conduct research (Silver, Strong, & Perini, 2000).

Variations for Emergent English Language Learners

- Differentiate the reading material for ELLs by using the "input plus next level" principle.
- Provide linguistic buddies or reading guides for ELLs.
- Try a coteaching model with the ESL teacher.

ASCD © 2007. All Rights Reserved.

Strategies for
SUCCESS
with English Language Learners

READING STRATEGIES FOR GRADES 3–12

Pen in Hand

Why use it?

Use of this strategy will help students to . . .

- Read grade-level text with comprehension and for different purposes.
- Use comprehension and self-monitoring strategies to clarify meaning of text.
- Recognize when comprehension has been disrupted and initiate self-correction.
- Use text features to understand text.
- Ask questions to clarify meaning of text.
- Identify the themes or message of a text.
- Use a variety of strategies to support understanding of text.
- Demonstrate comprehension of text though a range of responses.
- Make inferences and draw conclusions.
- Recognize the organizational format of text.
- Note and describe aspects of the writer's craft.
- Make connections between texts and own lives, the lives of others, texts read in the past, and the world at large.
- Take notes to record data, facts, and ideas.
- Take notes to record significant details about characters and events in stories.

How does it work?

The continuum of writing-reading interactions in the example is based on the degree of student involvement. The Pen in Hand tool focuses on two of these types of interactions to help students engage in the construction of meaning when reading textbooks: underlining/highlighting and margin notes. For the first, the teacher provides photocopies of text pages or transparencies to place on top of text pages to model how to interact with text. For the second, the teacher provides sticky notes and models writing notes in the margins of the texts (e.g., reactions, associations, questions, applications, examples, drawings, and symbols). This strategy thus provides an "entry point" for text interaction (Brown, Phillips, & Stephens, 1993).

Variations for Emergent English Language Learners

- Provide cues or partially completed transparencies and sticky notes to guide ELLs.
- Try alternative coteaching with the ESL teacher (i.e., one teaches underlining/highlighting and the other teaches margin notes, and then the groups of students rotate).

Example:

The following continuum of writing-reading interactions is based on the degree of student involvement:

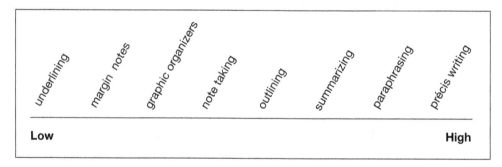

underlining   margin notes   graphic organizers   note taking   outlining   summarizing   paraphrasing   précis writing

Low   High

ASCD © 2007. All Rights Reserved.

READING STRATEGIES FOR GRADES 3–12

Proposition Support Outlines

Why use it?

Use of this strategy will help students to . . .

- Identify purpose for reading.
- Organize and categorize text information by using knowledge of a variety of text structures.
- Apply thinking skills to interpret data, facts, and ideas from multiple sources.
- Use organizational features of text to locate information.
- Use knowledge of text structures to support understanding.
- Support interpretations and explanations with evidence from text.
- Compare and contrast information on one topic from multiple sources.
- Condense, combine, or categorize new information from more than one source.
- Make inferences and draw conclusions.
- Distinguish between fact and opinion.
- Judge accuracy of content to gather facts.
- Evaluate the validity and accuracy of information, ideas, and opinions in texts by identifying statements of fact, opinion, and exaggeration.
- Distinguish verifiable statements from hypotheses and assumptions, and facts from opinions.
- Consider the writer's assumptions, beliefs, intentions, and biases.
- Identify propaganda.
- Identify differing points of view.
- Present clear analyses using examples, details, and reasons from text.

PROPOSITION SUPPORT OUTLINES

Section Two

- Take notes to record data, facts, and ideas by following teacher direction and working with peers.
- Use graphic organizers to record significant details from informational text.
- Use opinions of peers to evaluate interpretation of text.
- Use prewriting strategies to organize ideas and information to plan writing.

How does it work?

In large-group sharing, the teacher introduces a blank proposition support outline on an overhead and models for students how support for a proposition can be categorized as facts, statistics, examples, expert authority, logic, or reasoning. The teacher then assigns a text passage that follows the same framework, and pairs of students complete the outline as they analyze the author's arguments. This strategy is an excellent guide for independent research. See the following example (Buehl, 1992).

Variations for Emergent English Language Learners

- Ask the ESL teacher to preview the concept of proposition support beforehand.
- Differentiate the reading materials and the topics of investigation.
- Provide linguistic buddies for ELLs.
- Try a coteaching model with the ESL teacher.

Example:

Proposition Support Outline

Topic	_____
Proposition	_____

Support	
	1. Facts
	2. Statistics
	3. Examples
	4. Expert Authority
	5. Logic and Reasoning

Source: From *Classroom Strategies for Interactive Learning,* 2nd ed. (p. 102), by D. Buehl, 2001, Newark, DE: International Reading Association. Copyright 2001 by International Reading Association. Reproduced with permission.

ASCD © 2007. All Rights Reserved.

Strategies for
SUCCESS
with English Language Learners

SECTION: LITERACY STRATEGIES

QAR (Question-Answer Relationship)

Why use it?

Use of this strategy will help students to . . .

*   Identify purpose for reading.
*   Use self-monitoring strategies such as rereading, cross-checking, and answering questions to comprehend meaning.
*   Use prior knowledge and experience to understand ideas and support comprehension of text.
*   Make connections between text and own lives, the lives of others, and other texts.
*   Present a point of view or interpretation and support it with details.
*   Use knowledge of story structure and story elements to interpret stories.
*   Use specific evidence from stories to identify themes, describe characters (e.g., their actions and motivations), and relate a sequence of events.
*   Read grade-level texts and answer literal, referential, analytical, and critical/application questions.
*   Demonstrate comprehension of text through a variety of responses.
*   Infer underlying theme or message from text.
*   Recognize how authors use literary devices to create multiple levels of meaning.
*   Identify social and cultural context and other characteristics to enhance understanding and appreciation of text.
*   Identify author's point of view.
*   Recognize how one's point of view contributes to interpretation.
*   Interpret multiple levels of meaning in text.

Section Two

QAR (QUESTION-ANSWER RELATIONSHIP)

- Form opinions and make judgments about literary works by analyzing and evaluating texts from a critical perspective.

How does it work?

The teacher gives students four types of questions classified as follows:

1. Right There! (The answer is found directly in the text. The words in the question can usually be found in the same sentence with the answer.)
2. Think and Search! (The answer is in the text but the words are not in the same sentence. You must read the text, look for ideas that you can put together, and think about what the author is saying.)
3. You and the Author! (The author gave you some ideas and made you think, but you must figure out what you know and use it to answer the question.)
4. On Your Own! (You must apply what you know and what you have learned to answer the question.)

The teacher models some examples and then students apply QAR while reading (Raphael, 1984, 1986).

Variations for Emergent English Language Learners

- Have ELLs respond to the Right There! questions to provide an appropriate "entry point."
- Provide partially completed responses to all levels of questions to ascertain what ELLs are able to do.
- Use coteaching (parallel teaching for pull-out arrangement and peer teaching if ESL teacher comes into class).

ASCD © 2007. All Rights Reserved.

Strategies for
SUCCESS
with English Language Learners

READING STRATEGIES FOR GRADES 3–12

Q-SPACE

Why use it?

Use of this strategy will help students to . . .
- Engage in purposeful reading in small and large groups.
- Use self-monitoring strategies such as rereading and cross-checking to comprehend text.
- Employ a range of postreading practices to think about new learning and plan further learning.
- Use text structures and features to comprehend text.
- Demonstrate comprehension of and respond to grade-level text.
- Ask questions to focus reading.
- Answer literal, referential, analytical, and evaluative questions.
- Make predictions, draw conclusions, and make inferences.
- Analyze ideas on the basis of prior knowledge and experience.
- Identify information that is implied rather than stated.
- Participate in discussion about grade-level text by integrating multiple strategies.
- Use opinions of classmates to evaluate personal response to text.
- Evaluate content by identifying author's purpose and intent.
- Identify different perspectives on or responses to issues presented in text.

How does it work?

This strategy's acronym that stands for the following steps: (1) **Question**—the teacher poses a content-specific question for students to answer. (2) **Silence**—the teacher remains silent to allow time for students to generate

ASCD © 2007. All Rights Reserved.

Q-SPACE

ideas. (3) **P**robe—the teacher responds to students' answers with questions about the process they used to form their answers. (4) **A**ccept—the teacher communicates to students the positive aspects of their answers. (5) **C**larify—the teacher helps students make their answers clearer (when an answer is incorrect, the teacher states the question for which the student's answer would be appropriate). (6) **E**laborate—the teacher encourages students to look past answers to see where they may lead (Strong, Silver, Perini, & Tuculescu, 2002).

Variations for Emergent English Language Learners

- Use a cooperative learning strategy to have students go through the process in groups, then pairs, and then "elaborate" alone.
- Provide the ESL teacher with the questions beforehand to prepare ELLs.

Section Two

ASCD © 2007. All Rights Reserved.

Strategies for
SUCCESS
with English Language Learners

READING STRATEGIES FOR GRADES 3–12

Question Menu

Why use it?

Use of this strategy will help students to . . .

- Engage in purposeful reading.
- Use a variety of comprehension strategies to monitor own reading.
- Read grade-level texts and answer literal, inferential, and critical/application questions.
- Ask questions to clarify meaning and focus reading.
- Use specific evidence from stories to describe characters' motivations and actions and to relate sequence of events and importance of setting.
- Make predictions, draw conclusions, and make inferences.
- Use knowledge of story structure and story elements to interpret stories.
- Identify ways in which characters change over the course of a story.
- Make connections between text and own lives, the lives of others, other texts read in the past, and the world at large.
- Recognize how authors use literary devices to create meaning.
- Recognize how an author's use of language creates images or feelings.
- Interpret multiple levels of meaning in text.
- Generate a significant list of questions to assist with analysis of text.
- Work cooperatively with peers to comprehend text.
- Use opinions of classmates to evaluate personal interpretation of texts.

How does it work?

The teacher selects an appropriate text and, using the question stem menu, establishes at least one question for each level of understanding. Students

 © 2007. All Rights Reserved.

review the questions before reading. As they read, they collect the information needed to generate a response for each question. Students may meet with other students to discuss their responses. As students become more competent, the teacher fosters independence by encouraging them to ask their own style-based questions as a way to expose the multiple layers of a reading. See the example that follows (Silver, Strong, & Perini, 2000).

Variations for Emergent English Language Learners

- Ask the ESL teacher to generate the questions for ELLs.
- Prepare reading guides to support ELLs.
- Provide question spinners to cue ELLs so they can generate questions.

ASCD © 2007. All Rights Reserved.

Example:

Question Menu

Mastery questions ask students to . . .	Interpersonal questions ask students to . . .	Understanding questions ask students to . . .	Self-expression questions ask students to . . .
Focus on reading facts: • Who was involved? • Where did it take place? • When did it occur? • What happened? • How did it occur? Supply information based on observation: • What did you observe? • What is wrong with this? How would you correct this? • Can you describe the data? Establish procedures on sequence: • What are the steps? • How would you go about doing this? • What comes first? Next? • What is the correct order for this?	Empathize and describe feelings: • How would you feel if _____ happened to you? • How do you think _____ felt? • Can you describe your feelings? Value and appreciate: • Why is _____ important to you? • What's the value of _____? • What decision would you make? Explore human interest problems: • How would you advise or console _____? • What is the issue facing _____? • What would you do about it? • How would you help each side come to agreement?	Focus on making connections: • What are the important similarities and differences? • What is the cause? • What is the effect? • How are the parts connected? Make inferences and interpret: • Yes, but why? • How would you explain _____? • Can you prove it? • What can you conclude? • What experience do you have to support your position? Focus on understanding meaning: • What are the hidden assumptions? • What does this prove? • What have you discovered?	Rethink their ideas: • What comes to mind when you think of _____? • How is _____ like _____? Develop images, hypotheses, and predictions: • What would happen if _____? • Can you imagine _____? What would it look like? What would it be like? Focus on alternatives and original solutions: • How many possible ways can you _____? • What is another way to do this? • Is there a better way to design _____? Think metaphorically and creatively: • How is _____ like _____? • Can you create a poem, icon, or skit that represents this?

Source: From *Questioning Styles and Strategies: Procedures for Increasing the Depth of Student Thinking* (2nd ed.), by R. W. Strong, J. R. Hanson, and H. F. Silver, 1995, Woodbridge, NJ: Thoughtful Education Press. Copyright 1995 by Thoughtful Education Press. Adapted with permission.

Section Two

QUESTION MENU

Strategies for
SUCCESS
with English Language Learners

SECTION: LITERACY STRATEGIES

Questioning the Author

Why use it?

Use of this strategy will help students to . . .

- Identify a purpose for reading.
- Use comprehension strategies to monitor own reading and clarify meaning of text.
- Read grade-level texts and answer literal, referential, and evaluative questions.
- Engage in purposeful reading in small groups.
- Participate in discussions by integrating multiple strategies.
- Make connections between texts and own lives, the lives of others, other texts read in the past, and the world at large.
- State main ideas and support or elaborate on them with relevant details.
- Use specific evidence from stories to identify themes and to describe characters' actions and motivations.
- Use knowledge of story structure to interpret stories.
- Present a point of view or interpretation of a text, such as its theme or author's intended message, and support it with details.
- Determine how the use and meaning of literary devices conveys author's intent or message.
- Evaluate ideas, themes, and experiences to identify multiple levels of meaning in texts.
- Form opinions and make judgments by analyzing and evaluating text from a critical perspective.

 © 2007. All Rights Reserved.

How does it work?

This strategy is designed to assist students in their efforts to understand text as they read, especially for social studies or language arts texts. Select passages based on important concepts, develop queries that will prompt discussion and build understanding, instruct students to read the passage, facilitate a query-driven discussion about the passage, giving students the opportunity to grapple with ideas in small groups first, and be sure to model the strategy yourself by thinking aloud how you might grapple with ideas to build understanding around a passage (Beck, McKeown, Hamilton, & Kucan, 1997).

Variations for Emergent English Language Learners

- Provide a reading guide to ELLs to facilitate their understanding.
- Groups students into the small groups strategically so that ELLs have linguistic buddies in the discussion.
- Provide the material to the ESL teacher beforehand as a prereading strategy to build vocabulary and background knowledge.

ASCD © 2007. All Rights Reserved.

Strategies for
SUCCESS
with English Language Learners

READING STRATEGIES FOR GRADES 3–12

RAFT

Why use it?

Use of this strategy will help students to . . .
- Demonstrate comprehension of text through creative responses.
- Respond in writing to prompts that follow the reading of literary or informational texts.
- Understand the purpose for writing.
- Determine the intended audience before writing.
- Use tone and language appropriate for audience and purpose.
- Use the writing process.
- Adjust style of writing, voice, and language used according to purpose and intended audience.
- Review writing independently to revise for focus, development of ideas, and organization.
- Review writing independently to edit for correct language.
- Identify different perspectives on an issue presented in text.
- Evaluate information, ideas, opinions, and themes in texts by identifying central ideas, primary details, and multiple levels of meaning.
- Maintain a writing portfolio that includes RAFT writing.

How does it work?

The RAFT tool enhances understanding of informational text by encouraging creative thinking and reflection. The RAFT acronym stands for **R**ole of the writer (What is the writer's role—reporter, observer, eyewitness?); **A**udience (Who will be reading this writing—the teacher, other students, people in the

© 2007. All Rights Reserved.

Section Two

RAFT

community, an editor?); **Format** (What is the best way to present this writing—in a letter, an article, a report, a poem?); **Topic** (Who or what is the subject of this writing—a famous mathematician, a reaction to a specific event?) The teacher analyzes the information she wants students to learn from a reading. The students brainstorm possible roles they could assume in their writing, decide who the audience will be, and determine the format for the writing. After students have read, the teacher explains RAFT and lists the role, audience, format, and topic for the writing. The teacher may choose to have all students do the same or may offer choices. See the examples of RAFT assignments that follow (Santa, 1988).

Variations for Emergent English Language Learners

- Consult the ESL teacher on the design of RAFT assignments for ELLs and differentiate the assignments according to their interests and preferences.

ASCD © 2007. All Rights Reserved.

Example:

Role	Audience	Format	Topic
Newspaper	Readers in the 1870s	Obituary	Qualities of General Custer
Lawyer	U.S. Supreme Court	Appeal search	Dred Scott decision
Abraham Lincoln	Dear Abby	Advice column	Problems with his generals
Mike Royko	Public	News column	Capital punishment
Frontier woman	Self	Diary	Hardships in the West
Constituent	U.S. Senator	Letter	Gun control
News writer	Public	News release	Ozone layer is disappearing
Chemist	Chemical company	Instructions	Combinations to avoid
Wheat Thin	Other Wheat Thins	Travel guide	Journey through the digestive system
Plant	Sun	Thank-you note	Sun's role in plant's growth
Scientist	Charles Darwin	Letter	Dispute a point in evolutionary theory
Square root	Whole number	Love letter	Explain the relationship
Repeating decimal	Set of rational numbers	Petition	Prove you belong to this set
Cook	Other cooks	Recipe	Alcoholism
Julia Child	TV audience	Script	Wonders of eggs
Advertiser	TV audience	Public service	Importance of fruit
Lungs	Cigarettes	Complaint	Effects of smoking
Huck Finn	Jim	Letter	What I learned during the trip
Joseph Stalin	George Orwell	Letter	Reactions to *Animal Farm*
Comma	9th grade students	Complaint	How it is missed
Trout	Self	Diary	Effects of acid rain on lake

Source: From *Classroom Strategies for Interactive Learning* (p. 115), by D. Buehl, 1995, Schofield, WI: Wisconsin State Reading Association. Copyright 1995 by Wisconsin State Reading Association. Reprinted with permission.

Strategies for
SUCCESS
with English Language Learners

READING STRATEGIES FOR GRADES 3–12

Read Three Times

Why use it?

Use of this strategy will help students to . . .
- Identify specific words causing comprehension difficulties in written language.
- Use comprehension strategies to clarify meaning of text (e.g., attend to vocabulary).
- Ask questions to clarify understanding and to focus reading.
- Use self-monitoring strategies such as cross-checking and self-questioning to construct meaning.
- Read unfamiliar texts to collect, data, facts, and ideas.
- Locate information in a text that is needed to solve a problem.
- Understand written directions and procedures.
- Identify signal words that provide clues to meaning.
- Read the steps in a procedure in order to accomplish a task.
- Identify missing and irrelevant information.
- Apply corrective strategies, such as discussing with others and monitoring for misunderstandings, to assist in comprehension.
- Use knowledge of structure, content, and vocabulary to understand text.
- Identify missing, conflicting, or unclear information.
- Demonstrate task awareness by employing flexible strategies.
- Recognize unstated assumptions.
- Work cooperatively with peers to comprehend text.

READ THREE TIMES

Section Two

How does it work?

This strategy is a mathematics strategy for solving word and logic problems. Students read through a problem quickly, list the words they do not understand, and try to answer questions (What is the problem asking us to do? What do we need to know? What is unnecessary information? What materials do we need? What math operations will we use?), and review their responses to the questions (Sadler, 2001).

Variations for Emergent English Language Learners

- Pair ELLs with linguistic buddies to read problems and ask questions.
- Send questions to the ESL teacher beforehand to prepare ELLS.
- Differentiate the word problems by linguistic level or unpack the language to make them more comprehensible (e.g., divide complex sentences into simple sentences).
- Use a coteaching model with the ESL teacher.

ASCD © 2007. All Rights Reserved.

Strategies for
SUCCESS
with English Language Learners

READING STRATEGIES FOR GRADES 3–12

Reading for Meaning

Why use it?

Use of this strategy will help students to . . .

- Identify the purpose for reading.
- Use self-monitoring strategies such as rereading, cross-checking, and self-correcting.
- Read unfamiliar text to collect data, facts, and ides.
- Locate information in a text that is needed to solve a problem.
- Identify main ideas and supporting details in text.
- Skim material to locate information.
- Draw conclusions and make inferences on the basis of information from text.
- Present a point of view or interpretation of a text and support it with significant details.
- Recognize how new information is related to prior knowledge and experience.
- Identify information that is implied rather than stated.
- Identify missing, conflicting, unclear, and irrelevant information.
- Judge accuracy of content to gather facts.
- Use graphic organizers to record evidence from text.
- Work cooperatively with peers to comprehend text.
- Evaluate the validity and accuracy of information.
- Select, reject, and reconcile ideas and information in light of beliefs.

Section Two

How does it work?

This strategy helps students with difficulties they may have in getting meaning (literal meaning, important themes or ideas, ambiguous or symbolic language, and personally challenging texts). The teacher creates statements keyed to important information in the text and reviews the purpose and goals of the strategy with students by explaining the use of the organizer (see example). Students read the passage to collect evidence to support or refute the statements, form small groups to discuss the statements and share responses, and apply what they've learned to a writing task (Strong, Silver, Perini, & Tuculescu, 2002).

Variations for Emergent English Language Learners

- Highlight information in texts for ELLs so they can locate passages with specific information.
- Allow ELLs to have linguistic buddies to translate ideas.
- Use a coteaching model.

Example:

	Support	Refute
For Cherokees, moving west of the Mississippi is preferable to being oppressed in their homeland. ❏ Agree ❏ Disagree		"We wish to remain in the land of our fathers." "If we are compelled to leave, we see nothing but ruin before us."
Relocation is an inhumane policy. ❏ Agree ❏ Disagree	Cherokees would come into conflict with other tribes west of the Mississippi. The region was badly supplied with food and water, and they were forced to go against their will.	

ASCD © 2007. All Rights Reserved.

Strategies for
SUCCESS
with English Language Learners

SECTION: LITERACY STRATEGIES

READING STRATEGIES FOR GRADES 3–12

Reading-and-Writing-to-Learn Journals

Why use it?

Use of this strategy will help students to . . .

- Relate data, facts, and ideas to prior information and experience.
- Answer literal, inferential, and critical/application questions.
- Identify a conclusion that summarizes a main idea.
- Demonstrate comprehension of text through a variety of responses.
- Use journals to record significant ideas from text.
- Make predictions, draw conclusions, and make inferences.
- Understand the purpose for writing.
- Develop an idea with a brief text.
- Produce clear, well-organized accounts that demonstrate understanding of a topic.
- Support interpretations and explanations with evidence from a text.
- Present a point of view or interpretation of a text.
- Evaluate the validity and accuracy of information, ideas, themes, opinions, and experiences in texts.
- Participate in group discussions by integrating multiple strategies.
- Use opinions and reactions of classmates to evaluate personal interpretation of ideas, information, and experience.

How does it work?

The teacher thinks of reading selections that would go well with the types of journals that appear on the next page and asks students to share their ideas. The teacher then selects the type of journal that aligns with the specific subject area (e.g., double entry for literature, problem solution for math, meta-cognitive for science, speculation for social studies).

Variations for Emergent English Language Learners

- Allow ELLs to use primary language to write journals (and then have a bilingual student or staff member translate).
- Allow ELLs to illustrate their journals to show what they have understood.
- Ask the ESL teacher to do journal writing during ESL class so ELLs come to class with their journals to share.

Example:

Reading-and-Writing-to-Learn Journals

Double Entry Journal	Divide a sheet of paper in half. On the left side, copy a quotation or passage from the text. On the right side of the paper, you may respond, question, make personal connections, evaluate, reflect, analyze, and interpret. In other words, the left column is for note taking from the text and the right column is for your own note making.
Problem Solution Journal	Identify a problem, brainstorm possible alternatives, choose a probable solution, anticipate stumbling blocks, and propose arguments while writing in favor of a proposed solution.
Metacognitive Journal	Divide a paper in half. On the left side of the paper, record "What I learned." On the right side of the paper, record "How I came to learn it."
Synthesis Journal	Divide your paper into sections. Record "What I did," "What I learned," and "How I can use it."
Speculation About Effects Journal	Divide paper in half. On the left side, record "What happened." On the right side, record "What might/should happen as a result."
Reflective Journal	Divide paper into sections. Record "What happened" (or "What I did"); "How I felt"; "What I learned"; "What questions I still have"; and "Overall response."

ASCD © 2007. All Rights Reserved.

Strategies for
SUCCESS
with English Language Learners

READING STRATEGIES FOR GRADES 3–12

REAP

Why use it?

Use of this strategy will help students to . . .

- Read grade-level texts with comprehension and for different purposes.
- Use prior knowledge in concert with text information to support comprehension.
- Recognize when comprehension has been disrupted and initiate self-correction strategies such as rereading and adjusting rate of reading.
- Summarize main ideas and supporting details.
- Relate data, facts, and ideas from texts to prior information and experience.
- Draw conclusions and make inferences.
- State a point of view or interpretation of a text and support it with evidence.
- Recognize the theme or message of a text.
- Use knowledge of text or story features to interpret texts.
- Make connections between text being read and own lives, the lives of others, texts read in the past, and the world at large.
- Generate questions to further understanding.
- Identify information that is implied rather than stated.
- Distinguish between relevant and irrelevant information.
- Interpret multiple levels of meaning.
- Use graphic organizers to record ideas.
- Evaluate information, ideas, opinions, and themes by identifying the author's purpose; important and unimportant information; and the writer's assumptions, beliefs, stated ideas, and hidden agendas.

 © 2007. All Rights Reserved.

Section Two

REAP

How does it work?

REAP is an acronym for Read, Encode, Annotate, and Ponder. The teacher explains or models the following for students: read on your own; encode the text by putting the gist of what you read into your own words; annotate the text by writing down the main ideas and the author's message; and ponder what you read by thinking and talking with others to make personal connections, developing questions about the topic, and connecting this reading to other reading (Allen, 2004). See the example that follows.

Variations for Emergent English Language Learners

- Partner ELLs for reading text; differentiate the reading material if possible.
- Provide reading guides to assist ELLs with comprehension.
- Use coteaching (e.g., parallel teaching) to support the REAP process.

Example:

Read text.	**Encode text.**
Jot down title and author.	Put main ideas into own words.
Annotate text.	**Ponder text.**
Write a summarizing statement.	Why did the author write the text?

Section Two

ASCD © 2007. All Rights Reserved.

Strategies for
SUCCESS
with English Language Learners

READING STRATEGIES FOR GRADES 3–12

Reciprocal Teaching

Why use it?

Use of this strategy will help students to . . .

- Use comprehension strategies to monitor own reading (predict/confirm, reread, self-question) and clarify meaning of text.
- Summarize main ideas and supporting details from text.
- Support interpretations with evidence from text.
- Lead and participate in discussion about text by integrating multiple strategies (ask questions, clarify misunderstandings, support point of view, summarize).
- Make predictions, draw conclusions, and make inferences about events and characters.
- Use specific evidence from stories to describe characters and their actions and motivations, and to relate sequences of events.
- Ask questions to clarify understanding of texts.
- Read and interpret informational or literary texts.
- Present a point of view or interpretation of text and support it with evidence.
- Use prior knowledge to support comprehension, from forming predictions to making inferences and drawing conclusions.
- Use text structure and literary devices to aid comprehension and response.
- Generate a list of significant questions to assist with analysis of text.
- Seek opportunities for improvement in reading comprehension by choosing more challenging writers, topics, and texts.

Section Two

RECIPROCAL TEACHING

Section Two

How does it work?

This strategy is a four-step procedure (summarize, question, clarify, predict) that makes the reading process interactive between the teacher and the text. Initially, the teacher works with small groups of students to model the strategy— the teacher reads a paragraph or two and then summarizes. The teacher then poses questions for discussion, models how to clarify the meaning of the text, and asks students to make predictions about what happens next. After this modeling, it is time for students to reciprocate. A designated student-leader assumes the role of teacher and repeats the process. One by one, students take responsibility for the active, attend-read-think process of critical readers. The leadership role is reciprocal, turning over responsibility to the students, and in reciprocating, students eventually internalize the reading process (Palincsar & Brown, 1985).

Variations for Emergent English Language Learners

* Use parallel coteaching to allow the ESL teacher to work with ELLs on the same strategy.
* When ELLs become more proficient, use alternative coteaching.

ASCD © 2007. All Rights Reserved.

Strategies for
SUCCESS
with English Language Learners

READING STRATEGIES FOR GRADES 3–12

ReQuest

Why use it?

Use of this strategy will help students to . . .

- Identify purpose for reading.
- Engage in independent silent reading of text.
- Read grade-level texts and ask questions to self-monitor comprehension, clarify understanding, and focus reading of texts.
- Read grade-level text and answer literal, referential, and evaluative questions.
- Recognize the theme or message of a text.
- Use prior knowledge in concert with text information to support comprehension, from formulating questions to drawing conclusions to making inferences.
- State or summarize a main idea, and support or elaborate with relevant details.
- Use text features to understand and interpret texts.
- Recognize organizational formats to assist in comprehension of texts.
- Read and interpret literary texts from a variety of genres, in varying text formats, and by different authors for a variety of purposes.
- Identify opportunities for improvement of reading comprehension skills.
- Interpret multiple levels of meaning and subtleties in text.
- Lead and participate in discussion about text by integrating multiple strategies (e.g., ask questions, clarify misunderstandings).

REQUEST

Section Two

How does it work?

ReQuest is an abbreviation of reciprocal questioning, a strategy intended to help students (1) formulate their own questions about the text they are reading, (2) develop an active inquiring attitude toward reading, (3) acquire purposes for reading, and (4) develop independent comprehension abilities. ReQuest involves students and teacher silently reading portions of text and taking turns asking and answering questions concerning that material. It is the reciprocal nature of the questioning sequence that differentiates ReQuest from teacher-directed questioning strategies and provides the format for students' active involvement (Manzo, 1969).

Variations for Emergent English Language Learners

- Provide ELLs with questions, cues, or stems to assist.
- Prepare reading guides for ELLs.
- Use parallel, alternative, or team-teaching models to coteach with the ESL teacher.

ASCD © 2007. All Rights Reserved.

Strategies for
SUCCESS
with English Language Learners

READING STRATEGIES FOR GRADES 3–12

ROW

Why use it?

Use of this strategy will help students to . . .

- Read grade-level texts with comprehension and for different purposes.
- Organize and categorize text information by using knowledge of a variety of text structures (e.g., cause and effect, sequence).
- Summarize main ideas and details.
- Read unfamiliar texts to collect data, facts, and ideas.
- Use text structure to recognize differences among a variety of texts.
- Identify transitional words or phrases that provide clues to organizational formats.
- Condense, combine, or categorize new information to understand informational texts.
- Use graphic organizers to record significant ideas and details.
- Include relevant and exclude irrelevant information.
- Respond in writing to what is read in texts.
- Understand the purpose for writing.
- Use prewriting activities such as note taking and organizing.
- Use the writing process.
- Demonstrate comprehension of text through writing.
- Use organizational patterns for expository writing.
- Organize writing effectively to communicate ideas.

Section Two

How does it work?

ROW stands for Read, Organize, Write and is designed to help students with understanding different types of expository text. The teacher presents an expository text pattern using short, clear examples for the class to read. The class develops a working definition of the organizational pattern and a graphic organizer that represents it (e.g., sequence/direction, listing/description, definition/explanation, comparison/contrast, problem/solution, cause/effect). The students then write a selection using the text pattern (Stephens & Brown, 2000).

Variations for Emergent English Language Learners

- Ask the ESL teacher to preview the graphic organizer to be used for reading.
- Provide partially filled graphic organizers to ELLs as linguistic cues.
- Use writer's workshop as a differentiation strategy.
- Use coteaching models (e.g., station teaching) to implement writer's workshop.

ASCD © 2007. All Rights Reserved.

Strategies for SUCCESS with English Language Learners

READING STRATEGIES FOR GRADES 3–12

Save the Last Word for Me

Why use it?

Use of this strategy will help students to . . .

- Adjust reading rate according to purpose for reading.
- Infer underlying themes or messages.
- Analyze ideas and information on the basis of prior knowledge and experiences.
- Identify different perspectives—such as social, cultural, ethnic, and historical—on issues presented in text.
- Make connections between text being read and own lives, the lives of others, texts read in the past, and the world at large.
- Summarize a main idea, and support or elaborate with relevant details.
- Note and describe aspects of the writer's craft and explain the role that crafting techniques play in helping the reader comprehend the text.
- Identify information that is implied rather than stated.
- Identify how the author uses literary devices to make meaning.
- Analyze, contrast, support, and critique points of view in a wide range of genres.
- Identify poetic elements to interpret poetry.
- Interpret multiple levels of meaning in text.
- Present a point of view or interpretation and support it with significant details from text.
- Demonstrate personal response to text.
- Evaluate information, ideas, opinions, and themes by identifying author's purpose, and important and unimportant details.

 © 2007. All Rights Reserved. 319

SAVE THE LAST WORD FOR ME

Section Two

- Recognize development of central ideas or themes and the significance of language used by author.
- Take notes to record ideas and respond to reading.
- Engage in purposeful reading in small groups.
- Work cooperatively with peers to clarify meaning.
- Participate in discussion about grade-level texts by integrating multiple strategies (e.g., supporting point of view, summarizing ideas).
- Use opinions and reactions of peers to evaluate personal interpretation of ideas, information, and experiences.

How does it work?

This strategy helps students reflect on what they read and is especially useful with material that may elicit differing opinions. Reluctant speakers have an opportunity to be in small-group settings with time to rehearse. Using the strategy involves the following steps: (1) the teacher has students locate five statements that they find interesting while they read; (2) students write their statements on index cards and write comments about the statements on the other side; (3) in groups of four, students share their statements one at a time and help their team members locate the statement in the text; (4) students share comments after all group members have given their reactions—this gives the initial student the last word (Burke & Harste, described in Vaughan & Estes, 1986).

Variations for Emergent English Language Learners

- Be strategic in student groupings, appointing either linguistic buddies or nurturing friends.
- Ask the ESL teacher to preread the text before class so ELLs come prepared.

ASCD © 2007. All Rights Reserved.

Strategies for
SUCCESS
with English Language Learners

READING STRATEGIES FOR GRADES 3–12

Science Connection Overview

Why use it?

Use of this strategy will help students to . . .

- Identify purpose for reading.
- Use self-monitoring and comprehension strategies such as rereading, attending to vocabulary, and self-questioning.
- Relate data, facts, and ideas from informational texts to prior information and experience.
- Use knowledge of text features and organizational formats to assist comprehension.
- Read unfamiliar texts to collect data, facts, and ideas.
- Locate main ideas in texts.
- Skim material to gain an overview of content or locate specific information.
- Scan texts for particular information.
- Use text features such as headings, captions, and titles to understand and interpret informational texts.
- Recognize how new information is related to prior knowledge and experience.
- Identify missing, conflicting, unclear, or irrelevant information.
- Generate a list of significant questions to assist with analysis of text.
- Take notes to record significant information.
- Determine the meaning of unfamiliar words by using context clues, dictionaries, glossaries, and other resources.
- Work cooperatively with peers to comprehend text.

SCIENCE CONNECTION OVERVIEW

Section Two

How does it work?

This strategy, used in prereading, helps students make possible connections between the science in their texts and their understandings of the world around them. The teacher distributes a blank form and models on an overhead how to skim a portion of text and think aloud about familiar things that are mentioned, avoiding technical vocabulary. Students work with partners to survey the rest of the chapter. If the chapter has a summary, students read it to identify key topics that seem to be the focus of the chapter. Students then generate personal questions about the topic (the teacher may model the kinds of questions people normally have about science) and complete the "How is it organized?" section of the overview to become familiar with information to be found in the chapter. Students read the chapter, using the overview to remind them what the chapter is about. They complete 3 x 5 index cards for technical vocabulary (terms they need to "translate" into understandable language). See the example on the following page (Buehl, 1992).

Variations for Emergent English Language Learners

*   Ask the ESL teacher to model the strategy beforehand.
*   Pair ELLs with linguistic buddies.
*   Provide the stems of questions for ELLs.
*   Provide bilingual dictionaries for ELLs.

ASCD © 2007. All Rights Reserved.

Example:

What's familiar?	What's the Connection? Skim and survey the chapter for things that are familiar and that connect with your life or world. List them below: • mushrooms • mold on spoiled food • spores • yeast • plant rusts • fungi on rotting plants • lichens • penicillin • Dutch Elm disease
What topics are covered?	Read the Summary: What topic areas seem to be the most important? • How they look or are structured • How they reproduce • How they feed and stay alive

What questions do you have?	Questions of Interest: What questions do you have about this material that may be answered in the chapter? • Why do mushrooms grow in damp places? • Why does food get moldy when it spoils? • Why do they put yeast in bread doughs? • Why are some mushrooms poisonous? • How can you tell which mushrooms are poisonous and which are safe? • What do fungi eat? • Does the medicine penicillin come from a fungus?

How is it organized?	Chapter Organization: What categories of information are provided in this chapter?
	
	• Structure of Fungi
	• Nutrition
	• Reproduction
	• Variety of Fungi: molds imperfect
	                 yeast
	                 mushrooms
	                 lichens

Translate	Read and Translate: Use 3 x 5 cards for vocabulary.

Source: From "The Connection Overview: A Strategy for Learning in Science," by D. Buehl, 1992, *WSRA Journal, 36*(2), pp. 21–30. Copyright 1992 by Wisconsin State Reading Association. Reprinted with permission.

   © 2007. All Rights Reserved.   323

Strategies for
SUCCESS
with English Language Learners

READING STRATEGIES FOR GRADES 3–12

Scintillating Sentences and Quizzical Quotes

Why use it?

Use of this strategy will help students to . . .

- Adjust reading rate according to purpose for reading.
- Identify a conclusion that summarizes the main idea.
- Identify point of view.
- Infer underlying theme or message.
- Use prior knowledge and experience to understand.
- Distinguish between relevant and irrelevant information.
- Identify information that is implied rather than stated.
- Use established criteria to analyze the quality of information in text.
- Present a point of view or interpretation of a text, such as its theme or the author's intended message.
- Note aspects of the writer's craft.
- Draw conclusions and make inferences on the basis of explicit and implied information.
- Use text structure and literary devices to aid comprehension.
- Recognize how the author's use of language evokes feelings.
- Use reading strategies such as discussion with others to assist in comprehension.
- Identify statements that disrupt comprehension.
- Evaluate content by identifying the author's purpose; important and unimportant ideas; and statements of fact, opinion, and exaggeration.
- Engage in purposeful reading in small groups.
- Work cooperatively with peers to comprehend text.

Section Two

SCINTILLATING SENTENCES AND QUIZZICAL QUOTES

Section Two

- Use opinions of classmates to evaluate personal interpretation of ideas and information.
- Respond to text through writing.

How does it work?

While reading (in pairs), students find a sentence that represents a significant idea, illustrates a point of view, or has special meaning for understanding content, as well as a sentence that they don't understand or they find confusing. They record these on strips or chart paper along with the author, title, page number, and their initials. The papers are sent around the room so all class members can write their comments (Stephens & Brown, 2005).

Variations for Emergent English Language Learners

- Pair ELLs with linguistic buddies so they can translate.
- Highlight some sentences beforehand to facilitate ELLs' completion of the task.

ASCD © 2007. All Rights Reserved.

Strategies for
SUCCESS
with English Language Learners

READING STRATEGIES FOR GRADES 3–12

Scored Discussion

Why use it?

Use of this strategy will help students to . . .

- Listen respectively and responsively.
- Ask questions to clarify understanding.
- Present a point of view or interpretation, and support or elaborate with significant details.
- Demonstrate comprehension through oral presentations.
- Use previous reading and life experiences to understand and compare ideas from informational or literary text.
- Use evidence to describe characters and their actions and motivations.
- Distinguish between relevant and irrelevant ideas and details.
- Note and describe aspects of the writer's craft and explain the role that crafting techniques play in helping comprehension.
- Analyze, contrast, support, and critique points of view.
- Discuss how the use and meaning of literary devices conveys author's message or intent.
- Recognize how the author's use of language creates images or feelings.
- Form opinions and make judgments about literary works by analyzing and evaluating texts from a critical perspective.
- Select, reject, and reconcile ideas and information.
- Participate in discussions about texts by integrating multiple strategies (e.g., ask questions, clarify misunderstandings, support point of view, summarize information).
- Evaluate information, ideas, opinions, and themes in texts and discussions by identifying central ideas and themes, important and unimportant

 © 2007. All Rights Reserved.

Section Two

details, conflicting information, writer's assumptions, fallacies of logic, and multiple levels of meaning and subtleties.

- Use established criteria to analyze the quality of ideas and information in text.
- Use opinions of classmates to evaluate personal interpretation of ideas and information.

How does it work?

This strategy gives students the opportunity to practice and evaluate effective discussion skills. A small group (6–8 students) carries on a reading-related discussion while classmates listen. Meanwhile, the teacher and the rest of the class observe the small-group discussion and score individual contributions to it. Students are awarded points for contributing relevant information, using evidence, asking questions, making analogies, and encouraging others. Negative points are assigned for interruptions, irrelevant comments, and personal attacks. At the conclusion, the feedback is provided to the discussion group members. See the following example of a scored discussion rating sheet (Billmeyer & Barton, 1998).

Variations for Emergent English Language Learners

- Have ELLs listen and take notes the first few times.
- Tape-record the discussion and have ELLs listen afterwards at a listening center or for homework.
- Use coteaching with the ESL teacher (e.g., peer teaching).

328 □ · ASCD © 2007. All Rights Reserved. · · · · · · · · · · · · · ·

Example:

Discussion Score Sheet

SCORED DISCUSSION

Student: _____

Class: _____

Positive/ Productive Behavior	Points	Nonproductive Behaviors	Points
(1) Offers his/her position on a topic	___ x (1) = ___	(–2) Not paying attention or distracting others	___ x (–2) = ___
(1) Makes a relevant comment	___ x (1) = ___	(–2) Interruption	___ x (–2) = ___
(3) Uses evidence to support position	___ x (3) = ___	(–1) Irrelevant comment	___ x (–1) = ___
(2) Points out contradictions in another-person's statements	___ x (2) = ___	(–3) Monopolizing	___ x (–3) = ___
(2) Recognizes when another person makes an irrelevant comment	___ x (2) = ___	(–3) Personal attack	___ x (–3) = ___
(3) Develops an analogy	___ x (3) = ___		
(1) Asks a clarifying question	___ x (1) = ___		
(3) Uses active listening skills (e.g., rephrases or restates what another student says before commenting)	___ x (3) = ___		

Total Points:

Positive/Productive Behavior: _____

Nonproductive Behavior: _____

Overall Total: _____

Grade: _____

Source: Teaching Reading in the Content Areas: If Not Me Then Who? (2nd ed., p. 164), by R. Billmeyer and M. L. Barton, 1998, Aurora, CO: Mid-continent Research for Education and Learning. Copyright 1998 by Mid-continent Research for Education and Learning. Reprinted with permission

Section Two

 © 2007. All Rights Reserved.

Strategies for
SUCCESS
with English Language Learners

READING STRATEGIES FOR GRADES 3–12

Skimming & Scanning

Why use it?

Use of this strategy will help students to . . .

- Adjust the reading rate according to the purpose for reading.
- Use comprehension strategies to monitor own reading and clarify understanding (e.g., predict/confirm, reread).
- Summarize main ideas and significant details.
- Read unfamiliar texts to collect and interpret data, facts, and ideas.
- Use organizational features such as chapter titles, headings, and subheadings to locate information.
- Use text features such as captions, charts, tables, graphs, maps, notes, and other visuals to understand and interpret informational texts.
- Preview informational texts to assess content and organization.
- Skim material to gain an overview of content or locate specific information.
- Scan texts for particular information.
- Analyze ideas and information on the basis of prior knowledge and personal experience.
- Use prior knowledge in concert with text information to support comprehension, from forming predictions to making inferences and drawing conclusions.
- State a point of view or interpretation of a text.
- Identify information that is implied rather than stated.
- Distinguish between relevant and irrelevant information.
- Condense, combine, or categorize new information.
- Take notes to record data, facts, and ideas.
- Work cooperatively to comprehend text.

 © 2007. All Rights Reserved. 331

How does it work?

This strategy requires a reader to look quickly and find the most important features and information in a text. The teacher gives students a reading assignment from a textbook. Students work in pairs to skim and scan the reading by looking at the title, the headings and subheadings, the visuals, the boldface words, and the fist and last paragraphs in order to make predictions about what they think the reading is about. Using a three-columned form with "First Impressions," "Fast Facts," and "Final Thoughts," students each record their first impressions in the column. Next they skim and scan again, using the second column to write down several "fast facts" they discover in this limited reading. Finally, students look at the two columns they have filled in and determine what they believe will be the most important points. At that point they read the text to look for these "final thoughts." See the example that follows (Allen, 2004).

Variations for Emergent English Language Learners

- Pair ELLs with linguistic buddies for the initial skim and scan task.
- Provide a reading guide or differentiate the reading material.
- Use a coteaching model.

Example:

First Impressions	Fast Facts	Final Thoughts

ASCD © 2007. All Rights Reserved.

Strategies for
SUCCESS
with English Language Learners

READING STRATEGIES FOR GRADES 3–12

SMART (Self-Monitoring Approach to Reading and Thinking)

Why use it?

Use of this strategy will help students to . . .

- Adjust reading rate according to purpose for reading.
- Read grade-level texts with comprehension and for different purposes.
- Use self-monitoring strategies such as rereading, cross-checking, summarizing, and self-questioning.
- Apply corrective strategies using classroom resources such as peers, teachers, and reference tools.
- Use comprehension strategies to monitor own reading (e.g., attend to vocabulary) and clarify meaning.
- Recognize and use organizational features such as glossaries and chapter headings and subheadings to locate and interpret information.
- Use text features such as captions and other visuals to understand informational texts.
- Recognize when comprehension has been disrupted and initiate self-correction strategies such as discussing with others and monitoring for misunderstanding.
- Analyze information on the basis of new or prior knowledge and personal experience.
- Identify missing, conflicting, unclear, or irrelevant information.
- Combine multiple strategies to enhance comprehension.
- Identify opportunities for improvement of reading comprehension strategies.
- Demonstrate task awareness by employing flexible strategies.

 © 2007. All Rights Reserved.

Section Two

SMART

Section Two

How does it work?

This strategy helps students learn to carry on an internal monologue while they read, just as proficient readers naturally do. To use this metacognitive strategy, the teacher selects a challenging passage of about four or five paragraphs and enlarges it on an overhead. The teacher then models the process of thinking aloud while reading, directing students to place a check mark next to sentences or paragraphs they understand immediately and a question mark next to those they don't. After reading the passage, the teacher models the SMART protocol (see the example that follows). Students then practice the whole process on their own or with partners (Vaughan & Estes, 1986).

Variations for Emergent English Language Learners

- Use support or complementary coteaching for the modeling session.
- Pair ELLs with linguistic buddies for the practice session.
- Differentiate the level of challenge depending on ELLs' proficiency. Ask the ESL teacher to help if necessary.

Example:

READ SMART!

1. **Read.** Read a section of the text. Using a pencil, lightly place a check mark next to each paragraph that you understand and a question mark next to each paragraph that contains something you do not understand.
2. **Self-translate.** At the end of each section, stop and explain to yourself, in your own words or language, what you read.
3. **Troubleshoot.** Go back to each paragraph with a question mark and see if you can now make sense of the paragraph. Reread the trouble spot to see it now makes sense. If it still does not make sense:
   - Pinpoint a problem by figuring out why you are having trouble: Is it a difficult word or unfamiliar vocabulary? Is it a difficult sentence or confusing language? Is it a subject about which you know very little?
   - Try a fix-up strategy: Use the glossary or some other vocabulary aid, look over pictures or graphs to assist with meaning, examine other parts of the chapter (summary, review section, diagrams) to assist with meaning.
   - Explain to yourself exactly what you do not understand or what confuses you.
   - Get help. Ask the teacher or a classmate.

Source: From *Classroom Strategies for Interactive Learning,* 2nd ed. (p. 131), by D. Buehl, 2001, Newark, DE: International Reading Association, page 131. Copyright 2001 by International Reading Association. Reproduced with permission.

ASCD © 2007. All Rights Reserved.

Strategies for
SUCCESS
with English Language Learners

READING STRATEGIES FOR GRADES 3–12

SPAWN

Why use it?

Use of this strategy will help students to . . .

- Demonstrate comprehension of texts through creative responses.
- Support interpretations, explanations, and points of view with evidence from text.
- Express opinions and make judgments that demonstrate point of view.
- Use supporting evidence from texts to evaluate ideas, information, themes, or experiences.
- Make connections between text read and own lives, the lives of others, and the world at large.
- Analyze examples, details, or reasons used to support ideas.
- Evaluate the validity and accuracy of text information by identifying differing points of view in texts and identifying fallacies of logic that lead to unsupported conclusions.
- Form opinions and make judgments by analyzing and evaluating texts from a critical perspective.
- Select, reject, and reconcile ideas and information in light of prior knowledge and experiences.
- Respond in writing to prompts that follow the reading of literary and informational texts.
- Develop ideas through brief written texts.
- Vary the formality of language depending on audience and purpose of writing.
- Combine information when writing.
- Use resources such as peers and text information to stimulate writing.

SPAWN

- Produce imaginative responses that show development, organization, insight, and effective language.
- Exhibit personal voice when writing.
- Use a computer to respond to texts.
- Maintain a portfolio that includes imaginative and interpretative writing as a method of reviewing work with the teacher.
- Share the process of writing to respond to written text.
- Use opinions of classmates to evaluate personal interpretation of ideas and information.

How does it work?

SPAWN stands for **S**pecial powers, **P**roblem solving, **A**lternative viewpoints, **W**hat if, and **N**ext. This strategy encourages students to examine complex issues and extend thinking related to content reading. After reading a text, researching a topic, or working with a concept, students work collaboratively on one or more writing tasks in each of the five SPAWN areas; for example: (1) You have been granted special powers. How is this situation different because of the way you choose to use your powers? (2) How would you solve this problem differently than the way presented? (3) You are a journalist interviewing different people on this topic. What kinds of viewpoints are you hearing? (4) What if the events had been different? (5) What do you think should happen next? (Martin, Martin, & O'Brien, 1984).

Variations for Emergent English Language Learners

- Pair ELLs with linguistic buddies.
- Differentiate the number of tasks for ELLs.
- Use the station coteaching model to implement writer's workshop.

ASCD © 2007. All Rights Reserved.

Section Two

Strategies for
SUCCESS
with English Language Learners

READING STRATEGIES FOR GRADES 3–12

SQ3R

Why use it?

Use of this strategy will help students to . . .

- Adjust reading rate according to purpose for reading.
- Use comprehension strategies to monitor own reading and clarify meaning (e.g., predict/confirm, reread, self-question).
- Use organizational and text features to locate and understand texts (titles, headings and subheadings, captions, visuals).
- Relate data and facts from texts to prior information and experience.
- Use prior knowledge in concert with text information to support comprehension, from forming predictions to making inferences and drawing conclusions.
- Formulate and generate questions to be answered by reading and analyzing informational text.
- Read and answer literal, inferential, and critical/application questions.
- Summarize main ideas and supporting details.
- Skim material to gain an overview of content or locate information, and scan texts for specific information.
- Recognize how new information is related to prior knowledge or experience.
- Distinguish between relevant and irrelevant information.
- Present a point of view or interpretation of a text and support it with relevant details.
- Recognize unstated assumptions.
- Evaluate information, ideas, opinions, and themes in texts by identifying central ideas.

 © 2007. All Rights Reserved.

Section Two

SQ3R

How does it work?

This strategy, best used with nonfiction and textbooks, has five steps:
(1) **S**urvey—preview or note the format of the book and discuss students' previous knowledge about the topic. (2) **Q**uestion or make predictions and pose questions inspired by the preview. (3) **R**ead through a shared reading format. (4) **R**ecite or answer and discuss questions generated earlier. (5) **R**eview or state the main idea, recalling and revisiting the text to assure comprehension (Robinson, 1961).

Variations for Emergent English Language Learners

- Ask the ESL teacher to build background knowledge about the topic before ELLs come to class.
- Provide question cues to help generate higher-order questions.
- Use cooperative learning strategies for reciting or discussing.
- Use coteaching strategies (e.g., parallel, support, or complementary).

ASCD © 2007. All Rights Reserved.

Section Two

Strategies for
SUCCESS
with English Language Learners

READING STRATEGIES FOR GRADES 3–12

Story Grammars and Maps

Why use it?

Use of this strategy will help students to . . .

- Read, view, and interpret texts from a variety of genres.
- Engage in purposeful reading in small groups.
- Use previous reading and life experiences to understand and compare literature.
- Use knowledge of story structure and elements to identify plot, character, and events.
- Use specific evidence to describe characters and their actions and motivations, and to relate a sequence of events.
- Make predictions, draw conclusions, and make inferences about events and characters, plot, setting, theme, and dialogue using evidence from the text.
- Define characteristics of literary texts.
- Identify literary elements of different genres.
- Identify the ways in which characters change and develop throughout a story.
- Recognize how the author uses literary devices to create meaning.
- Compare film, video, and stage versions of a literary text to the written version.
- Read, view, and interpret texts and performances from a wide variety of authors, subjects, and genres.
- Read, view, and respond to literary works that represent a range of social, historical, and cultural perspectives.
- Use graphic organizers to record details about literary elements.

 © 2007. All Rights Reserved.

Section Two

STORY GRAMMARS AND MAPS

Section Two

How does it work?

A story grammar identifies the story's structure and literary elements, and their relationships to one another. A story map is a visual representation of the story structure. Students fill them out as they read in small groups and then share and discuss them as a class. See the example that follows (Beck & McKeown, 1981).

Variations for Emergent English Language Learners

- Differentiate the material to be read and then use this strategy as a during-reading strategy before literature circle.
- If using the same material, then show visuals or a film as the prereading strategy to build a context.
- Provide a partially completed story map for ELLs to help them locate information.
- Use coteaching strategies.

ASCD © 2007. All Rights Reserved.

Example:
Story Map

STORY GRAMMARS AND MAPS

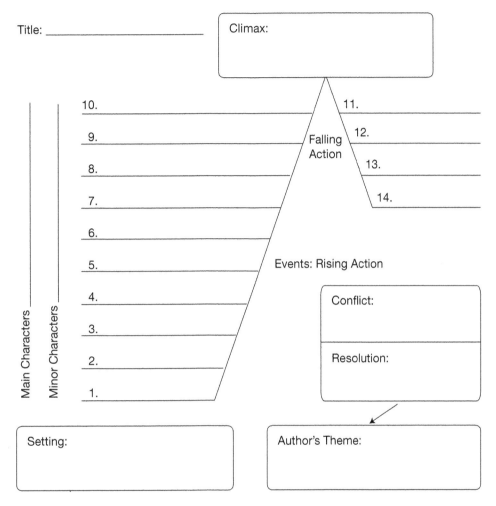

Title: _____

Climax:

10. _____

9. _____

8. _____

7. _____

6. _____

5. _____

4. _____

3. _____

2. _____

1. _____

Main Characters _____

Minor Characters _____

11. _____

12. _____

13. _____

14. _____

Falling Action

Events: Rising Action

Conflict:

Resolution:

Setting:

Author's Theme:

Source: From *Classroom Strategies for Interactive Learning,* by D. Buehl, 1995, Schofield, WI: Wisconsin State Reading Association. Copyright 1995 by Wisconsin State Reading Association. Reprinted with permission.

Section Two

Strategies for
SUCCESS
with English Language Learners

SECTION: LITERACY STRATEGIES

READING STRATEGIES FOR GRADES 3–12

Task Rotation

Why use it?

Use of this strategy will help students to . . .

- Demonstrate comprehension and response through a range of activities such as writing, drama, oral presentation, and mixed media performance.
- Show interest in a wide range of texts; select books independently to meet informational needs.
- Select literature on the basis of personal needs and interests from a variety of genres and by different authors.
- Read, view, and interpret texts from a variety of different genres.
- Use a variety of strategies (e.g., summarizing, forming questions, visualizing, and making connections) to support understanding of texts.
- Use classroom resources to learn the meanings of words causing comprehension difficulties.
- Use graphic organizers to record significant details from texts.
- Use strategies such as note taking, semantic webbing, and outlining to plan and organize writing.
- Respond in writing to the reading of literary and informational texts.
- Write in a variety of formats such as print and multimedia.
- Participate in reading-response activities by integrating multiple strategies (e.g., summarize information, support point of view).
- Use opinions of classmates to evaluate personal interpretation of ideas and information.
- Maintain a personal reading-response list to reflect reading accomplishments.

TASK ROTATION

Section Two

How does it work?

The teacher begins by finding a reading selection that implies "how to" and designs four tasks going from the literal and concrete to the highly abstract (e.g., defining terms, webbing a summary, creating an outline, and writing a response). The teacher then groups students so that some complete all four tasks and others just do the tasks they can. Alternatively, the teacher can require all students to complete all tasks but with differentiated time lines.

Variations for Emergent English Language Learners

- Confer with the ESL teacher and the ELLs to determine tasks, time lines, and partners.
- Differentiate the reading selection if necessary.
- Provide a reading guide for ELLs.
- Try a coteaching strategy.

ASCD © 2007. All Rights Reserved.

READING STRATEGIES FOR GRADES 3–12

Think-Aloud Self-Assessment

Why use it?

Use of this strategy will help students to . . .

- Use self-monitoring strategies such as cross-checking, visualizing, and self-questioning to construct meaning from text.
- Make, confirm, or revise predictions.
- Connect words and ideas in books to spoken language vocabulary and background knowledge.
- Use prior knowledge in concert with text information to support comprehension, from forming predictions to making inferences and drawing conclusions.
- Ask questions to self-monitor comprehension, to clarify understanding, and to focus reading.
- Combine multiple strategies (e.g., predict/confirm, question, visualize, summarize, monitor, self-correct) to enhance comprehension and response.
- Identify missing, conflicting, unclear, or irrelevant information.
- Recognize when comprehension has been disrupted and employ self-correction strategies such as rereading, adjusting rate of reading, and attending to specific vocabulary.
- Identify opportunities for improvement of reading comprehension skills.

How does it work?

The teacher selects a passage to read aloud that contains difficult points, unknown vocabulary terms, or ambiguous wording; develops questions that

© 2007. All Rights Reserved.

show what he thinks as he confronts these problems; and models the kinds of coping strategies he would use. Students then work with partners to practice this think-aloud method when reading short passages of text. The teacher should periodically revisit this strategy so that metacomprehension skills become second nature to the students. (Davey, 1983).

Variations for Emergent English Language Learners

- Ask the ESL teacher to guide ELLs through the think-aloud protocol on a regular basis.
- Pair ELLs with linguistic buddies.
- Differentiate the reading material but not the task.
- Use coteaching strategies.

Example:

Think-Aloud Strategy

Assessing My Use of the "Think-Aloud" Strategy

While I was reading, how much did I use these "think-aloud" strategies?

	Not much	A little	Most of the time	All of the time
Making and revising predictions				
Forming mental pictures				
Connecting what I read to what I already know				
Creating analogies				
Verbalizing confusing points				
Using fix-up strategies				

Source: From *Teaching Reading in the Content Areas: If Not Me Then Who?* (2nd ed., p. 141), by R. Billmeyer and M. L. Barton, 1998, Aurora, CO: Mid-continent Research for Education and Learning. Copyright 1998 by Mid-continent Research for Education and Learning. Reprinted with permission.

ASCD © 2007. All Rights Reserved.

Strategies for
SUCCESS
with English Language Learners

READING STRATEGIES FOR GRADES 3–12

T-Notes

Why use it?

Use of this strategy will help students to . . .
- Identify purpose for reading.
- Use comprehension strategies to monitor own reading and clarify meaning of text (e.g., reread, cross-check, take notes).
- Organize text information by using knowledge of a variety of text structures.
- Read unfamiliar texts to collect and interpret data, facts, and ideas.
- Use text organizational features to understand and interpret texts.
- Recognize when comprehension has been disrupted and initiate self-correction strategies such as adjusting rate of reading and attending to specific phrases.
- Skim material to gain an overview of content or locate specific information; scan material for specific information.
- Identify main ideas and supporting details in text to distinguish relevant and irrelevant information.
- Draw conclusions and make inferences on the basis of explicit and implied information.
- Support main ideas with significant details from the text.
- Use evidence from text to support statements, interpretations, and explanations.
- Identify missing, conflicting, or unclear information.
- Select, reject, and reconcile information.
- Evaluate information, ideas, opinions, and themes in texts by identifying

supporting details of central ideas and citing examples, details, and reasons used to support ideas.

- Use graphic organizers to record significant details from text.
- Take notes to record data, facts, and ideas independently.

How does it work?

This strategy is a simplified form of an outline to help students with reading comprehension and note-taking skills. T-notes have two columns: the left-hand side lists the main ideas of the reading, and the right-hand side is for students to complete details or examples of the main ideas (Reiss, 2005). See the example that follows.

Variations for Emergent English Language Learners

- Provide page numbers or partially completed notes for ELLs so they know where to locate information.
- Provide ELLs with the details and have them identify the main ideas.
- Differentiate the reading material for ELLs but not the topic.
- Use a coteaching strategy.

Example:

The Civil War: A Turning Point in American History	
Main Ideas	**Details/ Examples**
1. The Civil War was expensive in lives and money.	360,000 Union soldiers died. 250,000 Confederate soldiers died. $20 billion spent.
2. The Civil War was a turning point.	The Democratic party got weaker. The Republican party got stronger. States lost some power. The federal government got stronger.
3. The Civil War officially ended slavery.	African-Americans became free. Americans thought about the meaning of "free and equal."
4. The Civil War didn't end the struggle for equality.	In the Gettysburg Address, Lincoln said that the nation must work hard in the fight for equality. This struggle made the U.S. a stronger, freer country.

Source: From *Teaching Content to English Language Learners* (p. 58), by J. Reiss, 2005, Boston: Pearson Education. Copyright 2005 by Pearson Education. Reprinted by permission.

 © 2007. All Rights Reserved.

Strategies for
SUCCESS
with English Language Learners

READING STRATEGIES FOR GRADES 3–12

Two-Minute Preview

Why use it?

Use of this strategy will help students to . . .

- Use comprehension strategies to monitor own reading and to clarify understanding (e.g., predict/confirm, self-question, attend to vocabulary).
- Ask questions to self-monitor comprehension, to clarify understanding, and to focus reading.
- Recognize and use organizational features such as table of contents, indexes, chapter headings and subheadings, margin notes, and summaries to locate information.
- Use text features such as captions, charts, tables, graphs, maps, notes, and other visuals to understand text.
- Read unfamiliar text to collect data, facts, ideas, and information.
- Skim material to gain an overview, and to make, confirm, or revise predictions.
- Identify information that is implied rather than stated.
- Infer underlying theme or message of written text.
- Analyze ideas and information on the basis of prior knowledge and personal experience.

How does it work?

This strategy provides students with an overview of the reading and helps them develop a strategic plan for reading it. The teacher gives students an outline or checklist (see the example that follows), pairs students together, and gives them two minutes to preview the material and jot their responses. To be

Section Two

TWO-MINUTE PREVIEW

Section Two

effective, the teacher models several different ways of previewing and provides students with ongoing practice. This strategy is especially helpful with nonfiction reading passages (Stephens & Brown, 2005).

Variations for Emergent English Language Learners

- Pair ELLs with linguistic buddies.
- Differentiate the material but not the topic or task.
- Use coteaching strategies.

Example:

Textbook Preview

Introduction: What is the author talking about?

_____

_____

Headings and subheads: What are the topics of these sections?

_____

_____

Graphs, charts, maps, and tables: Do I understand how to interpret this information?

_____

_____

Margin notes: What kind of information do they provide?

_____

_____

Summary: Does it provide a clear overview of the chapter?

_____

_____

Questions: Do the questions cover major ideas in the chapter?

_____

_____

Source: From *A Handbook of Content Literacy Strategies: 125 Practical Reading and Writing Aids,* 2nd ed. (p. 71), by E. C. Stephens and J. E. Brown, 2005, Norwood, MA: Christopher-Gordon. Copyright 2005 by Christopher-Gordon Publishers. Adapted with permission.

  © 2007. All Rights Reserved.

Strategies for
SUCCESS
with English Language Learners

READING STRATEGIES FOR GRADES 3–12

Visual Reading Guide

Why use it?

Use of this strategy will help students to . . .
- Read unfamiliar texts to collect data, facts, and ideas.
- Locate information in a text that is needed to solve a problem.
- Use text features such as captions, charts, tables, graphs, maps, notes, and other visuals to understand informational texts.
- Relate data and facts from informational texts to prior information and experience.
- Identify and interpret facts taken from maps, graphs, and other visuals.
- Apply thinking skills such as define, classify, and infer to interpret data, facts, and ideas from informational texts.
- Recognize the defining features and structures of informational texts.
- Recognize unstated assumptions.
- Identify and evaluate the reliability and validity of informational sources.
- Identify a main idea and provide evidence to support or elaborate on it.
- Identify missing and irrelevant information.
- Make inferences and draw conclusions on the basis of information from text.
- Identify information that is implied rather than stated.
- Skim material to gain an overview, and scan text to locate specific material.

How does it work?

This strategy introduces students to a passage by predicting information based on graphics in a text. The teacher explains to students why some

VISUAL READING GUIDE

Section Two

graphics are more important than others by modeling the qualities that make one chart optional and another crucial. Students analyze what each graphic is depicting by answering questions: What is this showing us? How is this graphic organized? Why is this important to the topic? Is there anything that does not make sense? Students discuss the information to formulate a main idea, citing evidence to support their statements (Stein, 1978).

Variations for Emergent English Language Learners

- Provide translations of key terms used in the graphics, if possible, or allow ELLs to use electronic or buddy translations.

Example:

What is this showing us?	How is this graphic organized?	Why is this important to the topic?	Is there anything that does not make sense?

ASCD © 2007. All Rights Reserved.

Strategies for
SUCCESS
with English Language Learners

READING STRATEGIES FOR GRADES 3–12

X Marks the Spot

Why use it?

Use of this strategy will help students to . . .

- Read grade-level texts with comprehension and for different purposes.
- Identify specific words, phrases, or sentences causing comprehension difficulties in written language.
- Use comprehension strategies to monitor own reading and to clarify meaning of text.
- Use self-monitoring strategies such as rereading, cross-checking, and attending to vocabulary to determine meaning of a text.
- Recognize when comprehension has been disrupted and initiate self-correction strategies such as rereading, adjusting rate of reading, and attending to specific vocabulary.
- Use knowledge of structure, content, and vocabulary to understand text.
- Skim material to gain an overview of content.
- Ask questions to self-monitor comprehension, to clarify understanding, and to focus reading.
- Collect and interpret data, facts, and ideas from unfamiliar texts.
- Formulate questions to be answered by reading.
- Focus on key words and phrases to generate questions.
- Interpret information, ideas, opinions, and themes by identifying central ideas and supporting details, missing or unclear information, multiple levels of meaning, and relevant and irrelevant information.

 © 2007. All Rights Reserved.

Section Two

X MARKS THE SPOT

How does it work?

Students use a coding system to help them interact with their reading. The three-part reading response code helps them to identify significant information, new information, and information that is unclear. The teacher models the reading response code as follows: *X* means "I've found a key point," *!* means "I've found some interesting new information," and *?* means "This is confusing" or "I have a question about what this means." Students list the information on charts to serve as a guide for answering questions and reviewing the major text concepts (Stephens & Brown, 2005).

Variations for Emergent English Language Learners

- Pair ELLs with linguistic buddies to complete coding.
- Differentiate the material for ELLs but not the topic.
- Use parallel, support, or complementary coteaching.

ASCD © 2007. All Rights Reserved.

References

Allen, J. (2004). *Tools for teaching content literacy.* Portland, ME: Stenhouse Publishers.

Barton, M. L., & Heidema. (2002). *Teaching reading in mathematics* (2nd ed). Aurora, CO: Mid-continent Research for Education and Learning.

Beck, I., & McKeown, M. (1981, November). Developing questions that promote comprehension: The story map. *Language Arts, 58*(8), 913–918.

Beck, I. L., McKeown, M. G., Hamilton, R. L., & Kucan, L. (1997). *Questioning the author: An approach for enhancing student engagement with text.* Newark, DE: International Reading Association.

Billmeyer, R., & Barton, M. L. (1998). *Teaching reading in the content areas: If not me then who?* (2nd ed.). Aurora, CO: Mid-continent Research for Education and Learning.

Billmeyer, R. (2004). *Strategic reading in the content areas: Practical applications for creating a thinking environment.* Omaha, NE: Rachel & Associates.

Brown, A. L., Day, J. D., and Jones, R. (1983). The development of plans for summarizing texts. *Child Development, 54,* 968–979.

Brown, J. E., Phillips, L. B., Stephens, E. C. (1993). *Towards literacy: Theory and applications for teaching writing in the content areas.* Belmont, CA: Wadsworth.

Buehl, D. (1992). The connection overview: A strategy for learning in science. *WSRA Journal, 36*(2), 21–30.

Buehl, D. (1992). Outline helps students analyze credibility of author's premise. *WEAC News & Views, 28*(1), 8.

Buehl, D. (1995). *Classroom strategies for interactive learning.* Newark, DE: International Reading Association.

Buehl, D. (2001). *Classroom strategies for interactive learning* (2nd ed.). Newark, DE: International Reading Association.

Cutts, K. (2002). *Teaching reading in the content areas.* Presentation at area education agency, Cedar Falls, IA.

Davey, B. (1983). Think aloud: Modeling the cognitive processes of reading comprehension. *Journal of Reading, 27*(1), 44–47.

Devine, J. (1988). The relationship between general language competence and second language reading proficiency: Implications for teaching. In P. Carrell, J. Devine & D. Eskey (Eds.). (1998). *Interactive approaches to second language reading* (pp. 260–277). Cambridge, United Kingdom: Cambridge University Press.

Herber, H. (1978). *Teaching reading in content areas* (2nd ed.). Englewood Cliffs, NJ: Prentice Hall.

Klingner, J., & Vaughn, S. (2000). The helping behaviors of fifth graders while using collaborative strategic reading during ESL content classes. *TESOL Quarterly, 34*(1), 69–98.

Krashen, S. D. (1981). *Second language acquisition and second language learning.* New York: Oxford.

Manzo, A. V. (1969). The ReQuest procedure. *Journal of Reading, 13,* 123–126.

Martin, C. E., Martin, M. A., & 0'Brien, D. G. (1984). Spawning ideas for writing in the content areas. *Reading World, 24,* 11–15.

Palincsar, A. S., & Brown, A. L. (1985). Reciprocal teaching: Activities to promote "reading with your mind." In T. L. Harris & E. J. Cooper (Eds.), *Reading, thinking, and concept development* (pp. 147–158). New York: College Board Publications.

Pressley, M., Symons, S., McDaniel, M., Snyder, B., & Turnure, J. (1988). Elaborative interrogation facilitates acquisition of confusing facts. *Journal of Educational Psychology, 80*(3), 268–278.

Raphael, T. E. (1984). Teaching learners about sources of information for answering comprehension questions. *Journal of Reading, 27,* 303–311.

Raphael, T. E. (1986). Teaching question-answer relationships, revisited. *The Reading Teacher, 39,* 516–522.

Readence, J. E., Moore, D. W., & Rickelman, R. J. (2000). *Prereading activities for content area reading and learning* (3rd ed.). Newark, DE: International Reading Association.

Reiss, J. (2005). *Teaching content to English language learners: Strategies for secondary school success.* Boston: Pearson ESL, Pearson Education.

ASCD © 2007. All Rights Reserved.

Section Two

Robinson, F. (1961). *Effective study*. New York: Harper & Row.

Santa, C. M. (1988) *Content reading including study systems*. Dubuque, IA: Kendall/Hunt.

Sadler, C. R. (2001). *Comprehension strategies for middle grade learners: A handbook for content teachers*. Newark, DE: International Reading Association.

Silver, H. F., Strong, R. W., & Perini, M. J. (2000). *Discovering nonfiction: 25 powerful teaching strategies, grades 2–6*. Santa Monica, CA: Canter & Associates.

Silver, H. F., Strong, R. W., & Perini, M. J. (2001). *Tools for promoting active, in-depth learning* (2nd ed.). Ho Ho Kus, NJ: Thoughtful Education Press.

Stauffer, R. G. (1969). *Directing reading maturity as a cognitive process*. New York: Harper & Row.

Stein, H. (1978). The visual reading guide (VRG). *Social Education, 42,* 534–535.

Stephens, E. C., & Brown, J. E. (2000). *A handbook of content literacy strategies: Practical reading and writing aids*. Norwood, MA: Christopher-Gordon.

Stephens, E. C., & Brown, J. E. (2005). *A handbook of content literacy strategies: 125 practical reading and writing aids* (2nd ed.). Norwood, MA: Christopher-Gordon.

Strong, R. W., Hanson, J. R., & Silver, H. F. (1995). *Questioning styles and strategies: Procedures for increasing the depth of student thinking* (2nd ed.). Woodbridge, NJ: Thoughtful Education Press.

Strong, R. W., Silver, H. F., Perini, M. J., & Tuculescu, G. M. (2002). *Reading for academic success: Powerful strategies for struggling, average, and advanced readers, grades 7–12*. Thousand Oaks, CA: Corwin Press.

Vaughan, J., & Estes, T. (1986). *Reading and reasoning beyond the primary grades*. Boston: Allyn and Bacon.

Wood, K. (1988). Guiding students through informational text. *The Reading Teacher, 41*(9), 912–920.

ASCD © 2007. All Rights Reserved.

Writing Strategies
for Grades 3–12

Writing Strategies
for Grades 3-12

Strategy	Language Acquisition for ELLs			Writing Process			Content Areas				Page
	Input (Inter-pretive)	Intake (Inter-personal)	Output (Presen-tational)	Pre-writing	Drafting	Revising and Editing	LA	Sc	Math	SS	
Brain Writing	X	X	X	X			X	X	X	X	361
Conferring	X	X	X			X	X	X	X	X	363
Cubing	X	X	X	X			X	X	X	X	365
Discussion Continuum	X	X	X	X			X	X	X	X	367
Divorcing the Draft	X	X	X			X	X	X	X	X	369
Don't to *Do* List	X	X	X			X	X	X	X	X	371
Examples	X	X	X	X			X	X	X	X	373
4-2-1 Free Write	X	X	X	X	X		X	X	X	X	375
Guided Writing	X	X	X		X		X	X	X	X	377
Hennings Sequence	X	X	X		X		X	X	X	X	379

Section Two

Strategy	Language Acquisition for ELLs			Writing Process			Content Areas				Page
	Input (Inter-pretive)	Intake (Inter-personal)	Output (Presen-tational)	Pre-writing	Drafting	Revising and Editing	LA	Sc	Math	SS	
Journals	X	X	X	X			X	X	X	X	381
Looping	X	X	X		X		X	X	X	X	383
Pair Talking	X	X	X		X		X	X	X	X	385
Prewriting Chart											387
Publication	X	X	X			X	X	X	X	X	389
Rewording	X	X	X			X	X	X	X	X	391
Surprise!	X	X	X			X	X			X	393
Task-Based Rubrics	X	X	X	X	X	X	X	X	X	X	395
Two-Column Count	X	X	X			X	X	X		X	401
Writer's Notebook	X	X	X	X			X	X	X	X	403
Writing Workshop	X	X	X		X	X	X			X	405

ASCD © 2007. All Rights Reserved.

Strategies for
SUCCESS
with English Language Learners

WRITING STRATEGIES FOR GRADES 3–12

Brain Writing

Why use it?

Use of this strategy will help students to . . .

- Organize ideas and information.
- Understand the purpose of writing (e.g., to explain, describe, narrate, persuade, or express feelings).
- Engage in a variety of writing activities to respond to the reading of imaginative and informational texts.
- Write voluntarily to communicate ideas and emotions to a variety of audiences.
- Record ideas following teacher direction.
- Connect personal experiences to new information from subject areas.
- Compare and contrast ideas with others.
- Use resources such as personal experiences and elements from other texts to stimulate own writing.
- Express opinions and make judgments that demonstrate a personal point of view.
- Share the process of writing with peers.
- Write on a wide range of topics.
- Begin to develop a voice that allows a reader to get to know the writer.
- Work collaboratively with peers to plan written work.
- Write to share personal reactions to experiences, events, and observations.
- Maintain a portfolio of ideas for writing.

Section Two

How does it work?

Students work in small groups on an assigned topic. Each student writes for a few minutes, and then all students put their papers in the middle of the table. Each student reads another's paper and adds to it until all the papers have been read and added to by each group member. Each group develops a master list of ideas from all the papers to be used for drafting.

Variations for Emergent English Language Learners

- If possible, place ELLs of similar language backgrounds together so they can write in their primary language.
- Ask the ESL teacher to work with ELLs before they come to class.
- Allow ELLs to use illustrations.
- Act as a scribe, using the Language Experience approach to write what ELLs say.

ASCD © 2007. All Rights Reserved.

Strategies for SUCCESS with English Language Learners

WRITING STRATEGIES FOR GRADES 3–12

Conferring

Why use it?

Use of this strategy will help students to . . .

- Engage in a variety of writing activities.
- Learn and use revision strategies as a part of the total writing process.
- Present and discuss own writing in conferences with teachers and peers and respond with feedback.
- Develop a personal voice that enables the reader to get to know the writer.
- Work collaboratively with peers to revise written work.
- Identify and model the social communication techniques of published authors.
- Maintain a portfolio of writing that includes drafts needing revision.

How does it work?

Students divide a piece of paper into columns with one of the following sets of headings:

1. Questions the reader asked	1. I like
2. Comments the reader made	2. I wonder
3. Concerns the reader expressed	3. Questions I have
4. My plan of action to revise	

 © 2007. All Rights Reserved.

CONFERRING

Section Two

Students use these prompts in a teacher-student conference, a student-student conference, or alone.

Variations for Emergent English Language Learners

- Pair students with linguistic buddies so they can confer in the primary language if necessary.
- Use cooperative learning strategies for conference purposes.
- Use coteaching strategies for conference sessions.

ASCD © 2007. All Rights Reserved.

Strategies for
SUCCESS
with English Language Learners

WRITING STRATEGIES FOR GRADES 3–12

Cubing

Why use it?

Use of this strategy will help students to . . .

- Use a variety of prewriting strategies to organize ideas and information.
- Respond in writing to prompts that follow the reading of literary or informational texts.
- Develop an idea with a brief text.
- Plan a variety of compositions using different organizational patterns (e.g., cause/effect, compare/contrast).
- Use relevant examples, reasons, and explanations to support ideas.
- Use the tone, vocabulary, and sentence structure of informal conversation in initial writing.
- Write voluntarily to communicate ideas to a variety of audiences.
- Develop ideas by writing sentences.
- State a main idea and support it with details.
- Use relevant examples, reasons, and explanations to support ideas.
- Write on a wide range of topics.
- Use information and ideas from other subject areas and personal experiences to form and express opinions.
- Include relevant and exclude irrelevant information.
- Present a subject from more than one perspective.
- Understand the purpose for writing.
- Write and share personal reactions to experiences, events, and observations.

CUBING

Section Two

How does it work?

This strategy helps students construct meaning about a specific topic. Students write for 3–5 minutes on each of the six sides of a cube (describe something, compare it, associate it, analyze it, apply it, and argue for or against it). The intent of cubing is to have students generate more ideas or perspectives.

Variations for Emergent English Language Learners

- If possible, allow ELLs to orally cube about a topic in their primary language as a starting point.
- Provide linguistic cues or signal words to assist ELLs to put together their ideas and sentences.
- Provide linguistic buddies for ELLs so they can cube as partners in both languages.
- Have ELLs use cubing as a during-reading strategy to collect information about a topic that they can then use in prewriting.

ASCD © 2007. All Rights Reserved.

Strategies for
SUCCESS
with English Language Learners

WRITING STRATEGIES FOR GRADES 3–12

Discussion Continuum

Why use it?

Use of this strategy will help students to . . .

- Use a variety of prewriting strategies to organize ideas and information, such as keeping a list of topic ideas as a reference.
- Respond to prompts that follow the reading of literary or informational texts.
- Understand the purpose for writing (e.g., to explain, describe, narrate, persuade, or express feelings).
- Combine information from multiple sources when writing.
- Support interpretations and explanations with evidence from text.
- Write interpretive and responsive essays that express a personal response.
- Express opinions and make judgments that demonstrate a personal point of view.
- Share the process of prewriting with peers.
- Draw a conclusion about a topic.
- Use supporting evidence from text to evaluate ideas, information, themes, or experiences.
- Analyze the impact of an issue from personal and peer group perspectives.
- Engage in a variety of writing activities to respond to ideas and texts read.
- Respond to literature, connecting the response to personal experience.
- Identify an appropriate format for sharing information with an intended audience.
- Connect, compare, and contrast ideas and information from different sources.
- Present a subject from more than one perspective.

 © 2007. All Rights Reserved.

DISCUSSION CONTINUUM

Section Two

- Compose arguments to support points of view.
- Articulate one or more perspectives to summarize arguments on different sides of issues.
- Use strategies designed to influence or persuade in writing.
- Work collaboratively with peers to plan written work.

How does it work?

This strategy provides a structured format for a whole-class discussion of a topic to build background knowledge on an issue. The teacher writes two statements on opposite ends of the board—one for a position and one against. Students write their initials along the continuum to show where they stand and then explain their positions, often using references from reading to support their ideas. (All students must have a chance to speak before anyone has a second chance.) The ideas presented broaden students' perspectives on issues, give them ideas for their writing, and connect talking to writing.

Variations for Emergent English Language Learners

- Ask the ESL teacher to brainstorm opposing ideas before the class discussion.
- Provide cue cards with key words and phrases for ELLs.
- Wait until ELLs volunteer to speak before asking them to speak in front of the class (if they do not volunteer, just let them listen or take notes).

ASCD © 2007. All Rights Reserved.

Strategies for
SUCCESS
with English Language Learners

WRITING STRATEGIES FOR GRADES 3–12

Divorcing the Draft

Why use it?

Use of this strategy will help students to . . .

- Engage in a variety of writing activities during the revision stage of the writing process.
- Use revision strategies to develop writing, including conferring with teachers and peers, and cutting and pasting text.
- Use a variety of sentence types in writing.
- Review work for sentence variety.
- Use signal words that provide clues to organizational formats.
- Use a variety of organizational formats for writing.
- Adjust style of writing; write clear, concise, and varied sentences.
- Develop a personal voice that enables the reader to know the writer.
- Review work in order to revise for focus, development of ideas, and organization.
- Adjust style and language of writing according to audience.
- Use computer technology to create, manipulate, and edit text.
- Maintain a portfolio of writing that includes drafts needing revision.

How does it work?

This strategy gives writers an opportunity to detach themselves from a draft in its current form. Students (1) select a draft that needs revising; (2) use a pair of scissors to cut the draft by paragraphs or sentences; (3) mix the paragraphs or sentences out of the original order; (4) sift through the cut pieces looking for the one that best describes the message they want to convey; (5) continue

ASCD © 2007. All Rights Reserved.

sorting through the remaining pieces looking for those that relate to the central idea; (6) when the sorting is complete, lay out the saved items and reorder them; (7) tape the rearranged sentences and add new ones; and (8) retype the revision. Cutting and pasting is worth doing because it gives permission to writers to divorce the draft (Urquhart & McIver, 2005).

Variations for Emergent English Language Learners

- Pair ELLs and use a cooperative learning strategy.
- Use a coteaching strategy (e.g., parallel, supportive, team).
- Provide some cues for ELLs to follow when putting the pieces back together.

ASCD © 2007. All Rights Reserved.

Strategies for
SUCCESS
with English Language Learners

WRITING STRATEGIES FOR GRADES 3–12

Don't to *Do* List

Why use it?

Use of this strategy will help students to . . .

- Learn and use the editing stage of the writing process.
- Review work for mechanical errors.
- Use punctuation correctly.
- Write a variety of sentence types with correct tenses and agreements.
- Use spelling correctly.
- Use signal or transitions words to produce cohesive texts.
- Use dictionaries, thesauruses, and style manuals.
- Use word processing to support editing.
- Work collaboratively with peers to edit own and one another's writing.

How does it work?

Note: If students do not know how to edit their work using the symbols of an editing checklist, then an interim step might be needed. Students divide a paper into two columns—one labeled *Don't* and the other labeled *Do*. They invest some time in copying representative spelling, grammar, and usage errors they have made in previous papers in the *Don't* column, recording the errors exactly as the students wrote them originally. The teacher then groups students into pairs who have made similar errors; the pairs work together to turn the *Don't*s into *Do*'s, following the teacher's guidance. For example, they use dictionaries or word walls for the spelling errors, refer to readings for the grammar errors, and use a proficient peer to help with the usage errors. Once

 © 2007. All Rights Reserved.

DON'T TO DO LIST

students begin to explicitly grasp the concept of errors (the *Don'ts*) and the need for self-correction (the *Do's*), they will grow into the process implicitly (using an editing checklist). The time that both teacher and students invest will be worth the results.

Variations for Emergent English Language Learners

*   Have ELLs complete their lists under the guidance of the ESL teacher.
*   Use cooperative learning strategies.

ASCD © 2007. All Rights Reserved.

Strategies for SUCCESS with English Language Learners

WRITING STRATEGIES FOR GRADES 3–12

Examples

Section Two

Why use it?

Use of this strategy will help students to . . .
- Use a variety of prewriting strategies to organize ideas and information.
- Write in response to the reading of informational texts.
- Take notes to record data, facts, and ideas following teacher direction.
- Engage in a variety of writing activities in response to the reading of informational texts.
- Connect personal experiences and interpretations to new information.
- Write for a variety of purposes, with attention given to using the form of writing that best supports the purpose.
- Understand the purpose for writing (e.g., explain, describe, narrate, persuade, or express feelings).
- Support interpretations with evidence from texts.
- Understand and use writing for a variety of purposes.
- Analyze and evaluate authors' use of language in written and visual text.
- Use effective vocabulary in expository writing.
- Use tone and language appropriate for audience and purpose.
- Write labels or captions for graphics to convey information.
- Use paraphrasing and quotation correctly.
- Cite sources in notes using correct form.
- Incorporate aspects of the writer's craft, such as specific voice, into own writing.

How does it work?

The teacher selects a nonfiction text for students to read and highlight text features they find effective, modeling a couple with the class. Students pay close attention to the final column when planning their writing. See the example that follows (Urquhart & McIver, 2005).

Variations for Emergent English Language Learners

- After the modeling sessions, partner students for guided practice before they work independently.
- Ask the ESL teacher to practice this strategy with ELLs as a during-reading strategy so they come prepared to participate in this after-reading/prewriting activity.
- Differentiate the material or jigsaw the tasks for ELLs (see the differentiation tools in the Instructional Practices area of this section of the manual).

Example:

Sample text	Feature or craft	Effect	When will I use it?
"Folk Art Jubilee" by Brian Noyes (*Smithsonian,* October 2003)	Mixes photographs and sketches.	Photographs are precise; sketches leave more to the viewer's imagination.	I will use a photograph when I want my reader to see the exact features of an object and a sketch when the reader does not need a precise rendering.
"The typically taciturn Suddeth brightens as he recalls his breakthrough moment at age 7" (p. 80).	Uses alliteration.	Lets the writer be playful without having to use slang.	When I want to use slang or other commonly used words.

Source: From *Teaching Writing in the Content Areas* (p. 151), by V. Urquhart and M. McIver, 2005, Alexandria, VA: Association for Supervision and Curriculum Development. Copyright 2005 by Association for Supervision and Curriculum Development. Reprinted with permission.

ASCD © 2007. All Rights Reserved.

Strategies for SUCCESS with English Language Learners

WRITING STRATEGIES FOR GRADES 3–12

4-2-1 Free Write

Why use it?

Use of this strategy will help students to . . .

- Use a variety of prewriting tools to organize ideas and information.
- Engage in a variety of writing activities to respond to the reading of literary and informational text.
- Write on a wide range of topics.
- Write sentences in logical order and use paragraphs to organize topics.
- Develop an idea within a brief text.
- Combine information from multiple sources when writing reports.
- Take notes to record ideas.
- State a main idea and support it with details.
- Summarize literary or informational text in writing.
- Support interpretations and explanations with evidence from text.
- Write interpretive and responsive essays.
- Produce clear, well-organized responses to stories read.
- Use resources to stimulate own writing.
- State main ideas, themes, or opinions.
- Work collaboratively with peers to plan and draft written work.
- Compose arguments to support points of view.
- Include relevant and irrelevant information.
- Support ideas with examples, definitions, analogies, and direct references to the text.
- Understand the purpose for writing.
- Write clear, concise sentences.

Section Two

4-2-1 FREE WRITE

Section Two

How does it work?

This strategy makes the connection between reading and writing. Individually, students read and jot down four main ideas. In pairs, they share their ideas and together come up with two main ideas, selecting or synthesizing from among the eight ideas. Each pair of students joins another pair and, as groups of four, the students come up with one main idea, again selecting or synthesizing from among the four ideas. Finally, students write individually as much as they can about that one main idea. This strategy can serve as a prewriting or draft activity for students who complain about "not knowing what to write about" (Strong, Silver, Perini, & Tuculescu, 2002).

Variations for Emergent English Language Learners

- Ask the ESL teacher to preread the text with ELLs.
- Cue the four boxes for the first read so ELLs know what to look for.
- Allow ELLs to free-write in their primary language if possible.

Example:

1. Idea	2. Idea	3. Idea	4. Idea
1. Central Idea		2. Central Idea	
1 Big Idea			
Free Write			

Source: From *Reading for Academic Success: Powerful Strategies for Struggling, Average, and Advanced Readers, Grades 7–12* (p. 147), by R. W. Strong, H. F. Silver, M J. Perini, and G. M. Tuculescu, 2002, Thousand Oaks, CA: Sage Publications. Reprinted by permission of Corwin Press.

ASCD © 2007. All Rights Reserved.

Strategies for
SUCCESS
with English Language Learners

WRITING STRATEGIES FOR GRADES 3–12

Guided Writing

Why use it?

Use of this strategy will help students to . . .

- Engage in a variety of writing activities to respond to literary or informational texts.
- Determine the intended audience.
- Understand the purpose for writing.
- Begin to develop a voice in writing.
- Adjust style of writing, voice, and language according to purpose and intended audience.
- Write on a wide range of topics.
- Develop ideas with brief text.
- Write sentences in logical order and use paragraphs to organize topics.
- State a main idea and support it with facts and details.
- Connect personal experiences to new information.
- Produce accounts that demonstrate understanding of an idea or topic.
- Write clear, concise, and varied sentences.
- Produce responses to stories supporting understanding of characters and events.
- Write in a variety of styles, using different organizational patterns.
- Use grade-level vocabulary and sentence patterns in writing.
- Write voluntarily to communicate ideas and emotions to a variety of audiences, from self to unknown.
- Use word processing skills to create text.

 © 2007. All Rights Reserved.

Section Two

How does it work?

This strategy guides students from prewriting to drafting in stages. The teacher divides the prewriting plan into appropriate sections, and students write as much as they can for each section. The sections do not have to be followed in any order so if students get stuck while drafting, they should move on to another section.

Variations for Emergent English Language Learners

- Use coteaching tools to implement guided writing so both the classroom teacher and the ESL teacher can work with small groups of students.
- Use the prewriting plan to provide visual or linguistic cues on each section of the ELLs' drafts.
- Allow ELLs to draft using their primary language if they feel more comfortable at first.
- Act as a scribe, using the Language Experience approach to write what the ELLs say.

ASCD © 2007. All Rights Reserved.

Strategies for
SUCCESS
with English Language Learners

WRITING STRATEGIES FOR GRADES 3–12

Hennings Sequence

Why use it?

Use of this strategy will help students to . . .

- Write on a wide range of topics.
- Understand the purpose of writing (e.g., to explain, describe, narrate, persuade, or express feelings).
- Use a range of organizational strategies.
- Create paragraphs to develop ideas.
- State a main idea, theme, or opinion and support it with facts and details.
- Use relevant examples, reasons, and explanations to support ideas.
- Use a variety of organizational patterns for writing.
- Vary the formality of language depending on audience and purpose.
- Use personal experiences and knowledge to analyze and evaluate new ideas.
- Connect personal experiences to new information.
- Produce clear accounts that demonstrate understanding of an idea or topic.
- Use resources such as personal experiences and elements from others to stimulate own writing.
- Adjust style of writing, voice, and language use according to purpose and intended audience.
- Use grade-level vocabulary and varied sentence structures in writing.
- Use effective vocabulary in persuasive and expository writing.
- Present and discuss own writing in conferences with peers and respond with feedback.
- Work collaboratively with peers to draft written work.

 © 2007. All Rights Reserved.

Section Two

How does it work?

This strategy is inherently scaffolded since it takes students from context-embedded situations (i.e., concrete and visual) to context-reduced situations (i.e., abstract and text driven) and helps writers clarify the organization of information. "Fact storming" is a way to record students' knowledge after they have had a chance to become familiar with a topic through viewing films and slides, interviewing people, going on excursions, reading, talking, and observing. Students organize the concepts from fact storming by producing data charts in small groups (i.e., vertical and horizontal categories of information). Students then draft paragraphs by directly translating the information contained in the data chart columns, rows, or cells. They draft the introduction and conclusion as a teacher-guided group writing activity. The teacher guides students through reading similar pieces of discourse using the data chart concept as a postreading activity in addition to a prewriting one. Finally, students return to their writing to revise their drafts (Hennings, 1982).

Variations for Emergent English Language Learners

- Use a coteaching model, such as alternative, complementary, parallel, supportive, or team teaching.

ASCD © 2007. All Rights Reserved.

Strategies for
SUCCESS
with English Language Learners

WRITING STRATEGIES FOR GRADES 3–12

Journals

Why use it?

Use of this strategy will help students to . . .

- Use a variety of prewriting strategies.
- Write voluntarily to express ideas and emotions.
- Connect personal experiences to new information from school subjects.
- Use resources such as personal experiences and elements from other texts to stimulate own writing.
- Express personal opinions and make judgments that demonstrate a personal point of view.
- Respond in writing to prompts that follow the reading of literary or informational texts.
- Develop ideas by writing sentences.
- Write on a wide range of topics.
- Write for a variety of purposes.
- Use graphics to convey information.
- Take notes to record and organize relevant data, facts, and ideas and use the notes as part of prewriting activities.
- Connect, compare, and contrast ideas and information from one or more sources.
- Use paraphrasing to organize ideas and information.
- Respond to literature, connecting the response to personal experience.
- Express opinions and support them through specific references to the text.
- Use information and ideas from other subject areas and personal experiences to form and express opinions and judgments.

- Explain connections between and among texts to extend the meaning of each individual text.
- Write with voice to address varied topics across the curriculum.
- Engage in writing voluntarily on a range of topics for a variety of purposes.
- Present ideas for writing in conferences with teachers and peers.
- Maintain a portfolio of ideas for writing.

How does it work?

The teacher encourages students to jot down ideas in all their subject areas as a vehicle for informal writing to help them process and connect information, language, and problem-solving skills from one class to another.

Variations for Emergent English Language Learners

- Ask the ESL teacher to work with ELLs to use these ideas as starting points for assigned writing tasks by using ESL class time to write, share exemplars, and model think-aloud writing protocols.
- Act as a scribe, using the Language Experience approach to write what the ELLs say.

ASCD © 2007. All Rights Reserved.

Strategies for
SUCCESS
with English Language Learners

SECTION: LITERACY STRATEGIES

WRITING STRATEGIES FOR GRADES 3–12

Looping

Why use it?

Use of this strategy will help students to . . .

- Understand the purpose of writing (e.g., to explain, describe, narrate, persuade, or express feelings).
- Use a range of organizational strategies.
- Create paragraphs to develop ideas.
- State a main idea, theme. or opinion and support it with facts and details.
- Connect personal experiences to new information.
- Use personal experiences and knowledge to analyze and evaluate new ideas.
- Vary the tone, vocabulary, and sentence structure according to the audience and purpose of writing.
- Use details from stories and informational texts to predict, explain, or show relationships between information and events.
- Produce clear accounts that demonstrate understanding of a topic.
- Produce clear responses to stories read or listened to, supporting the understanding of characters and events with details.
- Develop ideas by writing sentences that are in logical order and organized into paragraphs.
- Review writing independently to revise for focus, development of ideas, and organization.
- Write on a wide range of topics.
- Present and discuss own writing in conferences with teachers and peers.
- Share the process of writing with peers and adults.

Section Two

LOOPING

- Use word processing skills.
- Maintain a portfolio of writings as a method of reviewing work with teachers and peers.

How does it work?

Students begin writing their ideas for a draft by writing nonstop for 10 minutes. They (or the teacher) read over the writing and circle one aspect to explore further. Students then write for another 10 minutes about the selected ideas. Again, characteristics or details from the second draft are circled, and students write for yet another 10 minutes. When students finish all the "looping" in this way, they have more and more ideas in their drafts and can begin the revising stage of the writing process.

Variations for Emergent English Language Learners

- Pair ELLs so they can take turns looping, using a cooperative learning structure.
- Ask the ESL teacher to work on looping in advance, or use a coteaching model (e.g., station teaching for writer's workshop or supportive teaching).
- Ask the ESL teacher to develop a text aid to guide ELLs through looping.
- Allow use of students' primary languages.
- Act as a scribe, using the Language Experience approach to write what the ELLs say.

ASCD © 2007. All Rights Reserved.

Section Two

Strategies for
SUCCESS
with English Language Learners

WRITING STRATEGIES FOR GRADES 3–12

Pair Talking

Why use it?

Use of this strategy will help students to . . .

- Understand the purpose for writing (e.g., to explain, describe, narrate, persuade, or express feelings).
- Use a variety of organizational patterns for writing.
- Develop a personal voice that enables the reader to get to know the writer.
- Write sentences in logical order and create paragraphs to develop ideas.
- Vary the formality of language depending on audience and purpose.
- State a main idea and support it with details.
- Support interpretations and explanations with evidence.
- Use relevant examples, reasons, and explanations to support ideas.
- Express opinions and make judgments that demonstrate a personal point of view.
- Compare and contrast ideas with assistance.
- Use resources such as personal experiences and elements from others to stimulate own writing.
- Adjust style of writing, voice, and language use according to purpose and intended audience.
- Use grade-level vocabulary and varied sentence structures in writing.
- Use effective vocabulary in persuasive and expository writing.
- Identify and model the social communication techniques of published writers.
- Present and discuss own writing in conferences with peers and respond with feedback.
- Work collaboratively with peers to draft written work.

PAIR TALKING

How does it work?

This strategy helps students work out vocabulary and linguistic structures that might impede their writing. In pairs, one student talks about what he or she wants to write in response to questions posed by the other student. Both then draft what was said.

Variations for Emergent English Language Learners

- Ask the ESL teacher to model this strategy for ELLs beforehand to prepare them with questions they might ask or be asked.
- Ask the ESL teacher to focus on the linguistic features of the particular genre being written as a during- or after-reading strategy before they write.
- Pair ELLs with students who represent the next level of competence (see Krashen's Input + 1 theory or Vygotsky's Zone of Proximal Development in the first section of this manual), using a cooperative learning strategy.
- Use a coteaching model.
- Act as a scribe, using the Language Experience approach to write what the ELLs say.

Section Two

ASCD © 2007. All Rights Reserved.

Strategies for
SUCCESS
with English Language Learners

WRITING STRATEGIES FOR GRADES 3–12

Prewriting Chart

Why use it?

Use of this strategy will help students to . . .

- Use a variety of strategies to plan and organize ideas for writing, such as keeping a list of topic ideas and purposes.
- Determine the purpose and audience for writing.
- Make plans for using the writing process.
- Write for a variety of purposes, selecting a form of writing appropriate to the function of the written communication.
- Vary the formality of language depending on audience and purpose.
- Present and discuss ideas for writing in conferences with teacher and peers.
- Write voluntarily for different purposes.
- Write on a wide range of topics.
- Maintain a portfolio that includes different types of writing (e.g., social communication, informational writing, etc.).
- Share the process of writing with peers (e.g., write a thank-you letter with a writing partner).
- Use the conventions of e-mail when writing informally.

How does it work?

The teacher and students develop a chart about the kinds of writing that will be expected in class or in a particular content area. The chart should help students distinguish three broad categories of school writing: writing without composing, writing to learn, and writing to demonstrate learning. This strategy

 © 2007. All Rights Reserved.

Section Two

helps students understand the purposes for different kinds of writing so they understand the processes or strategies used for each type. See the example that follows (Stephens & Brown, 2005).

Variations for Emergent English Language Learners

- Have ELLs keep two prewriting charts (one in the primary language and one in English) so they can begin to make the transfer from writing in one language to another.
- Have younger or academically underprepared ELLs keep a "driting" (drawings as writings) chart.
- Ask the ESL teacher to work on one type of writing each week as a connection between the mainstream and the ESL class.

Example:

Prewriting Chart

Writing Without Composing	Writing to Learn	Writing to Demonstrate Learning
Lists Note taking Brainstorming Fill-in-the-blank Outlining	Journals Logs Quick writes Rough drafts Short answers Content notebooks Response guides Lab notebooks	Essays Book reports & reviews Research papers Written projects Formal letters Newspaper writing Expository writing Narrative writing Creative writing

Source: From *A Handbook of Content Literacy Strategies: 125 Practical Reading and Writing Ideas* (2nd ed., p. 52), by E. C. Stephens and J. E. Brown, 2005, Norwood, MA: Christopher-Gordon Publishers. Copyright 2005 by Christopher-Gordon Publishers. Reprinted with permission.

ASCD © 2007. All Rights Reserved.

Strategies for
SUCCESS
with English Language Learners

WRITING STRATEGIES FOR GRADES 3–12

Publication

Why use it?

Use of this strategy will help students to . . .

- Write for an authentic purpose, including publication.
- Share the products of writing with peers and adults.
- Publish writing suitable for a variety of display purposes, such as within a classroom, for a school, or on the Internet.
- Publish writing for a variety of audiences.
- Distinguish between the conventions of published and nonpublished writing.
- Maintain a portfolio of writings from which to select for publication.

How does it work?

Student writing can be displayed on bulletin boards, in school showcases, or in waiting rooms. Students can formally share their writing in informal settings, much like "coffee house readings," or through formal settings such as writing contests or formal publications. Students come to understand that they are writing for real audiences outside the classroom through the publication of their writing.

Variations for Emergent English Language Learners

- Publish writing in the primary languages of ELLs.
- Use a coteaching model to publish writing.

Section Two

Strategies for
SUCCESS
with English Language Learners

WRITING STRATEGIES FOR GRADES 3–12

Rewording

Why use it?

Use of this strategy will help students to . . .

- Use revision strategies to develop writing, including conferring with teacher and peers.
- Develop an idea within a brief text.
- Use grade-level vocabulary and sentence structures in writing.
- Use effective vocabulary in expository or persuasive writing.
- Use signal and transitional words to clarify organizational format.
- Use precise vocabulary with assistance.
- Vary the formality of language depending on audience and purpose.
- Convey personal voice in writing.
- Present and discuss own writing in conferences with teacher and peers and respond to feedback.
- Use details to explain information.
- Adjust style of writing, voice, and language according to purpose and intended audience.
- Develop a personal voice that enables the reader to know the writer.
- Work collaboratively with peers to revise writing.

How does it work?

Students choose a selection of writing that needs revision. They switch papers with a partner; the partners read the selection, highlighting any words that are new to them. Partners then read each word to the authors, asking them to write a definition for each term using their own words. Partners substitute

REWORDING

Section Two

these definitions for the highlighted words and reread the sentences (Urquhart & McIver, 2005).

Variations for Emergent English Language Learners

- Provide ELLs with a personal word and phrase wall.
- Use a cooperative learning strategy or a coteaching model.
- Ask the ESL teacher to rehearse this strategy with ELLs beforehand.

ASCD © 2007. All Rights Reserved.

Strategies for
SUCCESS
with English Language Learners

WRITING STRATEGIES FOR GRADES 3–12

Surprise!

Why use it?

Use of this strategy will help students to . . .

- Engage in a variety of writing activities to revise work.
- Learn and use the revising stage of the writing process.
- Use revision strategies to develop writing, including conferring with peers.
- Write in a variety of styles, depending on the audience and purpose.
- Vary tone and language according to the audience and purpose.
- Review work in order to revise for focus, development of ideas, and organization.
- Develop a personal voice that enables the reader to know the writer.
- Select an organizational pattern that effectively communicates the topic and purpose of the text to the intended audience.
- Write clear, concise sentences.
- Write for a wide variety of audiences.
- Present and discuss own writing in conferences with teacher and peers, and respond to feedback.
- Maintain a portfolio of writings for revision purposes.

How does it work?

This strategy lets the writer know that the revision stage of the writing process can be used to reflect on whether or not the reader will be attracted to the piece of writing. Student writers come up with possible alternatives and then student readers select which alternative they prefer, providing a justification for the writer. For example, writers may come up with alternative introductions

Section Two

or conclusions, and readers select which they prefer; or writers may switch a point of view, and readers react accordingly. The strategy teaches that there are different ways to change a piece of writing, that the reader needs to be taken into consideration, and that readers sometimes have surprising suggestions.

Variations for Emergent English Language Learners

- Act as a scribe, using the Language Experience approach to write the ELLs' variations.
- Use interactive writing (groups of students writing together) to generate the alternatives.
- Use a cooperative learning strategy to have students generate alternatives.
- Use a coteaching model (e.g., peer or station teaching).

ASCD © 2007. All Rights Reserved.

Strategies for
SUCCESS
with English Language Learners

WRITING STRATEGIES FOR GRADES 3–12

Task-Based Rubrics

Why use it?

Use of this strategy will help students to . . .

- Learn and use the writing process (prewriting, drafting, revising, editing).
- Write in a variety of styles, using the writing process.
- Write on a wide range of topics.
- Write in response to the reading of literary or informational text.
- Understand the purpose for writing.
- Use prewriting strategies to organize ideas and information.
- Write sentences in logical order and use paragraphs to organize writing.
- Write with voice to address varied purposes, topics, and audiences across the curriculum.
- Combine information from multiple sources when writing reports.
- Vary tone, vocabulary, and sentence structure according to audience and purpose.
- Take notes to record data, facts, and ideas.
- Uses an organizational pattern for expository writing.
- Support interpretations and explanations with evidence.
- Write original literary texts.
- Write interpretative and responsive essays.
- Use and cite both primary and secondary sources of information for research.
- Define the meaning and understand the consequences of plagiarism.
- Revise independently for focus, development of ideas, and organization.
- Edit independently for correct spelling, grammar, capitalization, punctuation, and paragraphing.

 © 2007. All Rights Reserved.

Section Two

- Review writing with teachers and peers and be able to respond to feedback.
- Use teacher conferences and peer review to revise written work.
- Use word processing skills to support the writing process.
- Maintain a portfolio that includes all styles of writing.

How does it work?

A task-based rubric focuses on the writing process rather than the product (an analytical rubric). The rubric establishes clear criteria before the students begin each stage. The teacher can share the entire rubric with students or share each row as students progress through each stage of the writing process. Students can also sort pieces of writing to understand the criteria of each column of the rubric. Sample rubrics are provided on the following pages.

Variations for Emergent English Language Learners

- Allow use of the primary language for any or all stages of the process, and find someone to review or translate.
- Provide the ESL teacher with the rubrics so he can support ELLs' writing during ESL time.
- Pair ELLs up as much as possible using cooperative learning.

ASCD © 2007. All Rights Reserved.

TASK-BASED RUBRICS

Examples:

Grade 2 Task-Based Narrative Writing Rubric

	Exceeds Expectations	Meets Expectations	Approaches Expectations
Prewriting	I decide who will read my story and what I want to tell them in the beginning, middle, and end. I pick a prewriting strategy to help me organize what I want to say. I find words and phrases that I can use to make my reader more interested.	With help from my teacher, I decide who will read my story and decide what I want to tell them in the beginning, middle, and end. I make a list of words and phrases that I can use in my story.	I wait for the teacher to tell me what to write. When the teacher says I have to write more, I sometimes get ideas from my friends. I use words I already know.
Drafting	I use my prewriting tools to write a story that has a beginning, middle, and end. I use my notes (drawings) and my own experiences to help me write my story. I write what I want to say and what I think my readers will like to hear.	I use my ideas to write a story that has a beginning, middle, and end. I use what I know in my own life to help me with my story. I write what I want to say but I add extra ideas.	I write words when the teacher tells us to. I write one big paragraph. I copy ideas from books and friends because I don't know what to say.
Revising	I change words and phrases in my story so the readers will like it better. In writing conferences, I give ideas to others and I use others' ideas to make my story better.	I change some of my words and phrases to make my writing sound better. I change some of my sentences after other writers give me some ideas.	I copy my story again but make some changes with words and sentences because my teacher tells me to.
Editing	I check my stories and the stories of other writers for mistakes with capitals, punctuation, and spelling. I make sure that my writing and the writing of others is ready.	I use capitals, spaces, punctuation, and correct spelling in my writing. I make sure that my people, places, and things agree with action words.	I write my story again and change some words because my teacher tells me to.

ASCD © 2007. All Rights Reserved.

Grade 9 Task-Based Research Writing Rubric

	Exceeds Expectations	Meets Expectations	Needs Attention
Use writing process (informational writing)	❑ Justifies the use of a prewriting strategy to organize information into a plan.	❑ Selects a prewriting strategy to organize notes into a plan (e.g., graphic organizer, diagrams, outline).	❑ Copies information from the reading to start writing.
	Uses strategies to draft and revise as follows:	**Uses strategies to draft and revise as follows:**	**Uses strategies to draft and revise as follows:**
	❑ Follows organizational plan to ensure each thesis is supported with evidence, arguments, details, quotations, examples, analogies, anecdotes, visuals.	❑ Develops a thesis and provides supporting evidence, arguments, and details through paraphrasing, quotations, examples, comparisons, analogies, anecdotes, visuals.	❑ Writes one big paragraph and counts words to make sure there are enough.
	❑ Uses an organizational pattern that builds up to unified argument coherently and with mounting credibility.	❑ Uses an organizational format that provides direction, coherence, and unity.	❑ Copies words and sentences from material taken.
	❑ Provides references to verify accuracy and depth of information.	❑ Checks accuracy and depth of information.	❑ Copies a lot from books and the Internet.
	❑ Redrafts for readability and engagement of readers through transitional, cohesive, and stylistic devices.	❑ Redrafts for readability and needs of readers through transitional and cohesive devices.	❑ Copies draft again.
	❑ Expresses personal style and voice through a combination of techniques.	❑ Conveys a personal style and voice through a specific technique (e.g., sentence variety, multiple viewpoints, stream of consciousness).	❑ Makes some changes to words and sentences.

ASCD © 2007. All Rights Reserved.

TASK-BASED RUBRICS

Grade 9 Task-Based Research Writing Rubric (*continued*)

	Exceeds Expectations	Meets Expectations	Needs Attention
Use writing process (informational writing)	❏ Aligns form and function of message strategically and purposefully.	❏ Ensures that content and linguistic structure are consistent with purpose.	❏ Once text is written, sees no need to reread.
	❏ Uses rules of punctuation, capitalization, and spelling to review own and others' work.	❏ Uses the rules of punctuation, capitalization, and spelling to review work.	❏ Leaves errors unchanged.
	❏ Uses correct grammatical construction to review own and others' work.	❏ Uses correct grammatical construction to review work.	❏ Leaves out bibliography and citations.
	❏ Uses dictionaries, thesauruses, and style to support own and others' work.	❏ Uses dictionaries, thesauruses, and style manuals to support work.	❏ Types paper.
	❏ Cites primary and secondary sources in text and bibliography in own and others' work.	❏ Cites primary and secondary sources in text and bibliography in own work.	
	❏ Uses computer technology to create, manipulate, and edit own and others' text.	❏ Uses computer technology to create, manipulate, and edit text of work.	

Section Two

ASCD © 2007. All Rights Reserved.

Strategies for
SUCCESS
with English Language Learners

WRITING STRATEGIES FOR GRADES 3–12

Two-Column Count

Why use it?

Use of this strategy will help students to . . .

- Engage in a variety of writing activities during the revising stage of the writing process.
- Use a variety of sentence types in writing.
- Review work for sentence variety.
- Use grade-level sentence structures in writing.
- Use signal words that provide clues to organizational formats.
- Use a variety of organizational formats for writing.
- Adjust style of writing.
- Write clear, concise, and varied sentences, developing a personal writing style and voice.
- Vary tone, vocabulary, and sentence structure according to audience and purpose.
- Use computer technology to create, manipulate, and edit text.

How does it work?

Students do an exercise in which they list the first word of every sentence and then count the number of words in those sentences. By writing the results on a page with two columns—one column for the first words and one with the word totals—they see that some sentence variety is needed (or that some sentences are probably so long that they are run-ons).

ASCD © 2007. All Rights Reserved.

TWO-COLUMN COUNT

Section Two

Variations for Emergent English Language Learners

- Have ELLs practice changing words around in a sentence and then checking for verification with another student or with the ESL teacher.

ASCD © 2007. All Rights Reserved.

Strategies for SUCCESS with English Language Learners

WRITING STRATEGIES FOR GRADES 3–12

Writer's Notebook

Why use it?

Use of this strategy will help students to . . .

- Use a variety of prewriting strategies to organize ideas and information.
- Write on a wide range of topics.
- Understand the purpose for writing (e.g. to explain, describe, narrate, persuade, or express feelings).
- Determine the intended audience before writing.
- Write voluntarily to communicate ideas and emotions to a variety of audiences and for different purposes.
- Select a form of writing appropriate to the function of the written communication.
- Take notes to record ideas.
- Connect new personal experiences to new information from various content-area classes.
- Use resources such as personal experiences, knowledge from other content areas, and elements from other texts to stimulate own writing.
- Express opinions and make judgments that demonstrate a personal point of view.
- Use personal experiences and knowledge to analyze new ideas.
- Use relevant examples and explanations to support ideas.
- Write and share personal reactions to experiences, events, and observations.
- Maintain a portfolio that includes ideas for writing.
- Review writing ideas with teacher and peers.

WRITER'S NOTEBOOK

Section Two

- Use computer software (word processing, graphics) to support the writing process.

How does it work?

Students are asked to use notebooks to keep track of whatever they see, hear, or read. These serve as prewriting activities for focused writing later. Students may use questions such as the following to guide their thinking: Why am I writing about this topic? Why is this important to me? What do I really want to say about this topic and to whom do I want to say it? What details will help me communicate a clear message? What models can I use to guide the organization of my document? What will my final product have in common with my models?

Variations for Emergent English Language Learners

- Have ELLs use writer's notebooks to make connections between ESL and mainstream classes.
- Allow ELLs to use their primary language or to illustrate their writer's notebooks.
- Use cooperative learning strategies to have students model and share their writer's notebooks with ELLs.

ASCD © 2007. All Rights Reserved.

Strategies for
SUCCESS
with English Language Learners

WRITING STRATEGIES FOR GRADES 3–12

Writing Workshop

Why use it?

Use of this strategy will help students to . . .

- Learn and use the writing process (drafting, revising, editing).
- Engage in a writing of writing activities to respond to the reading of literary and informational texts.
- Use resources such as personal experience, knowledge from other content areas, and independent reading to create literary, interpretive, and responsive texts.
- Vary the formality of language depending on audience and purpose of writing.
- Write in a variety of styles using different organizational patterns.
- Write voluntarily for different purposes.
- State an opinion or present a judgment by developing a thesis and providing supporting evidence, arguments, and details.
- Develop a personal voice that enables the reader to get to know the writer.
- Demonstrate effective use of writer's craft techniques when writing.
- Use grade-level vocabulary and varied sentence structure in writing.
- Produce clear, well-organized reports and accounts that demonstrate understating of a topic.
- Produce clear, well-organized responses to literature.
- Analyze the author's use of literary elements and figurative language in written text.
- Produce written and multimedia reports using multiple sources.
- Present and discuss own writing in conferences with teacher and peers, and respond with feedback.

WRITING WORKSHOP

Section Two

- Work collaboratively with peers to use the writing process.
- Review work independently to edit grammatical constructions, spelling, capitalization, and punctuation.
- Use computer technology to create, manipulate, and edit text.
- Maintain a portfolio of writing at different stages of the writing process.

How does it work?

This strategy is effective during the drafting, revising, or editing phase of the writing process, depending on the focus and timing of the session. It allows for differentiation of the writing process so that students can work at their own pace, just as real writers usually do. The teacher gives a 5- to 10-minute minilesson focusing on a skill or concept. Students then write for 20–25 minutes. The last 10–15 minutes of the session are used for sharing. Areas to focus on in the revising/editing stage include vocabulary, content, conciseness, clarity, strength, introduction, connectors, conclusion, proofreading, and presentation.

Variations for Emergent English Language Learners

- Have ELLs write on topics that are culturally relevant to their lives; allow the use of the primary language when necessary.
- Use a coteaching model such as alternative, parallel, peer, station, or team teaching.

ASCD © 2007. All Rights Reserved.

References

Hennings, D. G. (1982). A writing approach to reading comprehension: Schema theory in action. *Language Arts, 59,* 8–17.

Stejnost, R., & Thiese, S. (2001). *Reading and writing across content areas.* Upper Saddle River, NJ: Pearson Education.

Stephens, E. C., & Brown, J. E. (2005). *A handbook of content literacy strategies: 125 practical reading and writing ideas* (2nd ed.). Norwood, MA: Christopher-Gordon Publishers.

Strong, R. W., Silver, H. F., Perini, M. J., & Tuculescu, G. M. (2002). *Reading for academic success: Powerful strategies for struggling, average, and advanced readers, grades 7–12.* Thousand Oaks, CA: Corwin Press.

Urquhart, V., & McIver, M. (2005). Teaching writing in the content areas. Alexandria, VA: Association for Supervision and Curriculum Development.

ASCD © 2007. All Rights Reserved.

Instructional Practices

Instructional Practices

Instructional practices that provide framework scaffolds to facilitate English language learners' access to content include cooperative learning, differentiation, and coteaching models. The Instructional Practices portion of this section of the Action Tool follows the same format as previous sections.

Section Two

Section Two

ASCD © 2007. All Rights Reserved.

Cooperative Learning Strategies

Cooperative Learning Strategies

Strategy	Language Acquisition for ELLs			Access to Content for ELLs			Page
	Input (Inter-pretive)	Intake (Inter-personal)	Output (Presen-tational)	Concept Exposure (Before)	Concept Development (During)	Concept Attainment (After)	
Carousel		X			X		417
Check and Compare in Pairs			X			X	419
Circle-the-Sage	X			X			421
Corners		X	X		X	X	423
Group-Pair-Individual			X			X	425
Inside/Outside Circle		X			X		427
Puzzle Pieces		X			X		429
Question Spinner		X			X		431
Roundtable		X			X		433
Send-a-Problem			X			X	435
Student Sharing		X			X		437
Team Stand and Share			X			X	439
Think-Pair-Share		X			X		441

ASCD © 2007. All Rights Reserved.

Section Two

COOPERATIVE LEARNING STRATEGIES

Carousel

Why use it?

Use of this strategy will help students to . . .

Language Arts
- Interpret information represented in pictures and illustrations.
- Connect information from personal experiences to information from texts.
- Identify main ides and provide supporting details.
- Offer feedback to others during conferences.

Science
- Refine and clarify questions so they are subject to investigation.
- Formulate hypotheses.
- Collect and organize data and use it to communicate a scientific idea.

Math
- Formulate problems and solutions from everyday situations.
- Use inductive reasoning to construct, evaluate, and validate conjectures and arguments.
- Translate from a picture or diagram to a numeric expression.
- Translate verbal expressions into algebraic expressions.

Social Studies
- Compare important events and accomplishments from different time periods.
- Interpret and analyze documents.

- Compare governmental structures.
- Suggest alternative solutions.

How does it work?

The teacher posts topics from a content area on chart paper around the room. Teams of students are assigned to discuss and record their thoughts (or give feedback) on each topic, and then discuss and move to the next topic. As students rotate, if they want to record similar ideas, they simply place a check mark next to the similar idea already recorded (Kagan, 1998).

Variations for Emergent English Language Learners

- Use visual icons to symbolize the meaning of the topic so ELLs have more than one way to obtain meaning.
- Assign a bilingual "translator" to the ELL groups as they move from topic to topic.
- Ask the ESL teacher to build background knowledge of the topic beforehand through the use of a prepared outline.

ASCD © 2007. All Rights Reserved.

Strategies for
SUCCESS
with English Language Learners

COOPERATIVE LEARNING STRATEGIES

Check and Compare in Pairs

Why use it?

Use of this strategy will help students to . . .

Language Arts
- Engage in reading activities.
- Discuss versions of text.
- Identify, explain, and evaluate ideas.
- Interview peers.

Science
- Interpret organized data.
- Observe, describe, and explain.
- Plan and build models.
- Discuss how to test solutions.

Math
- Compare the similarities and differences of mathematical ideas.
- Share mental images of mathematical ideas and understandings.
- Question the explanations heard from others.

Social Studies
- Compare characters and events described.
- Gather and organize information.
- Propose an action plan.
- Discuss newspaper articles or political cartoons.

How does it work?

Students work in pairs to complete a problem or task and then check or compare with another pair. The two pairs can see whether the answer was correct and how they each went about solving the problem or completing the task, or, as a foursome, they can come up with another response.

Variations for Emergent English Language Learners

- Pair ELLs together and differentiate the task and material accordingly.
- Allow ELLs to use the primary language when they work in pairs but instruct them to use English when they team up with a second pair.
- Ask the ESL teacher to preview the problems or task in advance to prepare ELLs.

ASCD © 2007. All Rights Reserved.

Strategies for
SUCCESS
with **English Language Learners**

COOPERATIVE LEARNING STRATEGIES

Circle-the-Sage

Why use it?

Use of this strategy will help students to . . .

Language Arts
*   Attend to a listening activity for an extended period of time.
*   Listen to comprehend or acquire information.

Science
*   Seek clarification and compare with own observations.

Math
*   Listen to solutions shared by others.
*   Gather data in response to questions posed by the teacher.

Social Studies
*   Gather information on an important event or turning point.
*   Form conclusions from multiple perspectives.

How does it work?

The teacher selects students who understand a concept or who can perform a particular skill as "sages" to model for their peers. Students gather around the sages to learn. Afterwards, students return to teams to share ideas. Students may also rotate from one sage to another to practice listening for information or to have sages give oral presentations on a topic (Kagan, 1998).

 © 2007. All Rights Reserved.   421

CIRCLE-THE-SAGE

Variations for Emergent English Language Learners

- Select a sage who can share the skill in the primary language if possible.
- Provide visual support to assist ELLs in understanding the main concept.
- Ask the ESL teacher to share the concept beforehand to build background knowledge or teach basic vocabulary.
- Ask the ESL teacher to come into class to participate, using a peer coteaching model.

Section Two

ASCD © 2007. All Rights Reserved.

Strategies for
SUCCESS
with English Language Learners

SECTION: INSTRUCTIONAL PRACTICES

COOPERATIVE LEARNING STRATEGIES

Corners

Why use it?

Use of this strategy will help students to . . .

Language Arts
- Present a short oral report (or retelling) and speak loudly enough to be heard by the audience.
- Share what they know, want to know, and have learned about a topic.
- Give book reviews.

Science
- Share research plans with others.
- Present results or findings of experimentation with others.

Math
- Communicate and reason mathematically.
- Explain to others how problems are solved.
- Justify claims or develop an argument.

Social Studies
- Consider different interpretations.
- Develop and present a multimedia report.
- Plan and execute an inquiry to answer questions about a region of the country or world.

How does it work?

English language learners are more comfortable sharing in small groups than in front of the entire class. In this strategy, students select or are assigned to a corner or classroom area where they can interact with small groups of other students. For example, students may give presentations over the course of a week rather than being required to do so individually at the front of the entire class. This procedure will also save time (Kagan 1992).

Variations for Emergent English Language Learners

- Allow ELLs to perform later rather than earlier in a group, so they have models to follow.
- Provide opportunities for ELLs to prepare and rehearse before performing.
- Ask the ESL teacher to come into the class so both teachers can assess the presentations using a station coteaching model.

ASCD © 2007. All Rights Reserved.

Strategies for
SUCCESS
with English Language Learners

SECTION: INSTRUCTIONAL PRACTICES

COOPERATIVE LEARNING STRATEGIES

Group-Pair-Individual

Section Two

Why use it?

Use of this strategy will help students to . . .

Language Arts
- Engage in reading activities or recognize the use of literary devices (group).
- Interpret, make inferences, or draw conclusions (pair).
- Construct a personal response to texts (individual).

Science
- Gather and process information (group).
- Generate and analyze ideas (pair).
- Present results using media (individual).

Math
- Interpret information from word problems (group).
- Identify a problem (pair).
- Generate solutions (individual).

Social Studies
- List analytical questions to guide investigations (group).
- Gather information in response to research questions (pair).
- Present results (individual).

GROUP-PAIR-INDIVIDUAL

Section Two

How does it work?

Students first work in small groups on a problem or task. Then each student pairs with one other student. Finally, students work or perform individually (Kagan, 1998).

Variations for Emergent English Language Learners

This strategy is inherently scaffolded because students progress from interdependence to independence (i.e., Vygotsky's zone of proximal development).

ASCD © 2007. All Rights Reserved.

Strategies for SUCCESS with English Language Learners

COOPERATIVE LEARNING STRATEGIES

Inside/Outside Circle

Why use it?

Use of this strategy will help students to . . .

Language Arts
- Learn and use new words.
- Engage in conversations.
- Speak in response to a variety of texts.
- Connect, compare, and contrast ideas and information.

Science
- Formulate hypotheses.
- Question the explanations heard from others.
- Describe patterns (e.g., weather) or cycles (e.g., life).

Math
- Use appropriate mathematical terms and language.
- Explain to others how problems are solved.
- Listen to solutions shared by others.

Social Studies
- Identify key turning points and important events.
- Discuss differences (e.g., governments).

 © 2007. All Rights Reserved.

Section Two

INSIDE/OUTSIDE CIRCLE

How does it work?

Students form concentric circles and communicate with their respective circle partner. After sharing is completed, the teacher directs either the inside or outside circle to move to the right or left so that partners are continually rotated. For younger children, it might be helpful to put cut-out feet on the floor ahead of time to facilitate the rotation process (Kagan, 1992).

Variations for Emergent English Language Learners

- For the first few rounds, keep ELLs in the middle of the circle so they can observe the dynamics; act as their partner.
- When ELLs are ready to participate with the circle, provide a cue card with some visual reminders of the topic under discussion.
- Preteach essential vocabulary words that are new to all students and use the inside/outside circle as an opportunity for students to practice using the vocabulary with one another.

Section Two

ASCD © 2007. All Rights Reserved.

Strategies for SUCCESS with English Language Learners

COOPERATIVE LEARNING STRATEGIES

Puzzle Pieces

Why use it?

Use of this strategy will help students to . . .

Language Arts
- Retell multiple pieces of information in sequence.
- Listen to and follow multistep directions.
- Connect, compare, and contrast ideas and information.
- Synthesize information from different perspectives.

Science
- Explore and solve problems.
- Generate ideas for possible solutions through a group activity.

Math
- Practice problem solving.
- Interpret information, identify a problem, and generate solutions.
- Identify independent and dependent variables in problems.

Social Studies
- Arrange events in chronological order.
- Suggest alternative solutions to problems or issues.
- Describe historical events through the eyes of others.

 © 2007. All Rights Reserved.

Section Two

PUZZLE PIECES

How does it work?

This strategy allows students to be responsible for material at their level of comprehension or parts of tasks that they can complete, so it is an inherently scaffolded strategy for all students. Each student has a part of the answer to a given problem. Teammates must put their information together to solve the problem (Kagan, 1998).

Variations for Emergent English Language Learners

- Ask the ESL teacher to help select material and tasks.

ASCD © 2007. All Rights Reserved.

Strategies for SUCCESS with English Language Learners

COOPERATIVE LEARNING STRATEGIES

Question Spinner

Why use it?

Use of this strategy will help students to . . .

Language Arts
- Ask probing questions to clarify interpretations or responses to stories or literature.
- Identify what they want to know about an informational topic.
- Ask follow-up questions.

Science
- Formulate questions about natural phenomena.
- Refine and clarify questions so they are subject to scientific investigation.
- Ask questions to seek greater understanding.

Math
- Formulate mathematically relevant questions.
- Pose questions to collect and record data.

Social Studies
- Ask geographical questions.
- Investigate important events by posing analytical questions.

Section Two

QUESTION SPINNER

How does it work?

In pairs, students generate questions from one of 36 question prompts produced by spinners. Spinners are available in English and Spanish from www.Kaganonline.com (Kagan, 2001).

Variations for Emergent English Language Learners

- Ask the ESL teacher to practice the forming of questions with content material beforehand.
- Allow students to make their own spinners in other languages.

Section Two

ASCD © 2007. All Rights Reserved.

Strategies for
SUCCESS
with English Language Learners

SECTION: INSTRUCTIONAL PRACTICES

COOPERATIVE LEARNING STRATEGIES

Roundtable

Why use it?
Use of this strategy will help students to . . .

Language Arts
- Retell multiple pieces of information in sequence.
- Identify or summarize main ideas and supporting details.
- Draft main ideas and supporting details.
- Present direct references to text to support ideas.

Science
- Participate in projects that require working together effectively.
- Gather and process information.
- Generate and analyze ideas.
- Present results.

Math
- Translate from a picture or diagram to a numeric expression.
- Practice problem solving.
- Use multiple representations.
- Use Venn diagrams to sort and describe data.

Social Studies
- Create historical time lines of major events and characters.
- Classify information by type of activity.
- Draw maps and diagrams.

 © 2007. All Rights Reserved. 433

ROUNDTABLE

- Present information by developing charts, tables, and diagrams.
- Write from varying points of view (journals, diary accounts, letters, or news accounts).

How does it work?

This strategy is inherently scaffolded for ELLs because they can complete a task interdependently that they might not be able to do independently. In teams of four, students take turns passing the same paper from one to the next in order to write or draw collectively. Only one paper and one pencil are used per team.

Variations for Emergent English Language Learners

- Seat the ELLs so they have the last turn in their group.

Section Two

ASCD © 2007. All Rights Reserved.

Strategies for SUCCESS with English Language Learners

COOPERATIVE LEARNING STRATEGIES

Send-a-Problem

Why use it?

Use of this strategy will help students to . . .

Language Arts
- Prepare and give presentations on informational topics.
- Present interpretations and support them through specific references to the text.
- Ask and respond to questions to clarify interpretations or responses to literature.

Science
- Consider constraints and generate ideas for alternative solutions using group ideation techniques such as discussion and brainstorming.
- Use logical reasoning to develop conclusions.
- Interpret organized data to answer research questions and to gain insight into a problem.
- Provide a correct, complete, coherent, and clear rationale for thought processes used in problem solving.

Math
- Represent problem situations verbally, numerically, algebraically, and graphically.
- Compare and discuss ideas for solving a problem.
- Apply a variety of strategies to solve problems.

Section Two

SEND-A-PROBLEM

Social Studies

- Suggest alternative solutions.
- Propose an action plan.
- Complete well-documented and historically accurate case studies.
- Investigate important events.

How does it work?

Teammates generate problems that are sent around the class for other teams to solve (Kagan, 1992).

Variations for Emergent English Language Learners

- Ask the ESL teacher to come to class to participate in station coteaching.
- Ask the ESL teacher to prepare the ELLs with vocabulary and background knowledge.
- Provide ELLs with cue cards (short phrases) so they can participate with their peers.
- Provide bilingual dictionaries for ELLs.

ASCD © 2007. All Rights Reserved.

Strategies for
SUCCESS
with **English Language Learners**

COOPERATIVE LEARNING STRATEGIES

Student Sharing

Why use it?

Language Arts
- Take turns speaking in a group.
- Share reading experiences.
- Share what they have learned about a topic.
- Communicate ides in an organized and coherent way.
- Participate in brainstorming sessions with peers.
- Contribute to group discussions by offering comments.
- Present reasons and examples from sources to support or defend opinions or judgments.

Science
- Interpret organized data.
- Formulate and defend explanations and conclusions.
- Explore and solve problems.
- Seek clarification and compare with own observations.
- Share research plans or results with others.
- Interpret organized data to answer questions.

Math
- Communicate and reason mathematically.
- Compare and discuss ideas for solving a problem.
- Question the explanations heard from others.
- Verbally support reasoning or explain rationale for strategy selection.

STUDENT SHARING

Section Two

Social Studies

- Listen to and participate in debates.
- Consider different interpretations.
- Make hypotheses about relevant issues.
- Interpret and analyze documents.
- Answer questions about regions of the world.

How does it work?

For each of a series of questions, students share and discuss their answers. Then they write answers in their own words (Kagan, 1992).

Variations for Emergent English Language Learners

- If possible, find someone who can translate the questions in advance for the ELLs so they have an idea of what will be discussed.
- Provide a partial script for ELLs to follow during the discussion.
- Ask the ESL teacher to prepare ELLs for the discussion.

ASCD © 2007. All Rights Reserved.

Strategies for
SUCCESS
with English Language Learners

COOPERATIVE LEARNING STRATEGIES

Team Stand and Share

Why use it?

Use of this strategy will help students to . . .

Language Arts
- Attend to a listening activity.
- Speak audibly and with expression appropriate for the audience and task.
- Retell stories.
- Role-play characters.
- Construct a personal response to literature.
- Report information to peers.

Science
- Form and defend a logical argument.
- Use logical reasoning to develop conclusions.
- Share findings with others.
- Describe, compare and contrast, or explain data.

Math
- Listen to claims others make.
- Listen to solutions shared by others.
- Justify claims.
- Develop and explain an argument or rationale for strategy selection.

Section Two

Social Studies:

- Form conclusions.
- Describe historic events through the eyes of others.
- Explain ideas embodied in a historical passage or primary source document.
- Present historical narratives that link together a series of events.

How does it work?

Teams stand with a list of ideas to share. The teacher selects one student to share an idea. Other teams either check the idea off their list or add it. Each team sits when all items on its list are shared (Kagan, 2001).

Variations for Emergent English Language Learners

- Have ELLs tape-record team responses and then listen to the responses later while completing a graphic organizer from which they can study.
- Have ELLs identify repetitive responses given by students or teams.

ASCD © 2007. All Rights Reserved.

Strategies for
SUCCESS
with **English Language Learners**

SECTION: INSTRUCTIONAL PRACTICES

Think-Pair-Share

Why use it?

Use of this strategy will help students to . . .

Language Arts
- Draw on prior experience to understand ideas.
- Learn and use new words.
- Recognize vocabulary used commonly in oral interaction experiences.
- Participate in small-group interactions.
- Synthesize information from different perspectives.

Science
- Gather and process information.
- Generate and analyze ideas.
- Observe common themes.
- Present results.
- Work toward reconciling competing explanations.

Math
- Interpret information.
- Identify a problem and generate solutions.
- Use appropriate mathematical terms, vocabulary, and language.
- Solve multistep equations.

Social Studies

- Discuss key turning points and important events.
- Listen to different perspectives.
- Debate various views.

How does it work?

Students think about their response to a question and then discuss their individual answers in pairs. Each pair of students then shares their ideas with another pair (Lyman, 1981).

Variations for Emergent English Language Learners

- Match ELLs with students who can use their primary language for the first round (pair).
- Provide ELLs with visual cues to help them generate language, or provide partial scripts for them to follow.
- Ask the ESL teacher to review information with ELLs beforehand.

ASCD © 2007. All Rights Reserved.

References and Resources

Kagan, S. (1992). *Cooperative learning resources for teachers*. San Juan Capistrano, CA: Resources for Teachers.

Kagan, S. (1998). *Kagan SmartCard of cooperative learning structures*. San Clemente, CA: Kagan Publishing and Professional Development.

Kagan, S. (2001). *Kagan SmartCard of cooperative learning structures,* 2nd ed.. San Clemente, CA: Kagan Publishing and Professional Development.

Lyman, F. (1981). The responsive classroom discussion. In A. S. Anderson (Ed.), *Main-streaming digest* (pp. 109–113). College Park, MD: University of Maryland College of Education.

© 2007. All Rights Reserved.

Section Two

Differentiation Strategies

Differentiation Strategies

Strategy	Differen-tiates Material	Differen-tiates Task (students do)	Differen-tiates Strategy (teacher designes)	Differen-tiates Student Groupings	Differen-tiates Language (level of Eng-lish or primary language)	Page
Activity Guides		X		alone	X	449
Agendas		X		alone	X	451
Alternative Assignments		X		alone	X	453
Anchor Activities	X	X		alone	X	455
Choice Boards	X	X	X	alone, pairs, or small groups	X	457
Group Investigations	X (topic)			small groups	X	459
Independent Studies	X	X		alone	X	461
Jigsaw	X			alone, pairs, or small groups	X	463
Literature Circles	X			total class or small groups	X	465

ASCD © 2007. All Rights Reserved.

Section Two

Strategy	Differen-tiates Material	Differen-tiates Task (students do)	Differen-tiates Strategy (teacher designes)	Differen-tiates Student Groupings	Differen-tiates Language (level of Eng-lish or primary language)	Page
Multiple Texts and Resource Materials	X				X	467
Schedule Chart or Work Board	X	X	X	alone	X	469
Think-Tac-Toe		X		alone, pairs, or small groups	X	471
WebQuests	X (topic)			alone, pairs, or small groups	X	473

ASCD © 2007. All Rights Reserved.

DIFFERENTIATION STRATEGIES

Activity Guides

Why use it?

Use of this strategy will help students to . . .

Language Arts
- Grade 9 example: Read, view, and interpret texts and performances in every medium from a variety of authors, subjects, and genres.

Science
- Grade 4 example: Describe how the structures of plants and animals complement the environment of the plants or animals.

Math
- Grade 1 example: Solve real-world problems involving addition and subtraction of whole numbers.

Social Studies
- Grade 6 example: Examine documents related to significant developments in world history and employ the skills of historical analysis and interpretation in probing their meaning and importance.

How does it work?

The teacher designs packets of materials so students can work on similar tasks but at different levels of complexity. These activity guides may contain any of the following: different sets of instructions, suggested steps for solutions,

 © 2007. All Rights Reserved.

ACTIVITY GUIDES

Section Two

partial models, performance criteria, options for presentations, and various resources.

Differentiated Components for Emergent English Language Learners

Activity guides inherently scaffold learning and potential for task completion by differentiating levels of complexity on similar tasks. The less English proficiency students possess, the more scaffolding they need, through either lower levels of linguistic complexity or the provision of comprehension aids. ESL and classroom teachers can use activity guides to equitably grade what English language learners know and can do.

ASCD © 2007. All Rights Reserved.

Strategies for
SUCCESS
with English Language Learners

SECTION: INSTRUCTIONAL PRACTICES

DIFFERENTIATION STRATEGIES

Agendas

Why use it?

Use of this strategy will help students to . . .

Language Arts
- Grade 1 example: Write voluntarily for different purposes (e.g., tell stories, share information, give directions, write to a friend).

Science
- High school example: Describe and explain the structures and functions of the human body at different organizational levels.

Math
- Grade 3 example: Organize and display data in simple bar graphs, pie charts, and line graphs.

Social Studies
- Grade 7 example: Compare several historical accounts of the same events in U.S. history, contrast the different facts included or omitted by each author, and determine the authors' points of view.

How does it work?

Agendas are personalized list of tasks that a particular student must complete in a specified time, possibly two to three weeks. A designated time of the day or period is set aside for this purpose. While students are working, teachers move about to coach and monitor progress.

Differentiated Components for Emergent English Language Learners

- Match the ELLs' agendas to their English proficiency levels as well as their background readiness in the primary language.
- Design tasks with familiar information and material, simple goals, and easy-to-follow directions.
- Design tasks together with the ESL teacher.

ASCD © 2007. All Rights Reserved.

Strategies for SUCCESS with English Language Learners

DIFFERENTIATION STRATEGIES

Alternative Assignments

Why use it?

Use of this strategy will help students to . . .

Language Arts
- Grade 10 example: Recognize and respond to historical and contemporary social and cultural conditions in presentation of literary texts.

Science
- Kindergarten example: Describe the effects of common forces (pushes and pulls) of objects, such as those caused by gravity, magnetism, and mechanical forces.

Math
- Grade 8 example: Create and use representations to organize, record, and communicate mathematical ideas (i.e., use physical objects, drawings, charts, tables, graphs, symbols, equations, or objects created using technology as representations).

Social Studies
- Grade 5 example: Participate in activities that focus on a classroom, school, or community issue or problem (e.g., brainstorm solutions, write letters, role-play, debate topics, hold a mock trial, develop a historic walking tour of a neighborhood).

 © 2007. All Rights Reserved.

ALTERNATIVE ASSIGNMENTS

Section Two

How does it work?

Alternative assignments can include various ways for students to represent their understanding of concepts or texts. Students might represent the main idea or message in the form of a drawing, a dramatic representation, or a written analysis. These can be assigned by the teacher or self-selected by the student.

Differentiated Components for Emergent English Language Learners

- Offer insights as to which assignments will be linguistically appropriate for individual students (e.g., those who have weak or strong literacy skills or those who can read English better than they can speak or write it).

ASCD © 2007. All Rights Reserved.

Strategies for SUCCESS with English Language Learners

DIFFERENTIATION STRATEGIES

Anchor Activities

Why use it?

Use of this strategy will help students to . . .

Language Arts
- Grade 7 example: Maintain a writing portfolio that includes imaginative, interpretive, and responsive writing.

Science
- Grade 5 example: Observe and describe developmental patterns in selected plants and animals (e.g., insects, frogs, humans, seed-bearing plants).

Math
- High school geometry example: Use synthetic (pictorial) representations and analytic (coordinate) methods to solve problems involving symmetry and transformations of figures (e.g., problems involving distance, midpoint, and slope and determination of symmetry with respect to a point or line).

Social Studies
- Kindergarten example: Create personal and family time lines to distinguish between the near and the distant past, or create a picture time line tracing developments in history.

Section Two

 © 2007. All Rights Reserved. 455

ANCHOR ACTIVITIES

Section Two

How does it work?

Anchor activities are tasks that students automatically undertake as soon as they complete assigned classroom work. The tasks are a good way to help students cultivate the habit of using time wisely and with a clear purpose. They should not be conceived of as "busy work" but must be important to the concepts and understandings of the content (Tomlinson, 1999).

Differentiated Components for Emergent English Language Learners

- Invite the ESL teacher to prepare some anchor activities specifically for the ELL students as a way of bridging what goes on in both classrooms.
- Ask the ESL teacher to develop anchor activities that ELLs can complete in the primary language to further conceptual development.

ASCD © 2007. All Rights Reserved.

DIFFERENTIATION STRATEGIES

Choice Boards

Why use it?

Use of this strategy will help students to . . .

Language Arts
- Grade 11 example: Read, view, and listen independently to literary works that represent a range of social, historical, and cultural perspectives.

Science
- Grade 8 example: Know characteristics and movement patterns of the planets in the solar system.

Math
- Grade 4 example: Understand that mathematical ideas and concepts can be represented concretely, graphically, and symbolically.

Social Studies
- Grade 2 example: Compare the characters and events described in historical fiction with primary sources (e.g., artifacts, journals, diaries, photographs) to judge historical accuracy and determine the variety of perspectives.

How does it work?

The teacher places changing assignments in permanent pockets or folders on a tack board. By asking a student to make a work selection from a particular pocket or folder, the teacher targets work toward student need and at the same time allows student choice.

Differentiated Components for Emergent English Language Learners

*   Work together with the ESL teacher to design assignments for ELLs using additional scaffolding strategies (e.g., time-honored ESL strategies and literacy scaffolds).

ASCD © 2007. All Rights Reserved.

Strategies for
SUCCESS
with English Language Learners

DIFFERENTIATION STRATEGIES

Group Investigations

Why use it?

Use of this strategy will help students to . . .

Language Arts

- Grade 3 example: Show interest in a wide range of grade-level texts, including historical and science fiction, folktales and fairy tales, poetry, and other imaginative and informational texts.

Math, Science, and Technology

- High school example: Participate in an extended, culminating mathematics, science, and technology investigation to solve interdisciplinary problems involving a variety of skills and strategies such as effective work habits, gathering and processing information, generating and analyzing ideas, and making connections among common themes.

Social Studies

- Grade 8 example: Undertake case studies to research violations of basic civil and human rights and case studies of genocide (e.g., mass starvation in Ireland, forced relocation of Native Americans, internment of Japanese Americans).

How does it work?

The teacher guides students through selection of topics and breaks the class into groups by learner interest. Then the teacher helps individual students and groups with planning the investigation, carrying out the investigation, presenting findings, and evaluating outcomes (Sharan & Sharan, 1992).

Differentiated Components for Emergent English Language Learners

- Allow ELLs to work in groups of their peers and to select topics of interest.
- Use group investigations as summative assessments to collect evidence of attainment of standards.

ASCD © 2007. All Rights Reserved.

SECTION: INSTRUCTIONAL PRACTICES

DIFFERENTIATION STRATEGIES

Independent Studies

Why use it?

Use of this strategy will help students to . . .

Language Arts
- Grade 9 example: Use resources such as personal experience, knowledge from other content areas, and independent reading to create literary, interpretive, and responsive texts.

Science
- Grade 7 example: Construct explanations independently for natural phenomena, especially by proposing preliminary visual models of phenomena; represent, present, and defend proposed explanations so they can be understood and assessed by others.

Math
- Grade 2 example: Explore and solve problems generated from school, home, and community situations, using mathematical analysis.

Social Studies
- Grade 5 example: Investigate the important achievements and accomplishments of the world's early civilizations (African, Greek, Roman, Egyptian, Indian, Chinese).

Section Two

INDEPENDENT STUDIES

Section Two

How does it work?

This strategy offers a tailor-made opportunity to help students develop talent and interest areas. Teachers systematically aid students in developing curiosity, pursuing topics that interest them, identifying intriguing questions, developing plans to find out more about those questions, managing time, setting goals and criteria for work, assessing progress, and presenting new understandings.

Differentiated Components for Emergent English Language Learners

- Use this tool to bridge the work between the ESL classroom and the mainstream classroom.
- Use a coteaching model with the ESL teacher.

ASCD © 2007. All Rights Reserved.

Strategies for
SUCCESS
with English Language Learners

DIFFERENTIATION STRATEGIES

Jigsaw

Why use it?

Use of this strategy will help students to . . .

Language Arts
- Kindergarten example: Compare characters and settings within stories (expert group) and between stories (home group).

Math, Science and Technology
- Grade 5 example: Solve interdisciplinary problems involving a variety of skills and strategies, including effective work habits, gathering and processing information, generating and analyzing ideas, realizing ideas, and making connections among the common themes of mathematics, science, and technology (expert group), and present results (home group).

Social Studies
- High school example: Research how leaders (expert group) fought for the rights of African Americans (home group).

How does it work?

This popular cooperative learning strategy easily doubles as a differentiation strategy. Students participate in two groups as follows: They start out in a *home* group. Within each home group, individual students choose or are assigned the responsibility of completing one facet of the group's overall task

 © 2007. All Rights Reserved.

JIGSAW

Section Two

or covering one section of content to be studied, thus becoming an "expert" in it. Home groups then disperse, and students reconfigure themselves so that all individuals pursuing the same facet of the overall task work together in an *expert* group. When the expert groups have all completed work, they disperse, and students return to their original (home) groups, where all the experts then take turns sharing until the original task is completed or the content is understood.

Differentiated Components for Emergent English Language Learners

- Divide the material to be studied or task to be completed into sections that match the linguistic proficiency levels of the ELLs.
- Ask the ESL teacher to help the ELL "experts," so that they can then share their work effectively when they return to their home groups.

ASCD © 2007. All Rights Reserved.

Strategies for
SUCCESS
with **English Language Learners**

DIFFERENTIATION STRATEGIES

Literature Circles

Why use it?

Use of this strategy will help students to . . .

Language Arts
- Grade 6 example: Recognize that the same story can be told in different genres (novels, poems, or plays); recognize how different authors treat similar themes; identify different perspectives presented in more than one text.

Science, Math, and Technology
- Grade 3 example: Know that people of all ages, backgrounds, and groups have made contributions to science and technology throughout history.

Social Studies
- Grade 1 example: Read and discuss how individuals have solved problems, made important contributions, and influenced the lives of others (e.g., historical stories, myths, legends, and fables).
- High school example: Draw upon literary selections to analyze the roles played by different individuals and groups during the major eras in U.S. history.

How does it work?

The teacher may assign students to read different texts connected by theme or genre, or may select a text from possible titles. Students perform specific roles

Section Two

LITERATURE CIRCLES

Section Two

(e.g., word searcher, discussion director, artist, connector) to prepare to participate in discussion groups. Students may produce assessment tasks such as reports or speeches as a result of their discussions.

Differentiated Components for Emergent English Language Learners

- Ask the ESL teacher to help select appropriate materials.
- Allow ELLs to shadow-read—that is, read a selection in their primary language while reading about the same topic in English.
- Assign emergent ELLs to complete the responsibilities of the artist or word searcher.

ASCD © 2007. All Rights Reserved.

Strategies for SUCCESS with English Language Learners

DIFFERENTIATION STRATEGIES

Multiple Texts and Resource Materials

Why use it?

Use of this strategy will help students to . . .

Language Arts
- Grade 10 example: Use both primary and secondary sources of information for research; use charts, graphs, and diagrams to support and illustrate informational texts.

Science
- Grade 3 example: Investigate problems and issues in science, technology, and society that affect their home, school, or community, and carry out a remedial course of action.

Math
- Grade 5 example: Collect and record data from a variety of sources (e.g., newspapers, magazines, polls, charts, and surveys).

Social Studies
- Grade 7 example: View history through the eyes of those who witnessed key events and developments by analyzing their literature, diary accounts, letters, artifacts, art, music, architectural drawings, and other documents.

MULTIPLE TEXTS AND RESOURCE MATERIALS

Section Two

How does it work?

Using multiple texts and combining them with a wide variety of supplementary materials increases teachers' chances for reaching all students. Through this tool, teachers develop valuable differentiation resources by building a classroom library of varied-level texts, magazines, newsletters, brochures, and other print materials. Additionally, teachers can investigate a rich array of materials available through the Internet, computer programs, manipulatives, audio and video materials, and so on.

Differentiated Components for Emergent English Language Learners

- Provide material in the primary languages of the ELLs.
- Work with the ESL teacher to identify materials that are appropriate to the linguistic levels of the ELLs. Students with less English proficiency will require material that provides meaning through context.

ASCD © 2007. All Rights Reserved.

Strategies for
SUCCESS
with English Language Learners

SECTION: INSTRUCTIONAL PRACTICES

DIFFERENTIATION STRATEGIES

Schedule Chart or Work Board

Why use it?

Use of this strategy will help students to . . .

Language Arts
- High school example: Read, write, listen, and speak for information and understanding.

Science
- Grade 1 examples: Ask *why* questions to seek greater understanding; develop and carry out plans for exploring phenomena; organize observations and measurements of objects and events through classification and the preparation of simple charts and tables; share findings.

Math
- Grade 7 example: Determine what can be measured and how, using appropriate methods and formulas (e.g., distance, volume, mass, proportions, prices, currency, angles).

Social Studies
Grade 4 example: Read historical narratives, literature, and many kinds of documents to investigate building tools, clothing, and artwork and to explore key events and issues in U.S. history.

Section Two

SCHEDULE CHART OR WORK BOARD

Section Two

How does it work?

The teacher uses schedule charts or work boards to help organize class time and to help students work independently as they follow. The teacher varies what individual students do in a particular task according to the students' interests or needs, assigning names of students accordingly on the chart. Students then work on their designated tasks in the designated order.

Differentiated Components for Emergent English Language Learners

- Work together with the ESL teacher to design the tasks and pacing for ELLs.
- Use a coteaching model (e.g., alternative or parallel coteaching).

ASCD © 2007. All Rights Reserved.

Strategies for
SUCCESS
with English Language Learners

DIFFERENTIATION STRATEGIES

Think-Tac-Toe

Why use it?

Use of this strategy will help students to . . .

Language Arts
- Grade 5 example: Publish writing in a variety of presentation or display media, for a variety of audiences.

Science
- High school examples: Understand and apply scientific concepts, principles, and theories pertaining to physical setting and living environment; recognize the historical development of ideas in science.

Math
- Grade 3 example: Represent problem situations in oral, written, concrete, pictorial, and graphic forms.

Social Studies
- Grade 8 example: Use a number of research skills (e.g., computer databases, periodicals, census reports, maps, standard reference works, interviews, surveys) to locate and gather geographical information about issues and problems.

 © 2007. All Rights Reserved.

Section Two

THINK-TAC-TOE

Section Two

How does it work?

This tool is a positive way to present a variety of assignments. The teacher arranges the assignments on the board by rows representing degree of difficulty or learning preferences. This tool is also useful for listing extension activities for students who have demonstrated the capacity to go beyond the core class assignments. Another variation is for students to complete three assignments, not necessarily in a row (Tomlinson, 2003).

Differentiated Components for Emergent English Language Learners

- Allow ELLs to self-select rather than assume that they can do only certain tasks.

ASCD © 2007. All Rights Reserved.

Strategies for
SUCCESS
with English Language Learners

DIFFERENTIATION STRATEGIES

WebQuests

Why use it?

Use of this strategy will help students to . . .

Language Arts
- Grade 7 example: Locate and use Internet resources independently to acquire information.

Science
- Grade 4 example: Access information from print media, electronic data-bases, and community resources; use the information to develop a definition of the problem and to research possible solutions.

Math
- High school example: Investigate how concepts of representation, random-ness, and bias in sampling can affect experimental outcomes and statistical interpretations.

Social Studies
- Grade 2 example: Investigate the importance of scientific and technological inventions such as the compass, steam engine, internal combustion engine, and computer chip.

 © 2007. All Rights Reserved.   473

Section Two

WEBQUESTS

Section Two

How does it work?

WebQuests are inquiry-based activities designed by teachers to help students negotiate the Internet to research a teacher-assigned or student-selected topic. When creating WebQuests, the teacher predetermines links that are connected to the topic. WebQuests support differentiated instruction because they can be based on student readiness and interest and can be conducted as group or individual inquiries (Dodge & March, as cited in Dodge, 1995).

Differentiated Components for Emergent English Language Learners

- Provide links that are appropriate to ELLs' language proficiency.
- Allow ELLs to conduct research in their primary language if it will facilitate their work.
- Ask the ESL teacher to use WebQuests as a basis for language development and for academic attainment either as a part of ESL instruction or as a bridge between the ESL and mainstream classroom.

ASCD © 2007. All Rights Reserved.

References

Dodge, B. (1995). *Some thoughts about WebQuests.* Retrieved January 5, 2007, from http://webquest.sdsu.edu/about_webquests.html

Sharan, Y., & Sharan, S. (1992). *Expanding cooperative learning through group investigation.* New York: Teachers College Press.

Tomlinson, C. A. (1999). *The differentiated classroom: Responding to the needs of all learners.* Alexandria, VA: Association for Supervision and Curriculum Development.

Tomlinson, C. A. (2003). *Fulfilling the promise of the differentiated classroom: Strategies and tools for responsive teaching.* Alexandria, VA: Association for Supervision and Curriculum Development.

Resources

Chapman, C., & King, R. (2003). *Differentiated instructional strategies for reading in the content areas.* Thousand Oaks, CA: Corwin Press.

Chapman, C., & King, R. (2003). *Differentiated instructional strategies for writing in the content areas.* Thousand Oaks, CA: Corwin Press.

Gregory, G. H., & Chapman, C. (2006). *Differentiated instructional strategies: One size doesn't fit all* (2nd ed.). Thousand Oaks, CA: Corwin Press.

Dodge King-Shaver, B., & Hunter, A. (2003). *Differentiated instruction in the English classroom: Content, process, product, and assessment.* Portsmouth, NH: Heinemann.

Smutny, J. F., & von Fremd, S. E. (2004). *Differentiating for the young child: Teaching strategies across the content areas (K–3).* Thousand Oaks, CA: Corwin Press.

Tomlinson, C. A., & Allan, S. D. (2000). *Leadership for differentiating schools.* Alexandria, VA: Association for Supervision and Curriculum Development.

Tomlinson, C. A., & Cunningham Eidson, C. (2003). *Differentiation in practice: A resource guide for differentiating curriculum (Grades K–5).* Alexandria, VA: Association for Supervision and Curriculum Development.

Tomlinson, C. A., & Cunningham Eidson, C. (2003). *Differentiation in practice: A resource guide for differentiating curriculum (grades 5–9).* Alexandria, VA: Association for Supervision and Curriculum Development.

Tomlinson, C., & McTighe, J. (2006). *Integrating differentiated instruction and understanding by design.* Alexandria, VA: Association for Supervision and Curriculum Development.

Tomlinson, C. A., & Strickland, C. A. (2005). *Differentiation in practice: A resource guide for differentiating curriculum (grades 9–12).* Alexandria, VA: Association for Supervision and Curriculum Development.

Section Two

Coteaching Strategies

Coteaching Strategies

Coteaching Model	Roles & Responsibilities	Perceived Owner-ship of ELLs	Planning Time	Instructional Capacities
Alternative Teaching	Each teacher works with different groups of students to teach different content using different methods. Students then switch from one group to the other.	Both teachers own all students.	Some coplanning time is needed to coordinate what students need to know and be able to do and to reach agreement on grading criteria.	Each teacher needs to have a repertoire of scaffolding tools for ELL students.
Complementary Teaching	ESL teacher scaffolds what the classroom teacher is teaching as a part of instruction.	Perception may be that ESL teacher is responsible for ELLs.	Some coplanning time is needed for ESL teacher to know what classroom teacher wants students to know and be able to do, as well as what strategies will be used.	ESL teacher needs to have a repertoire of instructional scaffolds to make content accessible to ELLs.
Parallel Teaching	Each teacher works with different groups of students to teach the same content using different methods. Not all students have both teachers; rather, each teacher has his or her own instructional group.	ESL teacher is responsible for ELLs (this is the closest model to the traditional ESL pull-out model).	Some coplanning time is needed for ESL teacher to know what classroom teacher wants students to know and be able to do.	Each teacher needs to have the instructional capacity to teach own group.

ASCD © 2007. All Rights Reserved.

Coteaching Model	Roles & Responsibilities	Perceived Ownership of ELLs	Planning Time	Instructional Capacities
Peer Teaching	Students learn together, using structured cooperative learning strategies. Both teachers are thus freed from direct instruction to observe, circulate, or assess.	Both teachers own all students.	Coplanning time is needed to coordinate what students need to know and be able to do, as well as to design the instructional experiences to facilitate peer teaching.	Teachers need to have a shared vision (namely, that peers can be as helpful for learning as teachers) and a solid repertoire of cooperative learning, differentiation, and time-honored ESL scaffolds.
Station Teaching	Both teachers may rotate among stations; one teacher may rotate while the other staffs a station; or both teachers may staff stations while students work independently at other stations.	Both teachers own all students.	Coplanning time is needed to coordinate what students need to know and be able to do, as well as to design the instructional experiences and materials for each center (work can be divided between teachers).	Teachers need to have a shared vision (i.e., peers can be as helpful for learning as teachers) and a solid repertoire of cooperative learning, differentiation, and time-honored ESL scaffolds.
Support Teaching	Classroom teacher maintains lead instructional role, and ESL teacher observes or circulates to assist ELLs.	Perception may be that ESL teacher is responsible for success of ELLs.	Minimal coplanning time is needed since classroom teacher works out what students need to know and be able to do.	ESL teacher needs to have a repertoire of moment-to-moment scaffolding tools.
Team Teaching	Both teachers assume responsibility of taking the lead instructional role.	Both teachers own all students.	Intensive coplanning time is needed to coordinate what students need to know and be able to do, and to plan the instructional experiences and scaffolds to enable all students to be successful.	Teachers need to have a shared vision of learning and teaching and a solid repertoire of scaffolding tools (time-honored ESL strategies, literacy tools, and instructional framework tools).

ASCD © 2007. All Rights Reserved.

Strategies for
SUCCESS
with English Language Learners

COTEACHING STRATEGIES

Alternative Teaching

Why use it?

Use of this strategy will help students gain skills such as those indicated in the following examples. Each example also suggests how teachers can assess what students have learned.

Language Arts: Grade 7 Example
- **English Language Arts:** Select content and choose strategies to write presentations on the basis of audience and purpose. Use the writing process to prepare a speech. Prepare and give oral presentations on informational topics. Credit sources of information and opinions accurately in presentations and handouts.
- **ESL:** Give formal oral presentations that focus on specified academic content, using appropriate vocabulary and syntax, recognizable organization, clear pronunciation, eye contact, and appropriate volume and intonation. Participate in creating scoring guides and use them to prepare, assess, and revise oral presentations.
- **Assessment**: Oral presentation with rubric.

Science: Kindergarten Example
- **Content**: The continuity of life is sustained through reproduction and development.
- **Science skills:** Describe the major stages of the life cycles of selected plants and animals. Describe evidence of growth, repair, and maintenance, such as nails, hair, and bone.
- **Language skills:** Use new vocabulary words to talk about life experiences.

Connect vocabulary and life experiences to ideas in books. Answer questions about text read aloud. Engage in prereading and reading activities and use illustrations to assist in understanding content and to anticipate what will happen next. Interpret information represented in simple charts and graphs.

- **Assessments:** Retellings, drawings, charts, graphs.

Math: Grade 9 Example
- **Content:** Statistics and probability.
- **Math skills:** Collect, organize, display, and analyze data.
- **Language skills:** Determine the meaning of unfamiliar words by using classroom and other resources. Recognize the organizational format of informational text (e.g., analyze published reports and graphs that are based on data). Use strategies such as discussing with others to assist in comprehension.
- **Assessments:** Vocabulary records, talking drawings, verbal explanations.

Social Studies: Grade 4 Example
- **Content:** Economics requires the development and application of skills to make informed and well-reasoned economic decisions in daily and national life.
- **Social studies skills:** Locate economic information using card catalogues, computer databases, indices, and library guides. Collect economic information from textbooks, standard references, newspapers, periodicals, and other primary and secondary sources. Make hypotheses about economic issues and problems. Present economic information by developing charts, tables, diagrams, and simple graphs.
- **Language skills:** Acquire information by locating and using library media resources with assistance. Collect and interpret data, facts, and ideas from unfamiliar texts. Use text and organizational features to locate information. Compare and contrast information on one topic from two different sources. Make inferences and draw conclusions. Use graphic organizers to record significant details.
- **Assessments:** Data gathering with references, display boards, solution-focused case studies.

How does it work?

The two teachers work with different groups of students. Each teaches different content at the same time, using different methods. The students rotate from one teacher to the other for instruction (e.g., the content teacher focuses on content concepts and understandings while the ESL teacher attends to language acquisition, language development, or literacy skills). The students can be heteroge-

ASCD © 2007. All Rights Reserved.

ALTERNATIVE TEACHING

neously grouped because all will be taught by both teachers in this model. Alternative teaching requires some coplanning time to coordinate what the students need to know (content) and be able to do (language or literacy skills), though each teacher uses different instructional strategies.

Variations for Emergent English Language Learners

- Use parallel coteaching to gather information for the writing and oral presentation of speeches so that ELLs have information to write about.
- Consider the learning style of ELLs when determining whether they participate in science (e.g., observation of living things) or language arts (e.g., vocabulary strategy Simon Says, Science Says) first.
- Use representational forms in mathematics because they are highly visual and contextualized and, therefore, comprehensible.
- Pair students appropriately for locating library resources and preparing case studies.

Section Two

Strategies for
SUCCESS
with English Language Learners

COTEACHING STRATEGIES

Complementary Teaching

Why use it?

Use of this strategy will help students gain skills such as those indicated in the following examples. Each example also suggests how teachers can assess what students have learned.

Language Arts: Grade 6 Example
- **Language skills:** Use similes and metaphors to infer the meaning of literal and figurative phrases.
- **ESL:** Locate and identify literary techniques in texts (e.g., metaphors and similes for imagery).
- **Assessments:** Right angle graphic organizer to sort similes and metaphors; visual interpretations and oral predictions about poems to be read.

Science: Grade 10 Example
- **Content:** Organisms inherit genetic information in a variety of ways that result in continuity of structure and function between parents and offspring.
- **Science skills:** Explain how the structure and replication of genetic material result in offspring that resemble their parents. Explain how the technology of genetic engineering allows humans to alter the genetic makeup of organisms.
- **Language skills:** Synthesize information from different sources (e.g., lectures, media, informational texts, science labs). Use reading strategies to comprehend text (e.g., skimming and scanning to locate

 © 2007. All Rights Reserved. 485

information, using reading guides and summaries). Articulate one or more perspectives such as one's own and those of a special-interest group to summarize arguments on different sides of issues.

- **Assessments:** Notes, charts, summaries.

Math: Grade 8 Example

- **Content:** Represent and analyze algebraically a wide variety of problem-solving situations.
- **Math skills:** Translate verbal sentences into algebraic inequalities. Write verbal expressions that match given mathematical expressions. Describe a situation involving relationships that matches a given graph. Create a graph given a description or an expression for a situation involving a linear or nonlinear relationship.
- **Communication skills:** Communicate mathematical thinking coherently and clearly to peers and teachers. Analyze the mathematical thinking of others. Use the language of mathematics to express ideas precisely.
- **Assessments:** Analyses, procedures, graphs.

Social Studies: Grade 3 Example

- **Content:** Establishing time frames, exploring different historical periods, examining themes across time and within cultures, and focusing on important turning points in world history help organize the study of world cultures and civilizations.
- **Social studies skills:** Distinguish between past, present, and future time periods. Develop time lines that display important events and eras from world history. Measure and understand the meaning of calendar time in terms of years, decades, centuries, and millennia. Compare important events and accomplishments from different time periods in world history.
- **Language skills:** Learn new vocabulary and concepts by reading books and other print sources. Read unfamiliar texts to collect facts and ideas. Organize and categorize text information in time sequence. Develop an idea with a brief written text.
- **Assessments:** A mural-size illustrated time line, explanations of key turning points and events.

How does it work?

In this model, one teacher enhances the instruction provided by the other. For example, one teacher may model a skill while the other teacher explains it. One teacher may take notes on the Smart Board while the other teacher lectures. The students are not split into separate instructional groups but are taught simultaneously by two teachers. Complementary teaching requires coplanning time to coordinate what the students need to know (content) and be able to do (e.g.,

486

COMPLEMENTARY TEACHING

language or literacy skills), as well as what instructional strategies will be used by both teachers.

Variations for Emergent English Language Learners

Complementary teaching is inherently scaffolded for emergent ELLs because the ESL teacher uses time-honored ESL strategies to provide access in real time.

Section Two

Strategies for SUCCESS with English Language Learners

COTEACHING STRATEGIES

Parallel Teaching

Why use it?

Use of this strategy will help students gain skills such as those indicated in the following examples. Each example also suggests how teachers can assess what students have learned.

Language Arts: Grade 1 Example
- **English Language Arts and ESL:** Use comprehension strategies (predict/confirm, reread, self-correct) to clarify meaning of a text. Work cooperatively with peers to comprehend text. Ask and answer questions in response to texts. Sequence events in retelling stories.
- **Assessments:** Guided reading group checklists.

Science: Grade 7 Example
- **Content:** The central purpose of scientific inquiry is to develop explanations of natural phenomena in a continuing, creative process.
- **Science skills:** Independently, formulate questions appropriate for guiding the search for explanations. Independently, construct explanations for natural phenomena. Represent, present, and defend proposed explanations of everyday observations so they can be assessed by others.
- **Language skills:** Use correct grammatical construction for generating questions and statements. Present a hypothesis and predict possible outcomes. Draw conclusions and provide reasons for them. Speak in grammatically correct sentences, communicating ideas in an organized and coherent manner. Use visual aids to assist in presentation of information.
- **Assessments:** Hypotheses, notes, summaries.

PARALLEL TEACHING

Math: Grade 2 Example

- **Content:** Apply and adapt a variety of appropriate strategies to solve word problems.
- **Math skills:** Use informal counting strategies to find solutions. Experience a teacher-directed questioning process to understand problems. Compare and discuss ideas for solving a problem with teacher or peers, to justify thinking. Use manipulatives to model the action in problems. Use drawings to model the action in problems.
- **Communication skills:** Verbally support reasoning and answers. Share organized mathematical ideas through the manipulation of objects, drawings, and pictures in written and verbal form. Use appropriate mathematical terms, vocabulary, and language.
- **Assessment:** Problem-solving rubric.

Social Studies: Grade 5 Example

- **Content:** Civics, citizenship, and government.
- **Social studies skills:** Explain what citizenship means in a democratic society. Understand the rights and responsibilities of citizenship. Discuss the role of an informed citizen in today's changing world.
- **Language skills:** Listen attentively to text read aloud. Take notes to record ideas. Use specific vocabulary to communicate ideas. Ask probing questions to interview. Use grammatically correct sentences when speaking. Compare and contrast information. Present reports to peers. Analyze an event or issue by using role-play as a strategy.
- **Assessments:** Definitions, interviews, notes, reports, political cartoons.

How does it work?

The two teachers work with different groups of students. Both teachers teach the same content at the same time, but they either use different methods or they may deem it necessary to have a lower adult-student ratio for reteaching, reinforcement, or skill practice. Most likely, the groups are homogeneously grouped for these activities. Parallel teaching requires some coplanning to coordinate what students need to know (content) and be able to do (skills), though each teacher uses separate instructional strategies.

Variations for Emergent English Language Learners

Parallel teaching assumes that the students who are grouped for separate instruction require specific scaffolding strategies that the other students do not, and that one of the teachers knows more about these scaffolds than the other. In the examples above, ESL teachers would pull out ELLs and scaffold as follows: use reading materials appropriate for guided reading instruction; teach sentence

ASCD © 2007. All Rights Reserved.

PARALLEL TEACHING

patterns needed to construct hypotheses, explanations, and conclusions before and after actual scientific investigations are conducted in class; unpack the language of mathematical word problems as part of the instructional process; build background knowledge of abstract and culturally unique concepts as part of an instructional unit.

ASCD © 2007. All Rights Reserved.

Strategies for
SUCCESS
with English Language Learners

COTEACHING STRATEGIES

Peer Teaching

Why use it?

Use of this strategy will help students gain skills such as those indicated in the following examples. Each example also suggests how teachers can assess what students have learned.

Language Arts: Grade 11 Example
- **Language skills:** Interpret multiple levels of meaning and subtleties in text. Engage in a variety of collaborative conversations (cooperative group discussions) to construct meaning. Recognize and analyze the relevance of literature to contemporary and personal events and situations. Share reading experiences with peers.
- **ESL:** Demonstrate comprehension of classroom discussions and interactions. Identify details that support the main ideas of literary text with assistance.
- **Assessments:** Double-entry journals, literature circle checklist.

Science: Grade 9 Example
- **Content:** Geologic history can be reconstructed by observing sequences of rock types and fossils to correlate bedrock at various locations.
- **Science skill:** Insightfully interpret organized data (e.g., use the Geological History Reference Table).
- **Language skill:** Discuss with others, and use reading guides and summaries to aid in comprehension.
- **Assessment:** RAFT (science students send teachers explanations answering a question such as, "How are rocks like clocks?").

PEER TEACHING

Section Two

Math: Grade 4 Example
- **Content:** Determine what can be measured and how, using appropriate methods and formulas (e.g., length, mass, capacity).
- **Math skills:** Become problem solvers by using appropriate tools and strategies.
- **Communication skills:** Work in collaboration with others to solve problems. Verbally explain rationale for strategy selection and provide reasoning in written and verbal forms. Use appropriate terms, vocabulary, and language.
- **Assessments:** Oral explanations of word problem solutions, metacognitive journals.

Social Studies: Grade 1 Example
- **Content:** Demonstrate understanding of the geography of the interdependent world we live in.
- **Social studies skills:** Draw simple maps of their communities or regions showing the major landmarks, industries, residential areas, business districts, transportation networks, health and educational facilities, and recreation areas.
- **Language skills:** Write data and facts gathered. Write words and draw pictures to capture important understandings. Share information, using appropriate visual aids, about what they know and have learned about a topic.
- **Assessments:** Data gathering, maps, descriptions.

How does it work?

When students are learning together, both teachers are essentially freed from direct instruction to observe, circulate, and assess as needed. This model is used when students are engaged in cooperative differentiated or peer-literacy learning experiences. Peer teaching requires a shared vision (i.e., peers can be as helpful for learning as teachers) and coplanning time to coordinate what students need to know (content) and be able to do (skills), as well as what instructional learning experiences will facilitate peer interaction.

Variations for Emergent English Language Learners

- Have ELLs shadow-read literary works in the primary languages if possible.
- Allow ELLs to read abridged versions or watch videos and read only certain sections.
- Preteach content obligatory vocabulary using parallel or alternative coteaching before having peers work together.
- Demonstrate measurement concepts as pre-activities to word problems in mathematics.
- Take all students on field trips for mapping activities of the community, or ask ELL parents to draw maps of communities in their countries to compare with U.S. communities.

ASCD © 2007. All Rights Reserved.

Strategies for
SUCCESS
with English Language Learners

COTEACHING STRATEGIES

Station Teaching

Why use it?

Use of this strategy will help students gain skills such as those indicated in the following examples. Each example also suggests how teachers can assess what students have learned.

Language Arts: Grade 3 Example
- **Language skills:** Select literature on the basis of personal needs and interests. Engage in purposeful oral reading in small groups. Read print-based and electronic literary texts on a daily basis. Recognize the differences among the genres of stories, poems, and plays. Relate the setting, plot, and characters in literature to own lives. Identify cultural influences in texts with assistance.
- **ESL:** Summarize information from a literary text. Support individual interpretations and conclusions, using evidence from a literary text. Identify and apply strategies to enhance comprehension of texts.
- **Assessments:** Journals, reading logs, self-assessments.

Science: Grade 6 Example
- **Content:** Energy and matter interact through forces that result in changes of motion.
- **Science skills:** Describe different patterns of motion of objects. Observe, describe, and compare effects of forces (gravity, electric current, and magnetism) on the motion of objects.
- **Language skills:** Determine the meaning of unfamiliar words by using content and classroom resources. Make or revise predictions, draw

 © 2007. All Rights Reserved.

conclusions, and make inferences. Take notes to record data. State a main idea and support it with details. Write a clear analysis using examples. Present reports using notes and visual aids.

- **Assessments:** Vocabulary records, notes, lab reports, oral presentations.

Math: Kindergarten Example
- **Content:** Describe characteristics and relationships of geometric objects (integrating shapes found in nursery rhymes such as "Humpty Dumpty," "Queen of Hearts," "Hickory Dickory Dock," "Hush-a-Bye Baby," "I Saw a Ship Sailing," "The Boy in the Barn"). Describe or make objects differently to fix or improve (e.g., "Humpty's Big Day").
- **Language skills:** Use mathematical vocabulary. Act out or model with manipulatives activities involving mathematical content from literature. Identify and produce spoken words that rhyme. Recite and respond to nursery rhymes. Retell or dramatize parts of stories.
- **Assessments:** Checklists, anecdotal records, puppet show, drawings.

Social Studies: U.S. History Example
- **Content:** Compare and contrast experiences of different ethnic, national, and religious groups, explaining their contributions to U.S. society.
- **Social studies skills:** Draw upon literary selections, historical documents, and accounts to analyze the roles played by different groups and individuals in U.S. history.
- **Language skills:** Analyze information from different sources by making connections and showing relationships to other texts and resources. Determine the significance and reliability of information. Take notes from written and oral texts. Use paraphrase and quotation in order to communicate information most effectively. Prepare and give presentations on informational topics.
- **Assessments:** Notes, diaries, graphic organizers, political cartoons, oral presentations.

How does it work?

Stations may be independent (students work alone or in groups to complete learning experiences) or dependent (students receive guided instruction from teachers to complete learning experiences). Both teachers may rotate among stations to observe or facilitate; one teacher may rotate while the other staffs a station; or both teachers may staff dependent stations while students work independently at other stations. Station teaching requires some coplanning time to coordinate what students need to know (content) and be able to do (skills), as well as to design the learning experiences (tasks, materials, strategies) to be used by students at each station. Teachers may divide the preparation of the centers.

ASCD © 2007. All Rights Reserved.

STATION TEACHING

Variations for Emergent English Language Learners

- Use literature that has universal themes.
- Make cultural connections with ELLs' backgrounds.
- Be sure one of the stations is always focused on vocabulary development, using interactive and conceptual strategies.
- Assign ELLs assessment tasks that align with their linguistic levels (e.g., drawings and graphic organizers for beginners, puppet shows and PowerPoint presentations for intermediates).
- Provide margin notes and reading guides for informational text.
- Help ELLs employ rehearsal strategies before oral presentations in front of small groups of peers.

Section Two

Strategies for
SUCCESS
with English Language Learners

COTEACHING STRATEGIES

Support Teaching

Why use it?

Use of this strategy will help students gain skills such as those indicated in the following examples. Each example also suggests how teachers can assess what students have learned.

Language Arts: Grade 8 Example
- **Language skills:** Formulate questions to be answered by reading informational text. Distinguish between relevant and irrelevant information. Find, condense, evaluate, and combine information from print and electronic sources for inquiries. Take research notes, using a note-taking process. Write accurate and complete responses to questions about informational material.
- **ESL:** Identify forms of informational and expository materials. Use knowledge of text and graphic features and organizational structures to determine purpose and meaning. Analyze main ideas, supporting ideas, and supporting details for purpose and meaning.
- **Assessments:** Note cards, outlines, summaries, essays.

Science: Grade 3 Example
- **Content:** Matter is made up of particles whose properties determine the observable characteristics of matter and its reactivity.
- **Science skills:** Observe and describe properties of materials, using appropriate tools. Describe chemical and physical changes, including changes in states of matter.

 © 2007. All Rights Reserved.

Section Two

- **Language skills:** Acquire information and understand procedures. Take notes to record data, facts, and ideas, following teacher direction. Use organizational patterns for expository writing. Summarize main ideas with supporting details. Identify a conclusion to support main ideas.
- **Assessments:** Hypotheses, notes, graphic organizers, conclusions.

Math: Grade 6 Example
- **Content:** Understand meanings of operations and procedures and how they relate to one another.
- **Math skills:** Add, subtract, multiply, and divide fractions and mixed numbers with unlike denominators. Decode and comprehend mathematical symbols to construct meaning. Explain the methods and reasoning behind the problem-solving strategies used.
- **Language skills:** Follow a sequence of instructions consisting of at least three steps when engaging in a task. Take notes to record data. Answer questions with supportive examples. Understand mathematical solutions shared by others.
- **Assessments**: List of procedures, problem-solving notebook, self-assessment checklist.

Social Studies: World History Example
- **Content:** Understand the development and connectedness of Western civilization and other civilizations and cultures in the world over time.
- **Social studies skills:** Analyze important events and developments through the eyes and experiences of those who were there.
- **Language skills:** Take notes from written and oral texts, such as lectures. Interpret and evaluate the validity of informational sources with guidance.
- **Assessment:** Summary chart.

How does it work?

The classroom teacher maintains the lead instructional role because he or she has the expertise for the lesson and the support teacher may not. The support teacher either observes to check on students' progress or circulates throughout the class to provide moment-to-moment scaffolding for students who may need assistance. Supportive teaching requires minimal coplanning time because the lead teacher determines what students need to know (content) and be able to do (skills), as well as the instructional strategies to be used. The model is frequently used for new coteaching situations.

ASCD © 2007. All Rights Reserved.

SUPPORT TEACHING

Variations for Emergent English Language Learners

- Model note-taking of informational text using various methods (e.g., Cornell and Pen in Hand). Have the support teacher circulate to assist students.
- Demonstrate science experiments or math operations and have the support teacher circulate to check comprehension.

Section Two

 © 2007. All Rights Reserved.

Strategies for
SUCCESS
with English Language Learners

COTEACHING STRATEGIES

Team Teaching

Why use it?

Use of this strategy will help students gain skills such as those indicated in the following examples. Each example also suggests how teachers can assess what students have learned.

Language Arts: Grade 4 Example
- **Language skills:** Use self-monitoring strategies to identify specific vocabulary that causes comprehension difficulty. Engage in purposeful oral reading in small and large groups. Identify literary elements such as setting, plot, and character. Recognize how authors use literary devices to create meaning. Read grade-level texts and answer literal, inferential, and evaluative questions. Participate in discussions about texts (e.g., use specific evidence to identify themes and describe characters' motivations). Demonstrate comprehension of grade-level texts through a variety of responses such as writing, drama, and oral presentations.
- **ESL:** Apply knowledge of context clues to determine the meaning of unfamiliar words. Demonstrate comprehension of classroom discussions and interactions when clarification is given. Respond to factual and inferential questions based on academic content. Summarize orally. Participate in small-group activities, playing a specified role. Analyze the elements of plot, character, and setting. Demonstrate understanding that dialogue develops the plot and characters.
- **Assessments:** Vocabulary records, story grammars, written and oral summaries, class plays.

Science: Grade 2 Example
- **Content:** Many phenomena that we observe on Earth involve interactions among components of air, water, and land.
- **Science skills:** Describe the relationship among air, water, and land (i.e., weather, water cycle, erosion and deposition, extreme natural events).
- **Language skills:** Understand oral and written directions. Collect information with assistance. Identify main ideas and supporting details in informational text with assistance. Compare and contrast information on one topic from two sources. Interpret facts taken from maps, graphs, charts, and other visuals with assistance. Describe a problem and suggest a solution. Share the process of writing with peers. Produce clear, well-organized short reports to demonstrate understanding of information. Maintain a portfolio that includes informational writing. Present a short oral report.
- **Assessments:** Charts, graphs, logs, experiments, graphic organizers, illustrated booklets, oral presentations.

Math: Grade 5 Example
- **Content:** Apply the knowledge and thinking skills of mathematics, science, and technology to address real-life problems and make informed decisions.
- **Math, science, and technology skills:** Solve interdisciplinary problems using a variety of skills and strategies, including effective work habits; gathering and processing information; generating and analyzing ideas; realizing ideas; making connections among the common themes of mathematics, science, and technology; and presenting results.
- **Communication skills:** Provide an organized thought process that is correct, complete, coherent, and clear. Share organized mathematical ideas through the manipulation of objects, numerical tables, drawings, pictures, charts, graphs, tables, diagrams, models, and symbols in written and verbal form. Answer clarifying questions from others. Understand mathematical solutions shared by others. Raise questions that elicit, extend, or challenge others' thinking. Increase use of mathematical vocabulary and language when communicating with others.
- **Assessment:** Rubric for an extended or culminating project.

Social Studies: Grade 7 Example
- **Content:** Demonstrate understanding of major ideas, eras, themes, developments, and turning points in U.S. history.
- **Social studies skills:** Use the skills of historical analysis to consider the sources of historical documents, narratives, or artifacts and evaluate their reliability. Understand how different experiences, beliefs, values, traditions, and motives cause individuals and groups to interpret historic events and issues from different perspectives. Compare and contrast different interpretations of key events and issues and explain reasons for the different

ASCD © 2007. All Rights Reserved.

accounts. Describe historic events through the eyes and experiences of those who were there.

- **Language skills:** Apply corrective strategies such as discussing with others, identifying transition words to assist with comprehension, and monitoring for misunderstandings to assist in comprehension. Form an opinion or judgment about the validity and accuracy of information, ideas, opinions, and experiences. Recognize multiple levels of meaning. Connect, compare, and contrast ideas and information. Identify missing, conflicting, or unclear information. Understand the purpose for writing (e.g., to explain, describe, narrate, persuade, or express feelings). Write accurate and complete responses to questions about material. Prepare and give presentations on informational topics. Present a subject from one or more perspectives. Recognize persuasive techniques, such as emotional and ethical appeals, in oral presentations.
- **Assessments:** Diaries, Venn diagrams, political cartoons, document-based essays, presentations, debates.

How does it work?

Two teachers assume responsibility for the lead instructional role by dividing the lessons in ways that capitalize on each teacher's curricular strengths and experiences. The team teachers codeliver lessons simultaneously and are comfortable alternately taking the lead and the supporter roles. Team teaching requires a shared vision of learning (i.e., ownership of all students) and teaching (i.e., two heads are better than one). Considerable coplanning time is needed to determine what students need to know (content) and be able to do (skills) as well as the instructional strategies and resources to be used.

Variations for Emergent English Language Learners

- Differentiate the texts or tasks ELLs will complete as part of a literature unit (e.g., assign roles and responsibilities ELLs will complete in the class play).
- Assign linguistic buddies to chart and graph science phenomena.
- Ensure that ELLs acquire mathematical vocabulary through hands-on applications.
- Provide reading guides for informational text.
- Group students strategically for pair and small-group work.
- Use cooperative learning, differentiation strategies, literacy strategies, and time-honored ESL strategies to construct a learning environment for all students.

References

Colorado State Department of Education. *Coteaching models* [handout].

Villa, R. A., Thousand, J. S., & Nevin, A. I. (2004). *A guide to coteaching: Practical tips for facilitating student learning.* Thousand Oaks, CA: Corwin Press.

Strategies for Working Together

SECTION THREE

Strategies for Working Together

ASCD © 2007. All Rights Reserved.

STRATEGIES FOR WORKING TOGETHER

Self-Assessment Checklist and Rating Scale

Scaffolding Success for English Language Learners

Research that characterizes responsive learning environments for English language learners specifies conditions that maximize second language acquisition and academic achievement. The three areas presented on this checklist for reflection include (1) responsive programs, (2) responsive schoolwide practices, and (3) responsive instructional strategies. For each statement, check the column that best portrays your school or district; in making your decision, consider the conditions that are suggested as evidence to support each statement's claim. Use staff responses to develop a plan for addressing the needs of English language learners.

Self-Assessment Checklist

Responsive Program Specifications	Exceeds	Meets	Needs Attention
1. We embrace our English language learners (ELLs) as an asset to our school and do not feel that they "pull down" our program, teaching, or learning standards. **Evidence:** • We have no quota system to limit enrollment. • Our ELLs are not considered remedial or special-needs.	☐	☐	☐
2. We have articulated language policies across the curriculum that honor additive bilingualism and emphasize language acquisition and development as lifelong processes for students. **Evidence:** • We have policy statements to which the community and staff assent. • We understand that students' primary languages are beneficial to and necessary for English language acquisition.	☐	☐	☐
3. We allow the use of students' primary languages as a tool for learning and are aware of and sensitive to variables that may cause students to use their primary language to avoid learning. **Evidence:** • Language usage self-assessments. • Primary language materials. • Linguistic autobiographies. • Conferences. • Counseling support.	☐	☐	☐
4. We understand how long peer-competitive English proficiency takes and how variable the process is, and we understand how different variables affect ELLs with distinct needs. **Evidence:** • Profiles of students are based on second language acquisition variables.	☐	☐	☐
5. We are sensitive to cultural identity issues among our learners. **Evidence:** • We have a bias checklist for materials selection. • We have awareness sessions on issues that could cause divisions among groups in school—students, teachers, or parents.	☐	☐	☐

514

ASCD © 2007. All Rights Reserved.

Responsive Program Specifications	Exceeds	Meets	Needs Attention
6. We have an ecological program model for our ELLs whereby *everyone* understands and embraces their roles and responsibilities as teachers of ELLs. **Evidence:** • We have a program whereby mainstream teachers are language sensitive and ESL teachers are content based. • Our program focuses on long-term efforts and not short-term fix-it solutions for a problem.	❐	❐	❐
7. We do not perceive the need for a separate ESL program as a safe haven for our ELLs because all classrooms in our school are safe learning environments for all our students. **Evidence:** • We have empathetic teachers and peers. • Striving for excellence and equity resonate as mutual goals.	❐	❐	❐
8. Our program allows English language learners access to grade-level content while they are learning English per the 2006 TESOL standards for English language learners. **Evidence:** • Our ESL program model is content based and supports grade-level core academic subjects. • We deliver one curriculum to all students by classroom and ESL teachers collaboratively.	❐	❐	❐
9. We use an assessment framework to collect data on language proficiency and academic achievement. **Evidence:** • We use diagnostic, formative, and summative classroom-based assessments. • We use standardized assessments that are valid and reliable for our population.	❐	❐	❐
10. We participate in ongoing staff development efforts in order to learn to help all students learn, and we reflectively transfer our knowledge to classroom practice. **Evidence:** We have or use • Study groups. • Courses and workshops. • Small-scale investigations. • Peer coaching and mentoring. • Assessment teams.	❐	❐	❐

ASCD © 2007. All Rights Reserved.

515

Responsive Schoolwide Practices	Exceeds	Meets	Needs Attention
1. We conceive of and implement literacy within a reading-and-writing-to-learn framework; reading and writing across the curriculum is a metagoal for acquiring and synthesizing information. **Evidence:** • All teachers use language development strategies as a part of their discipline. • Attention is explicitly paid to genre studies as a part of content in all subject areas. • All classrooms use the reading and writing processes for learning.	☐	☐	☐
2. We avoid the "twin sins" of schooling; that is, topics and activities in elementary school and curriculum coverage and transmission of information in upper-level classes. **Evidence:** • We focus on concepts and purposeful strategies in elementary school and depth of understanding and learning-centered strategies in upper-level classes.	☐	☐	☐
3. We use a backward planning curriculum model that identifies what we want students to know and be able to do (Stage I); how we will collect evidence of what they know and can do (Stage II); and how we will plan learning experiences and instructional strategies to facilitate their attainment of the evidence (Stage III). We then build scaffolds to support ELLs as a part of this process (Stage IV). **Evidence:** • We use Understanding by Design, assessment-driven planning.	☐	☐	☐
4. We conceive of assessment as informative (i.e., as assessment for learning) so students can show what they "got" though performance tasks; teachers can assist learners to "get more" because tasks are multistep and require coaching over time. **Evidence:** • We use a formative and summative complex assessment model.	☐	☐	☐
5. We provide expectations to students before instruction and feedback after instruction, along with instructional strategies to enable their progression. **Evidence:** • We use checklists. • We develop and use rating scales. • We use analytic, holistic, task-based rubrics.	☐	☐	☐

ASCD © 2007. All Rights Reserved.

Responsive Schoolwide Practices	Exceeds	Meets	Needs Attention
6. Our classes emphasize problem posing and solving through an inquiry model of learning. **Evidence:** • We use inquiry-based essential questions that are conceptual, overarching, open-ended, and succinct; require elaborated responses; and have an information gap or some tension. • We identify complex assessment tasks as evidence of responses to these questions.	❑	❑	❑
7. Our classes are learning centered—that is, it is the students who are doing the doing. **Evidence:** • Our model of learning gradually releases the responsibility of learning so that students do more than teachers to show what they know and can do.	❑	❑	❑
8. We hold high expectations for English language learners to use generated language and do not stop with scripted language tasks. **Evidence:** • We do not use ditto sheets. • We do not practice vocabulary or grammar skills out of context. • Lots of complex tasks integrate all four language skills.	❑	❑	❑
9. We—mainstream and ESL teachers—collaborate to ensure that all learning experiences of English language learners are scaffolded or supported as necessary. **Evidence:** • We use coplanning. • We use coteaching models. • We collaborate on assessments.	❑	❑	❑
10. We practice three-way communication among ELL parents, mainstream teachers, and ESL teachers. **Evidence:** We use the following vehicles: • Newsletters • Conferences • Meeting minutes • Translators	❑	❑	❑

ASCD © 2007. All Rights Reserved.

Responsive Instructional Strategies	Exceeds	Meets	Needs Attention
1. We develop language through content by focusing on linguistic features and discourse markers of our disciplines. **Evidence:** • Lessons have explicit content and implicit linguistic form and function.	☐	☐	☐
2. We plan instructional experiences and strategies only after we have designed evidence-based assessments. **Evidence:** • We use the backward design model of planning.	☐	☐	☐
3. We use the benchmarks or performance indicators from our curriculum to design our feedback tools, and we provide exemplars for learners to follow. **Evidence:** • We use assessment tasks with checklists, rating scales, or rubrics.	☐	☐	☐
4. We use portfolios to collect evidence of what students know and can do, and we conference with students to give them explicit strategies for improving their performance. **Evidence:** • Portfolios are full of projects, papers, checklists, rubrics, drafts, tapes, and self-assessments.	☐	☐	☐
5. We identify the content and language skills (benchmarks or performance indicators) students are to master as a result of completing the assessment tasks, and we are proficient at targeting instructional strategies to the skills. **Evidence:** • Lesson plans list content, and language skills are matched or aligned with instructional strategies.	☐	☐	☐
6. We use time-honored ESL scaffolds to make the content comprehensible to our ELLs. **Evidence:** We use the following: • Visuals • Demonstrations • Paraphrasing • Linguistic buddies • Active hands-on materials • Vocabulary previews • Comprehension checks • Graphic organizers	☐	☐	☐

ASCD © 2007. All Rights Reserved.

Responsive Instructional Strategies	Exceeds	Meets	Needs Attention
7. We consistently use 5–10 research-based instructional strategies to develop vocabulary that may be new for all students. **Evidence:** We use • Open word sorts or four-dimensional word study. • Vocabulary graphics. • Knowledge rating scales.	❑	❑	❑
8. We consistently use 5–10 research-based reading strategies to develop the comprehension skills of all students so reading becomes a tool for learning. **Evidence:** We use tools and strategies such as • Guided reading. • SSR (Sustained Silent Reading). • Collaborative Strategic Reading • Math Notes • SQR3 (Survey, Question, Read, Recite, Review). • DRTA (Directed Reading and Thinking Activity). • Pen in Hand. • T-Notes. • PORPE (Predict, Organize, Rehearse, Practice, Evaluate). • SPAWN (Special powers, Problem solving, Alternative viewpoints, What if, Next). • Proposition Support. • An array of graphic organizers.	❑	❑	❑
9. We consistently use research-based instructional strategies to develop the writing skills of all students so writing becomes a tool for learning. **Evidence:** We use strategies such as • Cubing. • 4-2-1 Drafting. • Hennings Sequence. • Exemplars. • Divorcing the Draft. • Writer's Workshop.	❑	❑	❑

ASCD © 2007. All Rights Reserved.

Responsive Instructional Strategies	Exceeds	Meets	Needs Attention
10. We use the instructional framework scaffold of cooperative learning to increase verbal interaction in our classes and to extend the classroom discourse beyond "teacher asks question and students respond one at a time." **Evidence:** • Students work together in structured groups so that they are talking to learn and are not passive recipients of teacher talk.	☐	☐	☐
11. We use the instructional framework scaffold of differentiation to provide multiple paths to learning for our diverse students. **Evidence:** • We differentiate material through jigsaw or literature circles. • We differentiate tasks through tiered activities or learning menus. • We differentiate instructional strategies through centers or curriculum compacting. • We differentiate classroom configuration through flexible student groupings.	☐	☐	☐
12. We use the instructional framework scaffold of coteaching with our ESL teachers in order to provide ELLs access to mainstream learning experiences. **Evidence:** We use • Parallel teaching. • Alternative teaching. • Station teaching. • Team teaching.	☐	☐	☐
13. We consistently work with and listen to students in small groups, whether it be a group that needs support or a group that needs to be extended. **Evidence:** We use strategies such as • Coteaching. • Conferencing records.	☐	☐	☐
14. We use multiple sources of information and materials including technology. **Evidence:** • The textbook is only one resource for learning. • We use instructional software, Internet investigations, SmartBoards.	☐	☐	☐

ASCD © 2007. All Rights Reserved.

Responsive Instructional Strategies	Exceeds	Meets	Needs Attention
15. We develop students' metalinguistic awareness focusing on English and primary language usage patterns and on language development strategies to assist our ELLs with language acquisition. We do not have punitive language usage policies in our classrooms, no matter how well intended they may be. **Evidence:** • We assign self-regulating tasks. • Students do self-assessments. • We use learning strategies checklists.	☐	☐	☐

ASCD © 2007. All Rights Reserved.

Self-Assessment Rating Scale: Responsive ELL Classroom

This rating scale assists classroom teachers and others involved in planning programming for English language learners to reflect on where they are on the continuum of submersion versus collaborative classrooms. Circle the number on the continuum that is closest to representing what happens now in your classroom serving ELLs. Share the results in discussion with colleagues and develop strategies together that will help your classrooms become models of collaborative sheltered immersion.

Unresponsive/Submersion				Responsive/Collaborative Sheltered Immersion
1	2	3	4	5
Ethos of subtractive bilingualism; that is, students' primary languages are perceived as detrimental to English language acquisition.				Ethos of additive bilingualism; that is, students' primary languages are honored as beneficial to and necessary for English language acquisition.
1	2	3	4	5
Parents are perceived as problematic or disinterested.				Parents are involved, especially in development of primary language.
1	2	3	4	5
Students' cultural backgrounds and experiences are perceived as irrelevant and at times are dismissed as inferior.				Connections between students' cultural backgrounds and experiences are made as bridges to development of new concepts, knowledge, and skills.

ASCD © 2007. All Rights Reserved.

Unresponsive/Submersion				Responsive/Collaborative Sheltered Immersion
1	2	3	4	5
ELLs are perceived as remedial or learning disabled and are expected to be "fixed" by specialists. "Fixing" can mean that students complete low-level tasks in tiresome contexts.				The ecology of the school provides a facilitating environment for ELLs' language acquisition and academic achievement; students are engaged in academically rigorous tasks in low-anxiety contexts.
1	2	3	4	5
Low expectations for achievement are evident in "watering down" of content, materials, or tasks as a means to provide equity.				High expectations for achievement are evident in providing access to grade-level content, materials, and tasks; equity is built into the instructional process.
1	2	3	4	5
There is little to no articulation between mainstream and ESL or bilingual programs, curriculum, and teachers.				Mainstream and ESL or bilingual teachers work collaboratively to provide inclusive instruction using one curriculum--from planning through implementation and reflection.

ASCD © 2007. All Rights Reserved.

523

Unresponsive/Submersion					Responsive/Collaborative Sheltered Immersion
1	2	3	4	5	
Content (what students know) and skills (what students can do linguistically) are separated and studied out of context with little to no understanding of the centrality of language to learning.					Content (what students know) and skills (what students can do linguistically) are integrated and placed in context with the understanding that learning and language are inseparable.
1	2	3	4	5	
Literacy is not conceived of and implemented within a learning-to-read-and-write framework; reading and writing are taught separately from content as skills prerequisite to the acquisition or sharing of new information and concepts.					Literacy is conceived of and implemented within a reading-and-writing-to-learn framework; reading and writing across the curriculum is a metagoal for acquiring new information and then synthesizing it to share new concepts with peers.
1	2	3	4	5	
Language development opportunities are provided through traditional language learning means (i.e., grammar and vocabulary as objects of study in hierarchically sequenced segments).					Opportunities for both informal and formal language development are systematically provided through the study of genres (i.e., linguistic markers and vocabulary for different types of text).

ASCD © 2007. All Rights Reserved.

Unresponsive/Submersion					Responsive/Collaborative Sheltered Immersion
1	2	3	4	5	
Assessment is conceived of as evaluative—that is, assessment of learning or a single piece of evidence to see who "got it"; assessments are often selected-response tests of passive knowledge.					Assessment is conceived of as informative—that is, assessment for learning so students can show what they "got" through open-ended performance tasks; teachers can assist learners to "get more" because tasks are multistep and require coaching over extended time.
1	2	3	4	5	
Feedback to students is often provided after instruction; students are assigned scores based on percentage correct, which are averaged over a specified period of time for a grade.					Feedback to students is provided before instruction through rubrics or checklists, which specify performance expectations along with instructional strategies to assist students to attain expectations; the achievement grade is based on the final level of performance.
1	2	3	4	5	
Instructional plans are disconnected from the assessment process; strategies might be related to learning targets, and activities might be unrelated to specific targets or be prescribed from texts.					A backward planning model for instruction is used in order to target strategies that will enable learners to complete previously designed performance assessment tasks.

ASCD © 2007. All Rights Reserved.

Unresponsive/Submersion				Responsive/Collaborative Sheltered Immersion
1	2	3	4	5
There is overreliance on teacher-centered and whole-class instruction; more often than not it appears that it is the teacher who is "doing" and the doing is through talking.				There is emphasis on learners as makers of meaning and builders of knowledge; instructional strategies are purposefully aligned with skills so that it is the students who are "doing" and the doing is through the negotiation of meaning.
1	2	3	4	5
English language learners are grouped by language proficiency level, thereby having limited opportunities for interaction with students of mixed proficiencies.				English language learners engage in collaborative learning through grade-level groupings with mixed language proficiencies and students who have English as their primary language.
1	2	3	4	5
Traditional instructional arrangements and methods are used, including use of a single text, single tasks for students to complete, and single instructional frameworks or strategies; students who do not "fit" do not do well.				A wide repertoire of instructional arrangements and methods is used, including multiple materials, a choice of tasks for students to complete, and a variety of instructional frameworks and strategies to support a range of knowledge and skill levels within the class.

ASCD © 2007. All Rights Reserved.

Section Three

Unresponsive/Submersion	1	2	3	4	5	Responsive/Collaborative Sheltered Immersion
Struggling learners fail or are referred to additional "fix-it" specialists for interventions.	1	2	3	4	5	Scaffolding strategies or ways of supporting struggling learners are built into the backward planning instructional model.
Students' language is characterized by literal-level discourse, often in response to yes/no, either/or types of questioning; responses are often *scripted*, indicating that students are parroting what teachers and texts say.	1	2	3	4	5	Students' language is characterized by descriptive, persuasive, and critical-level discourse produced in response to divergent, open-ended questions; responses are *generated* by students, indicating that students find ways to name their developing cognitive world.
Evidence of language performance is conceived of as students' capacity to recall what has been learned in a given context (i.e., it is coverage-focused).	1	2	3	4	5	Evidence of language performance is conceived of as students' capacity to transfer use to new situations and challenges (i.e., it is results-focused).

ASCD © 2007. All Rights Reserved.

Section Three

A Proposal for an Expanded Assessment Framework Tool to Monitor English Language Acquisition and Academic Achievement

The traditional framework for assessing second language acquisition and academic achievement of English language learners has overrelied on the use of standardized assessments as evidence of assessment of learning as the chart on the following page indicates.

Traditional Assessment Framework

		Language Proficiency				Academic Achievement			
		Listening	Speaking	Reading	Writing	Language Arts	Math	Science	Social Studies
Standardized Assessments	District State National	A language proficiency test—whether it is a district, state, or national measure—is used to determine English language learners' language proficiency in English (and perhaps in the primary language). Students who are identified below a specified cut-off score are identified as requiring services. The instrument is frequently used to determine a level of language proficiency, which determines the amount and type of service students will be given. Many of the tests used assess what is known as social skills (i.e., basic interpersonal communication skills), using topics that are often associated with a language-led curriculum (e.g., food, house, weather, body parts). Once students attain a determined score, they are generally exited from ESL or bilingual support services.				NCLB requires that all students be assessed on their academic achievement. English language learners are given an exemption period (up to one year) before they are to be included. They are then expected to take the scheduled tests and to show adequate yearly progress (AYP) thereafter.			

ASCD © 2007. All Rights Reserved.

This ASCD Action Tool recommends an expanded assessment framework to monitor language proficiency and academic achievement. This expanded framework emphasizes the use of classroom-based assessments in conjunction with a revised collection of standardized assessments that connect language proficiency and academic achievement and focus on assessment for learning.

Proposed Expanded Assessment Framework

		Language Proficiency				Academic Achievement			
		Listening	Speaking	Reading	Writing	Language Arts	Math	Science	Social Studies
Classroom-Based Assessments	Diagnostic	ESL teachers need to assemble and use types of classroom tasks that can be used to diagnose proficiency on these skills in an integrated and performance-based manner. The tasks are grounded in content-related expectations so the data can be used to determine how English language learners would cope with grade-level tasks in core subject areas.				Classroom teachers need to identify the summative assessments (i.e., evidence of standards) as well as the formative assessments (i.e., evidence of benchmarks) that lead students to the completion of the summative tasks. This process-to-product assessment path allows teachers to design scaffolds to support each step in a timely fashion. ESL teachers need to know in advance what products and performances English language learners will have to make and do in order to show attainment of content standards in these core subject areas. One example for each subject follows: *Language Arts* graphic organizers, drafts, revisions, peer edits = written paper *Math* vocabulary cards, data collection, data analysis, data presentation = math explanations *Science* hypotheses, experiments, observation notes, findings = lab reports *Social Studies* gathering information (notes), graphic organizer, rebuttal questions and answers, rehearsal = debate			
	Formative and summative	Once the diagnostic phase identifies students who need ESL support, a portfolio process is put into place to monitor English language acquisition and development. ESL and classroom teachers systematically collect sample formative and summative assessment tasks as evidence of benchmark and standard attainment. Most important, the data provides insight into the use of instructional strategies to support students' linguistic growth within the context of academic achievement. Aligning instructional tools with specific expectations (see the sample unit later) emphasizes the deliberate use of assessment as evidence *for* learning rather than *of* learning. The notion of moving English language learners into and out of ESL services to "fix" them gives way to a shared responsibility of ownership and effort for the amount of time that it takes for students to acquire academic English.							

© 2007. All Rights Reserved.

		Language Proficiency				Academic Achievement			
		Listening	Speaking	Reading	Writing	Language Arts	Math	Science	Social Studies
Standardized Assessments	District	Rubrics can be designed by districts to determine students' levels of performance on commonly developed classroom-based assessment tasks: *Task-based:* Task-based rubrics (see the sample on page 542) can be developed to equitably grade English language learners on classroom-based performance tasks and to determine and monitor language proficiency and academic achievement simultaneously. These rubrics are grounded in standards because grade-level benchmarks are used to describe the expected level of performance as well as levels of performance which either exceed or fall behind these expectations. The purpose of the task-based rubric is for classroom and ESL teachers to jointly assume responsibility to scaffold the learning experiences of English language learners so they are able to move toward higher levels of performance (i.e., march through the rubric). *Holistic:* Bonnie Campbell Hill's nationally used developmental language continuum can be systematically used to determine and monitor proficiency in oral reading and writing skills (by grade level). Some states have developed their own holistic rubrics to describe quantitative or qualitative levels of student performance. *Analytic:* The six traits writing rubric is one example of a nationally used analytic rubric that monitors language proficiency in the area of writing. Some states have developed their own analytic rubrics to describe quantitative or qualitative levels of student performance in all the skill areas of language proficiency.				A proposed alternative to the use of one test score—whether it be a district, state, or national test—to determine adequate yearly progress is to align or cross-reference test scores with a collection of evidence (i.e., a portfolio) that shows English language learners' academic growth. The portfolio collection should consist of a data-analysis overview of the aligned or cross-referenced items from each of the quadrants of this assessment framework.			

ASCD © 2007. All Rights Reserved.

		Language Proficiency				Academic Achievement			
		Listening	Speaking	Reading	Writing	Language Arts	Math	Science	Social Studies
Standardized Assessments *(continued)*	State or national rubrics	Newly developed language proficiency tests have been and are being designed to assess what is known as academic language (i.e., cognitive academic language proficiency) and are therefore more content- and standards-based than previous instruments. The data can be systematically used to verify or refute the information collected from classroom-based assessments and rubrics. Overreliance on one test score to determine support for English language learners is outdated.				Additionally, the scores of newly developed proficiency tests would provide useful instructional data if they were more criterion-referenced than norm-referenced. The criteria would be aligned with standards and benchmarks so that teachers and district staff could use the data to monitor students' progress on identified expectations.			

Source: From *Assessing English Language Learners: Bridges from Language Proficiency to Academic Achievement,* by M. Gottlieb, 2006, Thousand Oaks, CA: Corwin Press, and *Understanding by Design, 2nd ed.,* by G. Wiggins and J. McTighe, 2005, Alexandria, VA: Association for Supervision and Curriculum Development. Adapted with permission.

ASCD © 2007. All Rights Reserved.

References

Campbell Hill, B. (2001). *Developmental continuums: A framework for literacy instruction and assessment K–8.* Norwood, MA: Christopher Gordon Publishers.

Gottlieb, M. (2006). *Assessing English language learners: Bridges from language proficiency to academic achievement.* Thousand Oaks, CA: Corwin Press.

Wiggins, G., & McTighe, J. (2005). *Understanding by design* (2nd ed.). Alexandria, VA: Association for Supervision and Curriculum Development.

ASCD © 2007. All Rights Reserved.

Strategies for
SUCCESS
with English Language Learners

A Backward Design Unit Template and Example

Unit Planner

Stage 1: Identify expectations (standards & benchmarks)	Questions/ Expectations/ Understandings	Standards Addressed	Benchmarks Addressed
Mainstream teachers' responsibility to identify unit standards and benchmarks ESL teachers' responsibility to align TESOL standards and benchmarks (if different)			

ASCD © 2007. All Rights Reserved.

Stage 2: Determine acceptable evidence (evidence of standards)	Test Type		Assessment Tasks		Feedback Strategies
	Selected Response	Constructed Response	Product (students make)	Performance (students do)	Checklist
Mainstream teachers' responsibility to identify assessments					
ESL teachers' responsibility to designate modifications for emergent ELLs					Rating Scale
					Analytic Rubric
					Holistic Rubric
					Task-Based Rubric

ASCD © 2007. All Rights Reserved.

Stage 3: **Instructional Process/ Strategies (backward planning)** Mainstream teachers' responsibility to plan learning experiences	**Introduce/Expose**	**Develop/Practice**	**Master/ Assess**

ASCD © 2007. All Rights Reserved.

Stage 4: **Scaffolds Needed** (learners' needs) ESL teachers' responsibility to plan scaffolds for ELLs (time-honored ESL scaffolds, literacy scaffolds, and instructional framework scaffolds)	Language Proficiency	Literacy Skills
	Concept	Understanding

Source: Reprinted by permission of V. P. Rojas.

ASCD © 2007. All Rights Reserved.

Example: A 6th Grade Language Arts Unit

Stage 1: Mainstream Teacher Identifies Expectations		
Questions/ Expectations/ Standard	**Language Arts Benchmarks**	
How are myths, legends, and folktales unique? Why do they endure? *Expectation:* Distinguish similarities and differences of myths, legends, and folktales. *Standard:* Students will read, write, listen, and speak for literary response and expression.	*Listening and Speaking* Use strategies to enhance listening comprehension (e.g., take notes, paraphrase, summarize). Ask and answer questions. Play a variety of roles in group discussions. Speak with expression, volume, pace, and gestures appropriate for the topic, audience, and purpose of communication (oral sharing).	*Reading* Use reading skills and strategies to understand a variety of literary texts. Identify and interpret the defining characteristics of such texts, including the social and cultural context of the genre, to enhance understanding and appreciation. Understand the elements of character development, use of language to create images, setting, and conflict and resolution of plot.
	Writing Select an organizational pattern for writing appropriate to the audience and purpose (e.g., use literary elements of the genre). Use a variety of prewriting strategies to plan and organize writing (e.g., ask questions, list words and phrases to support topic). Use the writing process (prewriting, drafting, revising, and editing). Write original literary texts with well-developed characters, setting, and plot. Review writing with teachers and peers to revise sentences; to improve transitions; to add images and sensory details; and to edit for mechanics including spelling, punctuation, syntax, and usage.	

Stage 2: Mainstream Teacher Determines Acceptable Evidence	
Assessment Tasks	**Feedback Strategies**
Formative Assessments: Notes, story map, and Venn graphic organizers; drafts, revisions, and peer edits.	Teacher and peer conferences
Summative Writing Assessment: Over a four-week period of reading this genre, students will employ the writing process to develop one original myth, legend, or folktale. The work will contain literary structures and elements typical of the genre.	Writing process task-based rubric Six-traits analytic rubric
Summative Oral Assessment: Oral sharing with peers.	Checklist

Stage 3: Mainstream Teacher Plans Learning Experiences	Stage 4: ESL Teacher Plans Scaffolds for Varying English Proficiency Levels
Introduce/Expose	
Show films or vignettes of myths, legends, folktales to enhance listening comprehension, *or* read sections with whole class using Pen in Hand reading strategy (i.e., take notes), *or* do both of these—have students ask and answer questions about how the stories are the same and different using cooperative learning strategies.	Showing films is the time-honored scaffolding strategy of placing content in context. Pen in Hand is a modeling strategy. ESL teacher could also use cues to help ELLs take notes, or use a parallel coteaching strategy to work with ELL students on proficiency-appropriate texts. Write in names for ELL students of who they should find or pair with.
Students generate questions in groups using a cooperative learning strategy.	ESL teacher supplies question spinners so ELLs have linguistic prompts for generating questions, or uses a peer coteaching strategy if mainstream teacher wants to use spinners with all students.
Use a story impressions strategy for reading; use a word sort, word bank, or word chain vocabulary strategy to list words and phrases to support structure and meaning within and among paragraphs. Put up a phrase wall.	Pair ELLs with linguistic buddies who can translate, or ESL teacher previews the task with ELLs and helps them put words and phrases in writers' notebooks.
Use jigsaw strategy so students play a variety of roles in group discussions. Home groups (three students each) read a myth, legend, or folktale; expert groups complete story grammar maps to show elements of character development, use of language, setting, and conflict/resolution. Home groups share story maps to complete a triple Venn diagram as evidence of knowing defining characteristics of myths, legends, and folktales.	Use leveled readers to match ELL to reading level or provide shadow reading in mother tongue. Select folktales, myths, or legends that are universal or particular to ELL culture. Use a peer coteaching strategy for jigsaw groups so both teachers can assist groups. ELLs can complete triple Venn diagrams in primary language, or ESL teacher provides linguistic cues or illustrations to assist them.
Students can use any or all of several reading strategies: coding strategy, collaborative strategic reading, DRTA, elaborative interrogation, peer reading, etc. to understand and use dialogue and play a variety of roles in group discussion.	ESL teacher can use several reading strategies with ELLs simultaneously or beforehand: interactive reading guide, one-to-one tutoring, guided reading, REAP, SMART, think-alouds, two-minute preview, visual reading guide.
Develop/Practice	
Use vocabulary strategies involving word banks, word boxes, or word cards to help students generate specific and abstract words or phrases related to the writing task.	During pull-out time, ESL teacher reinforces vocabulary and models how these words can be used in writing a draft.
Use cooperative learning strategies to help students complete story maps to identify the structures and length of the writing task and to organize information into a multiparagraph format for their individual drafts.	Inherently scaffolded, because students do not have to work alone to complete story maps. Use alternative coteaching strategies for each teacher to model with groups. Use completed story maps to number paragraphs for ELLs during pull-out time.

ASCD © 2007. All Rights Reserved.

Stage 3: Mainstream Teacher Plans Learning Experiences	Stage 4: ESL Teacher Plans Scaffolds for Varying English Proficiency Levels
Students use completed story map and the writing process to draft a story with well-developed characters, setting, and conflict/resolution that includes sufficient descriptive detail.	Use station coteaching for writer's workshop, or ESL teacher modifies the length of the writing task for ELLs to include introductory, two or three supporting, and concluding paragraphs.
Use a writing strategy to help students generate dialogue into drafts.	Let ELLs work in pairs to draft story, or draft in mother tongue if they are able, or draft using a cartoon strip organizer with annotated text to accompany. Help ELLs focus on dialogue to develop character and plot and to work for more detail by using a graphic organizer or a coteaching strategy. Let ELLs revise color-coded drafts ESL teacher has prepared.
Hold writing conferences using exemplars with six traits analytic rubric to help students • Rearrange sentences, use a variety of sentence lengths and patterns, and combine sentences to make writing more clear or interesting to the reader. • Revise writing to ensure coherence and to improve transitions between ideas. • Add images and sensory details and incorporate idiomatic expressions that are relevant to the purpose of the writing.	ESL teacher uses guided writing and exemplars either in class or at a station for struggling students, or out of class with ELLs (station or parallel coteaching). ESL teacher provides explicit instruction on sentence types during pull-out time (parallel coteaching). ESL teacher provides ELLs a page with two columns as a strategy for sentence variety.
Use peer editing checklists to • Use knowledge of correct mechanics, spelling, and sentence structure and usage when editing.	ESL teacher uses explicit mediation editing strategy to help ELLs recognize and self-correct errors.
Master/Assess	
Use a cooperative learning strategy that lets students work in partners to rehearse oral sharing, focusing on expression, volume, pace, and gestures appropriate for the topic, audience, and purpose.	ESL teacher audiotapes self reading students' papers, then audiotapes ELLs practicing so they can listen to both over and over.
Orally present using a cooperative learning strategy for two voices; students of same story type get together to present to each other and use oral checklist with each other.	Inherently scaffolded, because ELLs will present to a small group and have a partner.

ASCD © 2007. All Rights Reserved.

Sample Rubric for 6th Language Arts Unit

The descriptors of the levels of performance are grounded in the identified language arts benchmarks of the unit. Qualitative differences are underlined in this copy so as to point out how explicit feedback is given to students about what they need to do in order to improve their performance (i.e., grade). Percentages are assigned for each task by the classroom teacher. The ESL teacher scaffolds the learning experiences of English language learners so they are able to secure a grade (it is the mission of the ESL teacher to ensure that no ELL ends up at the novice level of performance).

Task	A—Expert	B—Practitioner	C—Apprentice	D—Novice
Prewriting 25%	I *brainstormed and wrote* a series of questions about my audience and the purpose of my writing, including *specific* characteristics of a myth/legend/folktale that would help me develop my writing. I then provided, in writing, clear answers to these questions. Using previously read works of this genre as models, I created a list of words and phrases that might be useful in my writing. I *developed* an outline for my myth/ legend/ folktale and identified locations within the outline where the words and phrases I had generated might be used.	I *brainstormed and wrote* a series of questions about my audience and the purpose of my writing, including the *general* characteristics of a myth/legend/folktale that would help me develop my writing. I then provided, in writing, clear answers to these questions. Using previously read works of this genre as models, I created a list of words and phrases that might be useful in my writing. I *developed* an outline for my myth/ legend folktale and identified locations within the outline where the words and phrases I had generated might be used.	I wrote *a series of questions* about my audience and the purpose of my writing. I then provided answers to these questions. I created a list of words and phrases that might be useful in my writing. I *wrote* an outline for my myth/legend/ folktale, and *kept it with* the words and phrases I had generated.	I wrote *a few ideas* about my audience *or* the purpose of my writing. I created a list of words *or* phrases that might be useful in my writing. I *thought about* an outline for my myth/legend/folktale.

ASCD © 2007. All Rights Reserved.

Task	A—Expert	B—Practitioner	C—Apprentice	D—Novice
Drafting **30%**	*Following my outline,* I wrote the first draft of my myth/legend/ folktale. I included the appropriate elements of plot in a clear and balanced manner, and established *both* internal and external character traits for the protagonist, antagonist, and *other characters*.	*Following my outline,* I wrote the first draft of my myth/legend/ folktale. I included the appropriate elements of plot. The protagonist and antagonist possess *either* internal or external character traits.	I wrote the first draft of my myth/legend/ folktale. Minimal or sketchy elements of plot are included. *Characters not central to the plot* possess either internal or external character traits.	I *copied* a first draft of my myth/legend/ folktale. The plot contains gaps. *Minor characters* possess some character traits.
Revising **30%**	*In accordance with* the feedback I received from my teacher and from my peers on the peer feedback forms, I revised my writing, making *improvements* in organization, reader interest, coherence, transitions, sensory details, idiomatic expressions, formal versus informal language, and sentence length and variety.	*In accordance with* the feedback I received from my teacher and from my peers on the peer feedback forms, I revised my writing, making *changes* in organization, reader interest, coherence, transitions, sensory details, idiomatic expressions, formal versus informal language, and/or sentence length and variety.	I revised my writing, making changes in organization, reader interest, coherence, transitions, sensory details, idiomatic expressions, formal versus informal language, or sentence length and variety.	I decided not to make any changes in organization, reader interest, coherence, transitions, sensory details, idiomatic expressions, formal versus informal language, or sentence length and variety from my draft.
Editing **15%**	*Using a number of resources, including Spell Check, a dictionary, a thesaurus, my peers, and my teacher,* I proofread and edited my and others' work for accuracy in mechanics, spelling, and sentence structure and usage.	I proofread and edited my and *others' work* for accuracy in mechanics, spelling, and sentence structure and usage.	I proofread and edited my work for accuracy in mechanics, spelling, *and/or* sentence structure and usage.	I *reread* my work, and *made few or no corrections* for accuracy in mechanics, spelling, and/or sentence structure and usage.

Note: Rubric completed in collaboration with 6th grade language arts teachers, Ambrit International School, Rome, Italy.

ASCD © 2007. All Rights Reserved.

Lesson Task Planner Template for Coteaching

Content	Skills	Assessment	Strategies	Scaffolding
		Task:		

ASCD © 2007. All Rights Reserved.

Example 1: Lesson Task Planner--4th Grade Social Studies

This example depicts English language learners in a 4th grade social studies class going through the steps of gathering information about a selected country, for the purpose of writing a research report and giving an oral presentation. The ESL teacher uses the T-Notes reading strategy to scaffold English language learners' note-taking skills, either in English or in the primary language of the students, depending on their varying language proficiencies. The classroom teacher models how to put notes into a graphic organizer as a postreading or prewriting strategy. Because the two teachers decide that all students in the class can learn from using T-notes and the graphic organizers, they decide to use the alternative coteaching model. When it comes time to use the remaining steps of the writing process to finish the report, the teachers decide to use the differentiation strategies of writer's workshop and flexible groupings. Because the English language learners are not quite ready to do whole-class oral presentations, the teachers use the cooperative learning strategy Corners for small-group student presentations.

ASCD © 2007. All Rights Reserved.

Content	Skills	Assessment	Strategies	Scaffolding
Social Studies (Geography) Standard: Students will use a variety of intellectual skills to demonstrate their understanding of the geography of the interdependent world we live in, including the distribution of people, places, and environments. **Benchmarks:** Study about how people live, work, and use natural resources. Identify and compare the physical, human, and cultural characteristics of different regions and people. Investigate how people depend on and modify the physical environment. **Understanding:** Geography can be divided into six essential elements, which can be used to analyze important historic, geographic, economic, and environmental questions and issues.	**Language Arts Standard:** Students will read, write, listen, and speak for information and understanding. **Benchmarks:** Take notes to record data, facts, and ideas by following teacher direction and working independently. Use graphic organizers to record significant details. Use text features to understand and interpret text (e.g., main ideas and supporting details). Make inferences and draw conclusions. Compare and contrast information on one topic from different sources. Use the writing process (prewriting, drafting, revising, editing). Produce clear, well-organized, and well-developed reports. Communicate ideas in an organized and cohesive way. Speak with expression, volume, pace, and gestures appropriate for the audience and purpose. Offer feedback to others.	Questions Notes Graphic organizer Drafts, revisions, edited copy of report Use of rating scale to provide expectations and feedback Oral presentation	**Prereading:** View filmstrips depicting different countries. Generate research questions for focus. **During Reading:** T-Notes reading tool **After Reading/ Prewriting:** Graphic organizer **Drafting/Revising/ Editing:** Writer's Workshop and Flexible Groupings **Prepare for oral presentation:** Teacher models **Rehearse oral presentation:** Partners Check **Perform oral presentation:** Corners	ESL teacher previews filmstrips with ELLs, focusing on vocabulary development, and works on question formation in ESL class. Alternative coteaching strategy: ESL teacher works with group using T-Notes (in primary language if needed), and classroom teacher works with group on using notes to complete graphic organizer; groups switch. Teachers use differentiation strategies and station coteaching. ESL teacher models during ESL class. Teachers use cooperative learning strategies for small-group practice sessions and presentations rather than whole-class strategies.

ASCD © 2007. All Rights Reserved.

Example 2: Lesson Task Planner—Kindergarten

In this example, English language learners in a kindergarten language class do a picture walk of *The Hungry Caterpillar* during pull-out ESL time as a prereading strategy for an in-classroom read-aloud. The after-reading task requires students to draw the stages of a life cycle of a butterfly as a formative assessment task of a science concept. All children rehearse their oral explanation with one another using the cooperative learning strategy Inside/Outside Circle, not only to provide multiple opportunities for practicing with different partners but also to reinforce the concept of how a cycle works.

ASCD © 2007. All Rights Reserved.

Content	Skills	Assessment	Strategies	Scaffolding
Science Standard: The living environment (continuity of life) is sustained through reproduction and development. **Benchmark:** Describe the major stages in the life cycle of selected animals (e.g., butterfly). **Understanding:** Animals have life cycles, which include beginning of a life, development into an adult, reproduction as an adult, and eventually death.	**Language Arts Standard:** Students will read, write, listen, and speak for information and understanding. **Benchmarks:** Listen to text to match spoken words with pictures. Learn new words from books. **Language Arts Standard:** Students will read, write, listen, and speak for literary response. **Benchmarks:** Engage in prereading and reading activities to retell a story with assistance. Recall a sequence of events from a story. Use new vocabulary to talk about life experiences.	Comprehension checklist Drawings (life cycle) Retellings or oral explanations (life cycle)	**Prereading:** Picture walk of *The Hungry Caterpillar* **During Reading:** Read-aloud **After Reading:** Students work together to draw what each says. Inside/Outside Circle	Parallel coteaching: ESL teacher does picture walk with ELLs to teach vocabulary and sequence markers, using time-honored ESL scaffolds. Support coteaching: ESL teacher is in class to provide moment-to-moment scaffolds if needed. Cooperative learning tool: ELLs are paired with linguistic buddies or by proficiency levels (lower-proficiency student draws while higher-proficiency student retells). Cooperative learning strategy: All students have drawings in hand to serve as visual prompts for a second retelling. ESL teacher rehearses with ELLs in small-group setting. Peer coteaching strategy.

ASCD © 2007. All Rights Reserved.

Example 3: Lesson Task Planner—10th Grade Science

In this example, English language learners in a 10th grade science class are participating in a required science lab. To prepare the students during a pull-out class, the ESL teachers had English language learners semantically group essential vocabulary and then hypothesize what they thought might happen as a result of the experiment (an open word sort vocabulary tool). The ESL teacher also provided a sequence graphic organizer using mnemonic scaffolds to make sure that students could follow the steps. On the day of the lab, the classroom teacher models and the ESL teacher circulates (a support coteaching strategy). Students work as strategic cooperative partners: the job of beginning English language learners is to illustrate the lab report while the more proficient students are recorders of the findings. Students complete a self-assessment checklist and individual lab reports. The ESL teacher assists English language learners during a designated ESL pull-out class.

ASCD © 2007. All Rights Reserved.

Content	Skills	Assessment	Strategies	Scaffolding
Science Standard: Students will use scientific inquiry to pose questions, seek answers, and develop solutions. **Benchmarks:** Develop and present hypotheses to test explanations (i.e., predict what should be observed under specified conditions if the explanation is true). Carry out plan for testing explanations, including acquiring and building apparatus and recording observations as necessary. Use various means of representing and organizing data. Assess correspondence between the predicted result contained in the hypothesis and the actual result, and reach a conclusion as to whether or not the explanation on which the prediction was based is supported. Develop a written report that describes their proposed explanation, including the research and its result. **Understanding:** Scientific inquiry involves the testing of proposed explanations; the observations made provide new insights into phenomena.	**Language Arts Standard:** Students will . . . Read, write, listen, and speak for information and understanding. Ask questions about what they will need to know for their research. Read and follow written directions and procedures to accomplish tasks. Take notes and organize information from oral texts such as lectures or demonstrations. Use illustrations to support ideas. Analyze data, facts, and ideas to communicate information. Express a point of view, providing supporting facts and details. Maintain a portfolio that includes informational writing.	Predictions or hypotheses Checklist Illustrations and findings Draft lab report Final lab report	Demonstration—science teacher demonstrates steps of lab. Pairs Compare Rally Table	ESL teacher prepares students with vocabulary using open word sort vocabulary strategy and sequence graphic organizer, with mnemonic scaffolds so students can follow steps for the lab in class. Support coteaching strategy. Cooperative learning strategy—students conduct a science lab in pairs and then compare results with another pair. Peer coteaching strategy. Cooperative learning strategy: students write a draft lab report; each student then writes an individual report from the draft. Parallel coteaching strategy: ESL teacher works with ELLs in ESL class to complete lab report assignment.

ASCD © 2007. All Rights Reserved.

Example 4: Lesson Task Planner—7th Grade Math

English language learners in a 7th grade math class participate in the cooperative learning strategy Draw What I Say with a peer to show their understanding of the types of representational forms used to communicate statistical information, while the classroom and ESL teachers complete a checklist to monitor students' concept development and oral language proficiency. Later, the teachers decide to use the parallel coteaching model and the differentiation strategy of tiered activities to build different skills of English language learners and their English-proficient peers in communicating math concepts and understandings.

Content	Skills	Assessment	Strategies	Scaffolding
Mathematics Standard: Students will understand the concepts of and become proficient with the skills of mathematics; communicate and reason mathematically; and become problem solvers (data analysis). **Benchmarks:** Explain, describe, and defend mathematical ideas using representations. Recognize, compare, and use an array of representational forms. **Understanding:** Representations are used to organize, record, and communicate mathematical ideas.	**Language Arts Standard:** Students will read, write, listen, and speak for information and understanding. **Benchmarks:** Draw conclusions and make inferences on the basis of explicit information. Interpret data, facts, and ideas by applying thinking skills such as defining, classifying, and inferring. Use appropriate and precise vocabulary to convey ideas effectively. Participate actively and productively in group work.	Self-assessment checklist for new vocabulary Representational forms Problems Journals	Knowledge Rating Scale vocabulary strategy **Presentation of Information:** Modeling **Guided Practice:** Draw What I Say **Independent Practice:** Tiered activity of problems for students to choose from Journal writing (using new vocabulary)	Complementary coteaching strategy: ESL teacher scaffolds math teacher presentation with a preparatory vocabulary strategy. Use of SmartBoard to provide visuals and interactive problem-solving examples (data analysis). Cooperative learning strategy: students pair up; one describes a representational form while the other draws it. Peer coteaching strategy. Differentiation strategy. Time-honored ESL scaffolds of pictures or primary language journals.

ASCD © 2007. All Rights Reserved.

Section Three

Strategies for
SUCCESS
with English Language Learners

A Professional Development Rubric
for Sheltered Immersion

ASCD © 2007. All Rights Reserved.

Tasks	Exceeds Expectations	Meets Expectations	Approaching Expectations
Participate in professional development training for planning of sheltered immersion assessment and instruction.	Classroom and ESL teachers will actively collaborate with one another in pairs or small groups as they identify formative and summative assessment tasks they will use in an instructional unit, draft a task-based rubric explicitly grounded in the standards, and justify specific scaffolding strategies to support ELLs' language acquisition as well as the literacy needs and academic achievement of all students.	Classroom and ESL teachers will collaborate with one another in pairs or small groups as they identify formative and summative assessment tasks they will use in an instructional unit, draft a task-based rubric connected to the standards, and select specific scaffolding strategies to support ELLs' language acquisition, literacy, and academic achievement.	Classroom and ESL teachers will work with one another in pairs or small groups as they identify assessment tasks, draft a task-based rubric from expectations in their own heads, and identify scaffolding strategies that could be used as a part of the instructional unit.
Develop and implement a standards-based rubric and instructional planner for collaborative sheltered immersion.	Classroom and ESL teachers will implement the rubric for the unit of instruction, sharing the rubric with their students at the outset of the unit and using the rubric as an equitable grading instrument at the unit's conclusion. Scaffolding strategies will be adjusted throughout the course of the unit in accordance with students' performance on the formative assessments in order to improve ELLs' performance.	Classroom and ESL teachers will implement the rubric and instructional planner for the unit of instruction, sharing the rubric with their students at the outset of the unit and using the rubric as an equitable grading instrument at the end of the unit. Scaffolding strategies will be used to support ELLs' attainment of expectations.	Classroom and ESL teachers will implement the rubric and instructional planner for the unit of instruction, using the rubric as a grading instrument at the unit's conclusion.
Provide the school leadership team a copy of the rubric and instructional planner, along with a one-page reflection on the effect of the strategies on student learning.	Classroom and ESL teachers will provide a copy of the rubric and instructional planner along with a one-page reflection on the effect of the strategies. The reflection will include the modifications made during the implementation of the rubric and planner in ﹁ order to improve ELLs' performance.	Classroom and ESL teachers will provide a copy of the rubric and instructional planner along with a one-page reflection on the effect of the strategies on ELLs' attainment of expectations.	Classroom and ESL teachers may provide a draft copy of the rubric and instructional planner. The rubric or planner may be yet to be implemented.

Section Three

ASCD © 2007. All Rights Reserved.